Fragments for Fractured Times

Fragments for Fractured Times

*What Feminist Practical Theology
Brings to the Table*

Nicola Slee

scm press

© Nicola Slee 2020

Published in 2020 by SCM Press
Editorial office
3rd Floor, Invicta House,
108–114 Golden Lane,
London EC1Y 0TG, UK
www.scmpress.co.uk

SCM Press is an imprint of Hymns Ancient & Modern Ltd
(a registered charity)

Hymns Ancient & Modern® is a registered trademark of
Hymns Ancient & Modern Ltd
13A Hellesdon Park Road, Norwich,
Norfolk NR6 5DR, UK

British Library Cataloguing in Publication data

A catalogue record for this book is available
from the British Library

978 0 334 05908 0

Typeset by Regent Typesetting
Printed and bound by
CPI Group (UK) Ltd

Contents

For Stephen Burns, Ashley Cocksworth and Rachel Starr
colleagues, friends and companions at the table
with gratitude and delight

Acknowledgements

I am grateful for each of the invitations I have received from a wide variety of individuals and groups – to lecture, speak, preach, lead workshops, retreats or quiet days – that have occasioned the pieces that follow. I describe briefly the specific context out of which each piece arose in an introductory note that heads up each chapter, gladly acknowledging the gift of invitations that called out new work, as well as acknowledging where material has been previously published. While one frequently hears prophecies of doom about the future of theology in universities, I have been immensely heartened by the number and range of amateur theological societies and associations up and down the land, in places large and small, as well as lively groups in university settings I have had the pleasure of encountering. If people of all faiths and none, with varying levels of formal theological education, can pitch up in all weathers to hear talks on all subjects, there must be something good going on, and I'm glad to have been part of some of this informal, lay theological ferment as well as more formal, academic settings.

I am delighted that Jan Richardson gave permission to use her beautiful collage, *Christ among the scraps*, on the cover. I have come to know Jan's work, both as a writer and a visual artist, in recent years, and found it deeply resonant with my own work; it is therefore a great joy to be able to use an example of her work that I consider embodies both the spirit and material content of this book. Dede Tyndall experimented with an alternative cover image and, although we have not, in the end, used it, I hope there will be occasion to share Dede's vibrant image, based on Judy Chicago's *The Dinner Party* installation, with others – including readers of this book – in the future.

I owe much to David Shervington, senior commissioning editor at SCM Press, who has borne with the various delays to this book with gentle patience and then moved swiftly to bring the manuscript to publication. I am grateful to my old friend Hannah Ward for her painstaking and theologically astute copy-editing of the manuscript; her eagle eye, combined with an extensive knowledge of theology, has improved both the style and the substance of all that follows.

I owe much to a whole company of theologians – practical, feminist and otherwise, scholars and practitioners, living and departed – whose companionship, conversation and shared commitments have helped to form and shape my own feminist practical theological convictions and practice. First and foremost, my colleagues at Queen's over more than twenty years have been the best people to work, think, eat and pray with. Peter Fisher first invited me to Queen's as a scholar in residence in 1997 for a term and I have never managed (or wanted) to get away! Peter and Elizabeth's generous hospitality set a tone for all that has followed; I owe much to them, and more recently to David Hewlett for his wise and creative leadership as well as his unstinting personal support. As I write this, I am very much looking forward to continuing to work with my colleague Professor Clive Marsh in his new role as Principal of Queen's. While I never imagined I would remain at Queen's so long, it has been for me, almost always, a generous and supportive community within which my gifts have flourished and been widely shared. I am bound to miss out some at Queen's over the years who have been significant conversation partners, particularly since the list includes former students as well as staff colleagues, but I must pay tribute to at least some of them, including Dave Allen, Eunice Attwood, Al Barrett, Mukti Barton, Robert Beckford, Robert Bruce, Sarah Bruce, David Bryan, Stephen Burns, Rod Burton, Sue Burton, Helen Dixon Cameron, Stephen Canning, Clare Carson, Andrew Chandler, Ash Cocksworth, Paul Collins, Ann Conway-Jones, Naomi Cooke, Janet Corlett, Jane Craske, Deseta Davis, Jonathan Dean, Chris Dowd, Donald Eadie, Alison Earey, Mark Earey, Jess Foster, Simon Foster, Julian Francis, Michael Gale, Ray Gaston, Paula Gooder, Gary Hall, Ruth Harley, Jeanette Hartwell, Andrew Hayes, Adam Hood, John Hull, Omari Hutchinson, Michael Jagessar, Alison Joyce, Peter Kevern, Sin Ai Kim, Lee Longden, Andy Lyons, Rachel Mann, Dulcie McKenzie, Vincent Manoharan, Rosemary Maskell, Neil Messer, Ruth Midcalf, Christina Le Moignan, Jenny Morgans, Lynnette Mullings, Paul Nzacahayo, Val Ogden, Fran Porter, Judith Rossall, Andrea Russell, Sheila Russell, Anthony Reddie, Joshva Raja, Kerry Scarlett, Melusi Sibanda, Jennifer Smith (both of them), Susie Snyder, Ian Spencer, Dennis Stamps, Helen Stanton, Rachel Starr, Richard Sudworth, Evie Vernon, Jane Wallman-Girdlestone, Tom Walsh, George Wauchoup, David Wood, Kathleen Wood, Alison Woolley and Christine Worsley.

Former colleagues in other theological educational institutions – Roehampton University, the Southwark Ordination Course (SOC) and the Aston Training Scheme – have continued to inform my thinking and practice; some of the best theological conversations I have ever had took place at residential events on SOC or Aston, and I gladly pay tribute to Martin Baddeley, Bob Dickinson, Neil Evans, Peter Hammersley, Georgie Heskins, James Langstaff, Cathy Michell, Peter Privett, Alan Race, Ruth Shelton, Ian Shield, Roger Spiller and Ian Wallis for those free-ranging conversations. More recently, I have been delighted to form friendships with new colleagues at the Faculty of Religion and Theology at the Vrije Universiteit

(VU), Amsterdam. I owe a particular debt of gratitude to the former Dean of the Faculty, Wim Janse, and the present Dean, Ruard Ganzevoort, for their colleagueship and support, as well as to Dirk-Martin Grube who was, for a number of years, the Queen's–VU liaison professor with whom I have worked closely. Joep Dubbink, Manuela Kalsky, Miranda Klaver, Bert Jan Lietaert Peerbolte, Joke van Saan, Peter-Ben Smit, Gerdien Bertram-Troost and Arie Zweip have also offered me much valued support and friendship. I have been glad to become better acquainted with colleagues from the International Baptist Theological Seminary, which is partnered, like Queen's, with VU, and am particularly grateful to David McMillan, Mike Pears and Marianne van Zwieten for their hospitality. Since 2017 I have been a Visiting Professor at the University of Chester and have had the pleasure of working closely with Hannah Bacon, Elaine Graham, Dawn Llewellyn and Wayne Morris, at various times and in different capacities; I admire each of their work and have learnt much from each of them.

Having been involved in various theological establishments for several decades, I am glad to have made the acquaintance of theologians up and down the country and more widely in Europe and across the world who have, in different ways and at different times, been important conversation partners in the forming of my own convictions and practices. Through BIAPT (the British and Irish Association of Practical Theology), EFM (Education for Ministry), WIT (Women in Theology), the St Hilda Community, the Catholic Women's Network (now Women, Word and Spirit), the Movement for the Ordination of Women (now Women and the Church, of which I am proud to be an honorary vice-president), the European Society of Women in Theological Research, and the American Academy of Religion, I have enjoyed and appreciated meeting theologians of all persuasions and specialisms and learning from and with them; and also in broader church and theological education settings. I want to thank Jeff Astley, Stephen Barton, Elizabeth Baxter, Zoë Bennet, Tina Beattie, Carol Boulter, June Boyce-Tillman, Ruth Brown, Cláudio Carvalhaes, Beverley Clack, Megan Clay, Hannah Cocksworth, Doug Constable, Pamela Cooper-White, Susannah Cornwall, Jim Cotter, Hilary Cotton, Alison Le Cornu, Jenny Daggers, Maggi Dawn, Gloria Durka, Kevin Ellis, John Fairbrother, Bernadette Flanagan, Leslie Francis, Talitha Fraser, Bryan Froehle, Kathy Galloway, Courtney Goto, Mary Grey, Daphne Hampson, Maria Harris, Hans-Günter Heimbrock, Geoffrey Herbert, Mike Holroyd, Marilyn Hull, Mary Hunt, Jo Ind, Lisa Isherwood, Susannah Izzard, Tone Kaufman, Ramona Kauth, Maggie Keane, Gertraud Ladner, Brenda Lealman, Gillian Lever, Jake Lever, Gillian Limb, Renato Lings, Eric Lott, Joy MacCormick, Caroline Mackenzie, Pat Marsh, Katharine Massam, Joyce Mercer, Peter Middlemiss, Bonnie Miller-McLemore, Gabriel Moran, Mary Elizabeth Moore, Janet Morley, Mary Clark Moschella, Anne-Claire Mulder, Gordon Mursell, Diann Neu, Gary O'Neill, Mary O'Regan, Stephen Pattison,

Emma Percy, Martyn Percy, Callid Keefe-Perry, Pat Pierce, Myra Poole, Anne Pounds, Melissa Raphael, Bridget Rees, Christina Rees, Helen Richmond, Geoff Robson, Andrew Rogers, Susan Roll, Nigel Rooms, Nicky Roper, Brian Russell, Christian Scharen, Friedrich Schweitzer, Philip Sheldrake, Lynn Thomas, David Tombs, Sue Tompkins, Kristin de Troyer, Mairin Valdez, Heather Walton, Roger Walton, David Warbrick, Doff Ward, Hannah Ward, Pete Ward, Tess Ward, Brenda Watson, Clare Watkins, Hazel White, Jennifer Wild, John and Renate Wilkinson, Lucy Winkett, Pam de Wit, Claire Wolfteich, James Woodward, Ruth Yeoman and Frances Young.

The two poetry groups I belong to, a local 'Edge' group (Kathy Gee, Penny Hewlett and Rosie Miles) and a more dispersed group of poet theologians, the 'Diviners' (Gavin D'Costa, Eleanor Nesbitt, Mark Pryce and Ruth Shelton) are ongoing sources of inspiration, encouragement and critical friendship. The Symposium on the Faith Lives of Women and Girls, which I have convened (with the encouragement and assistance of colleagues) for more than ten years at Queen's, is a significant community that brings together the work of qualitative research with a feminist commitment to making female faith visible. Within that community of women researchers, I have received immense support and friendship from Hannah Bacon, Jan Berry, Helen Collins, Deseta Davis, Lindsey Taylor Guthartz, Manon Ceridwen James, Dawn Llewellyn, Eun Sim Joung, Sarah-Jane Page, Ruth Perrin, Anne Phillips, Fran Porter, Fran Rhys, Susan Shooter, Kim Wasey and Alison Woolley, among others.

St Mary's Abbey, West Malling, and the monastery at Glasshampton, Shrawley, have been for me places of friendship, prayer and renewal over many years and I am deeply grateful for the monastic life that is lived out faithfully in these and other such places. I rejoice in the rich ministry of All Saints, Kings Heath, and am glad to be part of such a vibrant and inclusive parish church. Further afield, Vaughan Park Retreat Centre on the outskirts of Auckland has become a significant place of friendship, study, prayer and welcome that has birthed a number of my writing projects. A little cell group that began meeting ten years ago at Holland House retreat centre, Cropthorne (which, itself, has been an immensely important place for me over many years), has become a source of absolute trust and deep wisdom: Philippa Garety, Clare Herbert, Rachel Mann, Rosie Miles and Lisa Waller are 'risen women' (as we call ourselves) who help me to live the risen life I know I am called to live.

Friends are the mainstay of one's life and I am glad that many of my work colleagues are also good friends. Almost all of the people I've listed above, I am glad to be able to call friends. There are a few who do not appear in those lists; they are the handful who have kept faith with me over many years and with whom I've probably had the most profound theological conversations, whether we've recognized it at the time or not: Jamie

Featherby, Jo Jones, Kate Lees, Peter Kettle and Sr Mary John Marshall OSB couldn't be more different from each other but have each proved their mettle many times over in my life (Gavin D'Costa does appear in the above lists, but I also want to name his faithful friendship here). Rosie Miles is the friend with whom I live my life, and without her companionship my writing life would not have flourished in the way that it has over the past twenty years or so. 'Are the cats going to appear in this book?' she asked me recently, and I can hardly conclude the long list without acknowledging the feline companions who share our home and garden; like me, they are getting older and slower and face us with the reality of our own mortality even as they leaven our daily routines with laughter. I can't imagine life without them.

While I have been working on this book, my colleagues Stephen Burns, Ashley Cocksworth and Rachel Starr have been working on a companion volume shortly to be published by SCM Press that circles around some of my own key commitments and concerns (entitled *From the Shores of Silence: Conversations in Feminist Practical Theology*). I could not be more blessed by their friendship, scholarship and many shared conversations around the table; they represent all that is best in the world of theological education and scholarship, as well as in the community of the Church. It gladdens my heart to know that their work will continue long after I hang up my hat and take to the life of a Christa crone.[1] I gladly dedicate this book to them.

Note

1 'Christa, crone', Nicola Slee, *Seeking the Risen Christa* (London: SPCK, 2011), p. 126.

PART I

Fragments for Fractured Times

Fragment
n. bit, chip, crumb, dollop, dose, fleck, fraction, grain, granule, morsel, part, particle, patch, piece, portion, potsherd, remnant, scrap, shiver, shred, sliver, spot, unfinished symphony, wedge, wisp.
v. break, break up, come apart, come to pieces, crumble, disintegrate, disunite, divide, shatter, shiver, splinter, split, split up.

Fracture(d)
n. breach, break, cleft, crack, crevice, frission, fissure, gap, opening, rent, rift, rupture, schism, scissure, split.
v. break, burst, crack, craze, crumble, flake, grate, impair, rasp, rupture, shear, shatter, snap, splinter, split.[1]

Note

1 *Roget's Thesaurus* (Hardmondsworth: Penguin, 1966) and *The New Collins Thesaurus* (London: Collins, 1984).

Introduction

This book brings together a collection of articles, talks, sermons, papers, poems and a few prayers, from the last ten to fifteen years, broadly addressing key questions in contemporary feminist and practical theology. They circle around and interrelate questions of faith and practice (or lived religion), including gender, spirituality, liturgy, preaching, faith development, pedagogy (specifically, adult theological education), poetics, ethnography and qualitative enquiry. About half of the material is previously unpublished.

I regard the occasional, contextual and fragmentary nature of this collection as a virtue rather than a problem! Like much British theology, my own work eschews the large-scale, systematic or comprehensive approach typical of Germanic theology of the first half of the twentieth century and favours the small-scale, the incidental, the narrative and metaphorical, the particular. I am drawn to poetry and liturgy, as well as homiletics, as primary forms of theology-in-the-making, where religious practice and the language of poetry and prayer shape and articulate the sense of God and the ways of the Spirit in the contemporary church and world. I realize that my own shaping of theological forms, texts, language and convictions has very often come about in response to specific invitations from different groups and individuals – to preach, pray, conduct retreats, lecture or engage in conversation. Maybe this is partly because I work well when there is an external demand or deadline set by a speaking engagement or performative piece; but it is more than that. It speaks of the invitational, conversational and contextual nature of all theology, which is created anew out of the confluence of time and space, place and social-political moment, calling new truths out of the givenness of scripture and tradition.

To speak of the givenness of scripture and tradition should not suggest that scripture and tradition themselves are stable, unchanging categories. As new discoveries of the past are constantly made, including the discovery of ancient scriptural manuscripts and the emergence of new interpretations of old texts and traditions, so the 'givenness' of the past is constantly unsettled and reformed by the creative breath of the Spirit and the emergence of new human knowledge and wisdom. Invitations from diverse groups in different settings and places can help to unearth such new knowledge and therefore give expression to new theologies. This is perhaps particularly so when those who consider themselves to be marginal to the mainstream – however we might construe the 'mainstream' and whoever it is who decides – invite fresh tellings of the Christian gospel in response to their own marginalization and their urgent needs for justice and inclusion. At least some of the theology in this book has arisen out of such invitations from those at the margins; and even to speak of 'margins' may unhelpfully reinforce the unjust power dynamics between margins and centre, those with less and those with more power. For the place that is often regarded as marginal is, I suspect, much closer to the centre of God's heart than places colonized by those who claim to represent the mainstream, or who behave as if they are at the centre of power.

What I offer in this book is therefore a gathering of fragments collected from diverse times, places, settings and occasions; fragments that do not necessarily make a whole, in the sense of a comprehensive, systematic, 'finished' article, but might, together, add up to more than the sum of its many parts.

The metaphor of 'fragments' is, in fact, one that has appealed to and been used by a number of theologians over the past century, as the lead essay in the book explores, and continues to attract contemporary writers.[1] I use the metaphor in conjunction with other, more domestic metaphors drawn from women's lives, craft and art – metaphors of the web, tapestry, knitting and sewing, as well as metaphors of the table, all of which have been employed by a range of feminist theologians and thinkers to reflect the artistic, creative, material and embodied work of women down the ages. What feminist theology brings to the table of scholarly thinking and embodied practice is, I want to suggest, something creative, artful, prophetic as well as playful – a resource for Christian living and thinking in times when coercive, patriarchal religion is rightly rejected and condemned by many who are all too well aware of the harm it has done to women, children, ethnic minorities, LGBTQI+ folks, those who are differently abled, and many more.

I offer fragments, morsels, grains, scraps, plates of diverse cuisine and ingredients, some of which may appear very slight and small, while others are more substantial; perhaps this book is rather like a meal composed of many small courses, meze or tapas. Like such a meal, the pieces can be dipped into and out of in any order the reader fancies; some may be lingered over to appreciate their flavour, while others may be passed over. I offer these fragments into times I describe as 'fractured' – cracked, broken, split apart, crazed, ruptured, fissured – in which grand narrative and shared ideologies have broken down irreparably in favour of local, contextual and multiple narratives and ways. In the period during which I have been bringing this book together, such a description may take on new force and resonance as the world reels from the deadly coronavirus and continues to seek to respond to the climate catastrophe which surely represents the greatest threat to life on earth in our time. It is too soon to know what lasting impact these crises are going to have on humanity and on theological enquiry; maybe there is a chance that the global pandemic of Covid-19 will bring the different nations, cultures and religions of the world together in a way that we have not seen previously, to share knowledge and expertise and to support one another in this common threat to our humanity. Whether the fragments I offer in this book can speak into this new global reality remains to be seen; yet I am hopeful that feminist and practical theologies have both the characteristics and the courage to meet the challenges of our time. Both feminist and practical theologies have shown themselves willing to dive into the depths of human experience at the extremities of agonizing suffering and oppression, on the one hand, and in the celebration of divinely resourced human capacity, creativity and compassion on the other. Eschewing essentialisms and dogmatic certainty, both feminist and practical theologies represent lived wisdom for our time, which can adapt and respond creatively to new situations and global crises, continually drawing out new treasures from ancient depositories of scripture and tradition.

The unearthing of fragments of sometimes painful and traumatic experience, as well as of neglected (broken?) treasure, is costly, often laborious work. In her profound offering of what she names 'a spirituality of survival', Barbara Glasson uses the metaphor of excavation to speak of raising up what has been buried, 'sous vivre', in individual or collective trauma, in order that it may become a resource for 'sur vivre' or survival:

> The process associated with survival, 'sur vivre', entails excavation, raising things that 'sous vivre'. Sometimes these things are dug up, sometimes they emerge over time. This process involves the bringing into the light of those occurrences that we are too ashamed to name or too remiss to remember. What emerges among the soiled and discarded rubbish are a lot of tiny fragments. Shards and oddments, disjointed, broken remnants, strange garbled histories. But, as the story surfaces, there can also be the piecing together of things, a reconstruction, a remembering of broken bodies, histories and communities.[2]

A theology of fragments is both realistic about human frailty and hopeful about human creativity, under the inspiration of the creative Spirit of God who faithfully works to redeem all that is broken and maimed. Mark Oakley suggests that 'in and of ourselves ... our resources are limited and the human material we are made from is fractured, volatile and unique, but full of inheritance as well as potential'.[3] I am under no illusions about the partial, fragmentary, limited nature of the offerings in this book, and yet I do not want to masquerade under the banner of false humility for I know that what is offered here, partial and incomplete though it is, has been hard won from a lifetime of study, struggle, prayer and wrestling with my own Christian inheritance. I also know that every writer (as well as preacher, teacher, accompanist) relies on the generosity and creativity of her readers, who bring their own unique, partial and peculiar insight and experience to the text. In the meeting and melding of minds, with their motley collection of fragments of lived experience, knowledge and intuitions, something can be pieced together, reconstructed and re-membered that is greater than what any one person brings to the table. Yet I want to say more than this: the piecing together of fragments and the poetic process of making them into something much more than the sum of the parts is not only human work; it is the work of God in creation and most particularly in redemption. As Jan Richardson (whose lovely image of *Christ among the scraps* forms the cover image of this book) puts it:

> God takes everything: experiences, stories, memories, relationships, dreams, prayers – all those pieces, light and dark, rough and smooth, jagged and torn – and creates anew from them. I have learned to think of God as the consummate recycler: in God's economy, nothing is wasted. Everything – everything – can be transformed. Redeemed.[4]

Jan goes on to speak of the work of 'visible repair' in which the artist – whether human or divine – does not seek to hide 'what is broken, damaged, cracked, frayed, torn' but rather to work with it, 'bringing attention and care'.[5] Her own artistic work, particularly in collage but also in her poems and blessings, embodies this core conviction powerfully. This conviction – that, in the final analysis, nothing of human or indeed cosmic experience is wasted but is taken up into the creative and redemptive work of God – is perhaps the belief that, of all others, distinguishes persons of faith from those who do not believe. And many who do not think of themselves as believers do indeed share such a conviction, however haltingly expressed. Artists, similarly, are those who know how to take every shard and fragment of experience, knowledge, pain, disaster and wisdom and somehow weave them into their work, not discarding or rejecting anything, even if its part in the work may not be visible.

The book proceeds in six parts. Although the themes and issues throughout overlap and blur, there are distinct foci. Part 1 comprises an introduction to the book as a whole. The lead article, 'Fragments for Fractured Times', sets out a rationale for my approach to feminist practical theology and functions as a broad-ranging introduction to all of the key themes and concerns that follow. Each of the following five parts then picks up a key area of my work and offers a variety of pieces on that theme. Part 2 focuses on public and private prayer, including explorations of the nature of feminist prayer and liturgy, different forms of prayer, the significance of the body in prayer, the poetic within prayer discourse, and so on. Part 3 focuses on spirituality, offering diverse analyses and perspectives. Pieces here explore the particular challenges to Christian feminist spirituality in our time, and offer a range of metaphors that might illuminate the nature and practice of spirituality, from the metaphor of 'multiple overwhelming' to that of cartography, and embodied metaphors of standing, sitting and dancing. What is the difference between prayer and spirituality? This is not a question I set out to answer in the pieces that follow; clearly the practice of prayer and the embrace of spirituality are profoundly interconnected. If I see a distinction between them, it might be that prayer is a more focused, intentional activity of the praying individual or group (although in at least one of the pieces in Part 2 I stretch such a definition of prayer beyond the specific activity of offering verbal or mental prayers), while spirituality is the embrace of an entire way of living which includes prayer within the totality of faithful discipleship.

Part 4 picks up the theme of poetry and the nature of poetic discourse, exploring the political and theological significance of poetry for feminist liberation and for the practice of theological reflection. I reflect on the kind of language that poetic discourse is and why I consider it essential for faith, as well as its particular significance as a locus for feminist theological work. I include a case study of poetry as a form of 'benign witness'[6] in the traumatized country of Bosnia as a way of insisting that poetry and theology may function as forms of political protest, testimony and solidarity as well as of personal faith and spirituality. Part 5 explores the nature of work, particularly the vocation and practices of teaching, research, reading and writing, which have been the primary fora of my own scholarly, pedagogic and theological endeavour. I explore the ways in which the practices of teaching, reading and writing, in and of themselves, can be understood as spiritual practice; likewise, I describe the various methods of qualitative research, such as interviewing, transcribing and analysing data, as primary forms of prayer and spirituality. Part 6 is concerned with feminist theological exploration of the nature, images and discourse for God. In particular, the pieces in this section circle around the significance of naming, conceptualizing and praying to God in feminine terms, and the range of ways in which this can be done. Although an old theme in feminist theology, I bring fresh perspectives to this well-worn theme through a range of poetic, visual and metaphoric tropes, presenting the notion of Christ as the coming girl, the risen Christa, the crucified Christa and the feisty crone.

Throughout, I seek to acknowledge and highlight the particular context out of which each piece in the book emerged, not as an afterthought but rather as a way of holding up each particular fragment to the light and examining its size, shape, texture and pattern – or, to return to the metaphor of the meal, as a way of remembering the particular tables at which these dishes were cooked up, presented and shared. Just as a mosaic or patchwork brings together pieces that are very different in provenance, age, texture, colour and style, and the beauty of the whole is enhanced by this diversity and range, so I revel in the unevenness – or, as I would rather say, the 'thickness' – of the varied offerings here. Rather than seeking to flatten them all to one dimension or style, I point up the differing genres, accents and tongues. I relish the many different ingredients, cuisines and tables around which many morsels have been shared. Poems are peppered throughout the text, as well as introducing each section. Nor have I attempted to iron out inevitable overlap and a certain amount of repetition between the chapters. I note that there are favourite books and articles that I quote repeatedly! Simone Weil's little essay on 'Reflections on the right use of school studies in view of the love of God',[7] for example, is a favourite which crops up in quite a few of the chapters – it was only in working on this collection that I recognized how significant that little essay has been in my life. I hope readers will forgive such idiosyncrasies and regard them more like reappearing friends than annoying intruders – or as the staple bread or wine that accompanies every course!

Notes

1 To give two examples, Robert Atwell employs the metaphor of fragments to speak of the fragmented memories of those living with dementia in *God in Fragments: Worshipping with Those Living with Dementia* (London: Church House Publishing, 2020), while Clare Herbert speaks of piecing together a theology of same-sex marriage from fragments drawn from conversations with those who are in same-sex partnerships, in *Rethinking the Theology of Same-Sex Marriage: Squaring the Circle* (London: Jessica Kingsley, 2020). For other examples of the use of the metaphor of fragments in practical theology, see note 1, pages 22–3 below.

2 Barbara Glasson, *A Spirituality of Survival* (London: Continuum, 2009), p. 47.

3 Mark Oakley, *My Sour-Sweet Days: George Herbert and the Journey of the Soul* (London: SPCK, 2019), p. 122.

4 Jan Richardson, *What the Light Shines Through: A Retreat for Women's Christmas 2020*, at http://sanctuaryofwomen.com/blog/womens-christmas-retreat-2020-what-the-light-shines-through/: 7 (accessed 24.4.20).

5 Richardson, *What the Light Shines Through*, p. 16.

6 I owe this phrase to the Revd Dr Jane Tillier, as well as much wisdom in piecing together the fragments in my own experience and seeing the activity of the Spirit therein.

7 Simone Weil, 'Reflections on the right use of school studies with a view to the love of God', *Waiting on God* (Glasgow: Collins Fount, 1977).

I

Fragments for Fractured Times: What Feminist Practical Theology Brings to the Table

This chapter is the substance of my inaugural lecture, delivered on the occasion of my inauguration to the Queen's Chair in Feminist Practical Theology on 13 September 2017, at what was then the Faculty of Theology and is now the Faculty of Religion and Theology of the Vrije Universiteit Amsterdam. On 2 October 2017 I repeated the lecture at Queen's Birmingham as part of the celebrations to mark the opening of Frances Young House, at which Frances preached and formally opened the new building. A little later again, I was able to repeat the lecture at Luther King House, Manchester, at the kind invitation of the then Principal of the Open College, the Revd Dr Jan Berry, a long-time friend and colleague. These three events, collectively, represent something of a highlight of my professional life, and were occasions of great joy, surrounded by colleagues new and old and many students and friends, as well as members of the Symposium on the Faith Lives of Women and Girls. I make no apology for naming and thanking many to whom I owe much in the text that follows, in a manner that is common in inaugural lectures, although of course there is always the danger that one will miss someone out (and I have in fact included one or two more names in this version than were in the original lectures).

Introduction

In this inaugural lecture, I want to speak of my vision of the theological task. I shall focus in particular on the contributions of feminist and practical theologies, gathering fragments[1] from their endeavours to bring to the table of theological enquiry. I do so in order to address the larger vocation of theology represented by those of you gathered here who would not identify as either feminist or practical theologians. For I see practical and feminist theologies not so much as discrete species of theology as theology in particular mode or perspective. They highlight the vocation of *all* theology to be concerned with the lives and practices of ordinary believers and with the imperative of gender justice.

First, I shall locate the theological task in the context of times that I shall describe as fractured. Within the range of possible theological responses to such fracturing, I shall highlight what I see to be distinctive stances of feminist and practical theologies. I shall then offer a series of metaphors of theology that have been common in both practical and feminist theologies: metaphors of the web, tapestry and quilt, drawn from women's age-old crafts (which have, themselves, been marginalized from patriarchal traditions of the 'high arts' and reclaimed by contemporary feminists).[2] I shall take what I regard as one worked example of feminist practical theology, Judy Chicago's iconic art installation, *The Dinner Party*, which incorporates women's craft work of various kinds within the conceit of a dinner party for women from across millennia. *The Dinner Party*, I will suggest, can highlight key features of what feminist practical theology brings to the table of theological practice. The notion of 'table theology' has been a key concern in feminist theology and liturgy (for example, in Letty M. Russell's *Church in the Round*,[3] in which she develops the metaphor of the 'round table', the 'kitchen table' and the 'welcome table' as alternatives to the hierarchical 'master's tables' which have governed the church); it has also been a recurrent motif in my own work.[4] The table is, of course, a eucharistic image of ancient lineage and calls to mind many classic images such as Rublev's famous icon of the Trinity and Leonardo da Vinci's *Last Supper*. As I seek to gesture towards the table that Wisdom sets in our midst,[5] I shall aim to bring a variety of dishes to the banquet in the form of particular examples of feminist practical theological scholarship that have been significant in my own journey. I will raise a number of toasts to particular individuals who have meant much to me. Finally, I shall speak of some of my own distinctive methods in theology, highlighting the use of qualitative research, poetry and liturgy as tools for dismantling and reconfiguring the patriarchal symbolic imaginary. While this particular combination of genres is personal, there are many others whose work employs a similar, if not greater, range; and here I raise my first toast to Revd Professor Frances Young, who has been closely associated with Queen's for many years, and whose work demonstrates the ways in which systematic and practical theological concerns can enrich each other.[6]

I am not going to offer definitions of either feminist or practical theology at this point, as I hope that my understanding of both will emerge as I proceed. I will simply say that my hope for this chair is that it will promote and strengthen practical theology in the academy and in the churches, from the perspective of feminism and related discourses. While I am well aware of many forms of religious feminism outside the church and beyond Christianity, my own commitment is to work within a confessional context, in critical as well as constructive mode, functioning as 'the irritant in the eye/ Of the church', 'the cracked lens through which it needs to see',[7] reflecting back its own brokenness.

Feminist practical theology – formed out of the meeting and mingling of feminist and practical theologies – has been slow to emerge, only becoming established in the English-speaking world in the past few decades. Professor Riet Bons-Storm, now retired, held a chair in women's studies and pastoral studies at Groningen, but, as far as I know, the Queen's Chair in Feminist Practical Theology is the only current chair of its kind in Europe. Nevertheless, it stands in an honourable line of European chairs of feminist theology – held, for example, by Catherina Halkes (Nijmegen), Mary Grey (Nijmegen, Southampton and Lampeter), Ann Loades (Durham) and Lisa Isherwood (Winchester) – as well as chairs in practical theology, represented by our own Dean, Ruard Ganzevoort and by prominent European and American theologians such as Duncan Forrester (Edinburgh),[8] Elaine Graham (Manchester, Chester), Stephen Pattison (Birmingham), Friedrich Schweitzer (Tübingen), Bonnie Miller-McLemore (Vanderbilt), Mary Elizabeth Moore (Boston) and many others. I am deeply conscious of my dependence on both streams of scholarship and on many of these individuals' work and colleagueship.

Fractured times

Perhaps all times between Eden and the eschaton are fractured, but it seems to be a particular characteristic of our own era. Whichever way we turn, we witness the dismembering and fracturing of many previously taken-for-granted realities, what Rowan Williams has graphically described as 'a nervous breakdown in the body politic'.[9] The powerful state–church compact we have known as Christendom has long been in decline, the Protestant Reformation only one obvious historical marker of its fatal wounding. Old political alliances and global power dynamics are dismantled before our eyes. The maps and borders are being rewritten in complex, shifting ways, Brexit and parallel movements in other European countries constituting one obvious, local manifestation. Larger systems such as patriarchy and colonialism, those centuries-old rule of the masters, are in global decline even while they refuse to lie down, manifesting in ever new forms. The strong yet fragile body of the earth itself is in grave danger from daily rape and pillage.

Such ecological, religious and political fracturing is mirrored in the academy. Rapid expansion of the university sector in the UK has been followed by retraction in the light of austerity measures that threaten to unmake public services as we have known them. Academic disciplines themselves partake of this fracturing. Once the queen of the sciences, guaranteeing and exemplifying the unity of all knowledge under God, theology – where it exists at all in modern universities – is fragmented into ever-multiplying forms, many of which do not seem to want to talk to each other. Systematic, dogmatic, philosophical, historical, biblical, practical, public, liberation, feminist, LGBTQI+, queer, post-colonial – these are only a few of the myriad forms that theology now takes. To narrow the focus to my own field of feminist theology itself, the forms bifurcate and multiply at a dizzying rate: womanist, mujerista, Asian and African women's theologies have been joined by new discourses around gender and the search for new masculinities. There have been backlash, post-feminism, post-Christian and post-denominational feminist theologies.

All these different kinds of fracturing are symptomatic of the breakdown of grand narrative itself, the loss of a unifying symbol system which commands widespread assent, and an accompanying loss of confidence in rationality and institutional authority. Nor is the brokenness only outside us. Speaking personally, I am well aware that I come from a people of brokenness and carry their wounds within me, manifested in a series of fissures and gaps between who I am, what I say and what I do – the lack of integrity which is a condition of humanness. The gradual disintegration of my ageing body is only one of the more obvious signs of this lack. I name such personal dissolution not as an embarrassing addendum to the larger political and ecclesial brokenness I have been describing but because I regard it as central to the vocation of theology. Only the 'wounded researcher', the 'failed poet',[10] can inhabit the 'broken middle' of which philosopher Gillian Rose speaks,[11] which is the only site of authentic theological practice. This is something that theologians writing out of various experiences of impairment witness to in their writings as well as their lives, calling all theology to recognize its grounding in a 'disabled God'.[12]

Theology's response to the fracturing of knowledge and borders

Do we regard fragmentation as a 'predicament or an emancipation', something to be resisted or welcomed?[13] And how might theology respond to such fractured times? One, reactionary response to multiple fragmentation is to seek to reinstate a grand, meta-narrative upon the disorder. This is essentially a response of denial, frequently motivated by fear and a refusal to give up the iron grip of control. We see such a response in many forms of political and religious backlash. At the other extreme is a response which, far from denying the reality of fragmenting discourses, positively embraces the breakdown of monolithic structures. Queer and post-colonial theologies best typify this approach, in which those who have been most disadvantaged by the religiously endorsed grand narrative rejoice in its breakdown and revel in the fissures of the broken system, seeking not to reconcile the contradictions but to exploit and enlarge them.

I have some sympathy for both of these approaches. I recognize within myself a strong desire to fix what is broken and find security in some overarching system or story. At the same time, I am also attracted by the anarchic stance of queer theology, and my own theology is not a little informed by it. However, neither of these approaches will quite do. On the one hand, as Zygmunt Bauman asserts, 'No recipes of repairing the fissure are to be trusted; the more radical they are, the more they need to be suspected.'[14] On the other hand, as Kate Soper has suggested, to 'give up on the grand narrative idea of a single truth' does not compel us to give up 'on the idea of truth as a regulative ideal'.[15] Thus I want to suggest a 'third way' as the modus operandi of feminist practical theology – not so much a classic middle way between the two extremes as a form of oscillation, a dynamic toing and froing between them.[16]

Without imposing some kind of uniformity where there is none, I think one can see some family resemblances between the diverse expressions of feminist and practical theology, which allow some generalizations to be made. Feminist and practical theologies acknowledge the fragmentation of human knowledge and systems. Indeed, feminist theology has played its own part in demolishing the superstructure of patriarchal religion that has legitimized Christendom's grand narrative (practical theology has, on the whole, been less iconoclastic, although not without critique of the church it seeks to serve). Yet, feminist practical theology looks to reconstruct from the rubble of what is fallen, gathering the scattered fragments of what diners at the tables of power have discarded, seeking to make bread out of stone.[17] A characteristic stance of both feminist and practical theologies is the search for connections between the fragments within an epistemology of relationality and interconnection, a kind of toing and froing between the overarching claims of systematic theologies, on the one hand, and an acute listening to the neglected margins, on the other. This is a theological approach that is modest yet visionary: attentive to the diversity and particularity of things. It seeks to hold each fragment up to the light for critical scrutiny but also for appreciation, finding joy in the small, fragile thing. It analyses and responds to brokenness with realism and hopefulness, not looking to fix things so much as to hold and bear them. Refusing to impose an artificial unity upon the many fractured parts, such theologies nevertheless seek a larger whole that might be assembled from the fragments – a whole that is always ahead of us, never fully envisaged or realized.

Feminist practical theological responses

Both feminist and practical theologians of the past few decades have coined metaphors of the web to express such an epistemology and methodology of interconnectedness. Bonnie Miller-McLemore adapted Anton Boisen's metaphor of the 'living human document' to speak of the 'living human web'[18] as the basis of pastoral theology. This was an attempt to broaden pastoral theology's focus on the interpersonal dimensions of pastoral care towards a greater recognition of the socio-political contexts in which the pastoral encounter is rooted. Miller-McLemore's metaphor of the living web was itself indebted to the work of feminist philosophers, theologians, artists and psychologists who were developing the notion of the web in a range of ways.

Catherine Keller's *From a Broken Web*[19] is a fine example of such feminist metaphorical re-visioning. Keller surveys western philosophy and culture from classical to contemporary times, and deconstructs the model of the separative male self, made in the image of the all-sufficient male God, upon which western thought and culture have been based. Building on the research of Gilligan,[20] Dinnerstein[21] and Chodorow,[22] Keller charts patterns of early child-rearing which establish the male drive towards separation and autonomy, and the female self, nurtured in connection and relationship. Male fear of intimacy and female fear of autonomy have tended to result from these developmental pathways, fixing gender relations in unequal and anxious co-dependence. Employing the classical myth of Arachne, the great Spider or Spinner who defeats the goddess Athena in a contest of looms, Keller offers a 'hermeneutics of connection' – not to replace Ricœur's hermeneutics of suspicion[23] upon which it depends, but to set it within a larger vision of restoration and whole-making.[24] The image of the web, Keller argues, may 'claim the status of an all-embracing image, a metaphor of metaphors, not out of any imperialism, but because, as a metaphor of interconnection itself, the web can link lightly in its nodes an open multiplicity of images'.[25] She affirms the work of repairing the broken web as essentially religious, the tying together and binding up of 'the wounds of breaking worlds',[26] 'the passion to make and make again/ where such unmaking reigns'.[27]

Many feminist theologians and philosophers have taken up the metaphor of the web[28] and related metaphors of the tapestry, quilt and patchwork, employing them to illuminate feminist spirituality,[29] human and divine personhood,[30] redemption and atonement theologies,[31] violence against women,[32] pastoral care,[33] feminist preaching,[34] and feminist practical research methodology.[35] The relational theologies of Carter Heyward,[36] Rita Nakashima Brock[37] and Mary Grey[38] demonstrate how the metaphor of the web can be extended to a more comprehensive model of God and divine–human relations.[39]

Whether we are speaking of the web-making of the internet and social media, or of traditional female arts of tapestry, quilt-making and spinning, these metaphors enshrine a number of characteristics that are significant in feminist and practical theologies, beyond the core assertion of relationality and interconnectedness. They point to the materiality, artistry and collaborative nature of feminist and practical theological study. They affirm women's participation in the theological work of repairing the fabric of the world, sharing with God the work of sustaining and redeeming creation. Such metaphors also conjure feminist and practical theological ways of thinking and working that proceed via associative, evocative and lateral perspectives rather than systematic, deductive and linear thought.

Of course, metaphors of the web and the tapestry for the work of theology are not beyond criticism. Their very malleability and wide-ranging application may be both a weakness and a strength. More problematically, an emphasis on relationality and connectedness can obscure the differences and conflicts between women, and it is not insignificant that relational theologies have largely been created by white women. Black and Asian women may feel less of a need to connect with others who have been the source of their exclusion from the table. Mukti Barton's account of the racism and rejection that first-generation black and Asian immigrants experienced when they arrived in Britain in the late 1950s, and turned up at churches they expected would welcome them, makes painful reading.[40] Any account of relationality fit for purpose must grapple with the refusal of relations represented by racism, homophobia and every other exclusionary practice. As Keller herself says, 'we must avoid any naïve glorification of connection'; 'spiders remind us of … the dangers and tragedies of relation – it can ensnare, strangle, swallow and devour'.[41]

What feminist practical theology brings to the table

Judy Chicago's iconic feminist art installation, *The Dinner Party*,[42] may serve as a model of the kind of approach to knowing, thinking and creating that feminist and practical theologies embody. Integrating metaphors of the web, the tapestry and the mosaic with the image of a feminist eucharistic table, *The Dinner Party* provides a rich and evocative model of feminist practical theology.

A pioneering feminist artist who has constantly broken new ground throughout her long career, Chicago came to fame through her *Dinner Party* installation, created over five years with a collective of more than four hundred volunteers.[43] Chicago regarded the installation as a reworking of, or a 'female counterpart' to, the Last Supper, especially as visualized in Da Vinci's famous painting. The work consists of six tapestry entry banners welcoming visitors to the space, leading into the main area dominated by a massive three-sided ceremonial banquet table (the triangle chosen as a symbol of equality and one of the earliest symbols of the goddess). Place settings for 39 women are arranged in three groups of 13, one for each wing of the table. The first wing of the table features women from pre-history up to classical Rome;[44] the second wing women from Christianity up to the Reformation,[45] and the third wing, women from the American revolution to the feminist revolution.[46] Each place setting consists of an embroidered runner, a gold chalice and utensils, and a china-painted porcelain raised plate. The whole installation sits on a mosaic floor of tiles, 'the heritage floor', consisting of 2,300 hand-cast porcelain tiles commemorating 999 mythological and historical women of achievement.

The Dinner Party is a huge achievement in its own right (although it was savaged by critics of the time for its 'vapid prettiness', 'explicit sexual references', 'titillation', 'crass' and 'solemn vulgarity').[47] It can also serve to highlight many features of feminist practical theology: its collaborative, collective nature; its critique and dismantling of patriarchal tradition and ways of working; its forging of an alternative tradition of repressed and neglected female lives; its recovery and retrieval of a feminine symbolic imaginary rooted in the female body and ancient archetypes of the goddess; its artistry, painstaking labour and skill, its attention to detail as well as its vision and daring.

Yet *The Dinner Party* is also notable for what is missing, and this absence may shine a light on what feminist practical theology can bring to the table. For all its materiality, Chicago's dinner party has an oddly stylized and disembodied quality to it. We may watch at this table, we may approach within inches, yet we may not handle or touch. This is a not a table such as we might sit around to have a real dinner party. Its plates are sculptures to be admired rather than crockery to be used (and many of them took repeated firings to achieve Chicago's technically difficult design); and would we dare to set down a goblet, even spill a few drops of wine, on those exquisite runners? In its dark, hushed space, it is a museum piece, testifying to lives that are remembered, but absent. Above all, there are no living, breathing bodies at this table – except for those of visitors who view and observe, at a slight distance.

This absence is, of course, intentional. The women Chicago envisages at this dinner table can never meet in actuality; we, the viewers, have to bring our own work of imagination to realize the vision in our mind's eye. Their absence also points up women's absence in almost all depictions of the Last Supper and protests against women's exclusion from patriarchal ritual and religion.[48] Furthermore, Chicago's dinner guests, for all their relegation to the margins of history, remain the singular heroines of the past. They are exceptional achievers, whose lives or work broke new ground for women (even if their achievements were not recognized in their own time). Behind each of these women stand an invisible multitude of unnamed women and girls, who are even further removed from access to the table. Chicago's *Dinner Party* both is and is not a dinner party such as the Gospels envisage for the outsiders, the poor, the lepers, the prostitutes and tax-collectors. Insofar as she has widened access to the table, her vision marks only the beginning of the work of inclusion with which feminist practical theology is concerned.

It is precisely the living, breathing bodies of 'ordinary' women and girls (who are, of course, very far from ordinary) that feminist practical theology brings to the table, insisting on their right to be at the dinner party and lifting up the particular gifts they bring – gifts that have been disregarded, counted as no more than crumbs under the table. Practical theology looks to the lives and experience of ordinary seekers and believers, rather than to professional theologians, formally trained clerics or exceptional holy ones, as the main source and norm of theological enquiry. Far from being the application of an already worked-out doctrinal theology, practical theology insists that the practice *is* the theology and the theology is the practice. Maria Harris, a much-loved teacher and mentor, suggests five primary practices, drawn from the account of the early church in Acts, which characterize the life of the church.[49] She names them forms of curricula through which the church learns to be the church: the curricula of community, prayer, teaching, proclamation and service, respectively. Practical theologians in recent times have offered their own accounts of the classic or historic forms of religious practice that are regarded as normative for Christians (prayer and Bible reading, hospitality, tithing, fasting, the keeping of Sabbath, and so on) as well as probing contemporary practices that shape individuals' lives and the corporate expression of faith in new, and sometimes challenging, ways (for example, watching TV and film, the use of social media, changing habits of eating, shopping and other forms of consumption).[50] Both kinds of practice – historical and contemporary – are primary forms of faith, in at least a twofold sense: first, in the sense that practice *forms* thinking, belief and doctrine and, second, in the sense that practice has its own complex, intricate *forms* which are as worthy of scholarly attention as the complex systems of thought of great theologians.

Thus, much contemporary scholarship in practical theology focuses on the study of lived religion,[51] especially the faith lives of ordinary believers. James Fowler's research into adult faith development,[52] though rather out of favour now, laid theological foundations for this kind of approach in the United States, while Elaine Graham's insistence on the primacy of 'transforming practice'[53] helped to set a direction for British practical theology beyond the remit of pastoral care to a wider set of contexts and discourses that shape living (contexts including the city and the public square, to which Graham has made significant contributions).[54] Stephen Pattison's wide-ranging interests in the relation between belief and practice in contexts as diverse as health care and chaplaincy, and around notions of shame, face and visual art,[55] demonstrate the breadth and richness of such approaches. Heather Walton's range of concerns around materiality, aesthetics, gender and different forms of literature and creative writing remind us that 'lived religion' includes cultural practices such as reading, writing, making and viewing art.[56] Empirical work such as Jeff Astley's study of 'ordinary theology',[57] Linda Woodhead's sociological studies of spirituality within and beyond the churches,[58] and a variety of action research projects conducted by Helen Cameron and her colleagues,[59] have all been significant in fleshing out an approach committed to the study of faith as it is actually lived in people's everyday lives. Here at Vrije Universiteit (VU), the Amsterdam Centre for the Study of Lived Religion[60] draws together an impressive range of research and scholarship examining the changing face of religious practice within a contemporary intermingling of cultures and communities. I am excited to be joining this lively research culture.

Where practical theology shines a light on ordinary believers' faith lives, *feminist* practical theology focuses specifically on the neglected voices, experiences and practices of women and girls, critiquing, subverting and expanding androcentric accounts of religion – and, at the same time, helping to sensitize awareness to other neglected voices. For, as Teresa Berger puts it, 'women's real presence continues to be veiled'[61] in the life of the churches, despite the fact that women form the majority in most congregations (the eucharistic reference is, of course, intentional). Feminist practical theologians such as Elaine Graham, Heather Walton and Zoë Bennett in the UK, Bonnie Miller-McLemore, Jeanne Stevenson-Moessner and Carol Lakey Hess in the USA, as well as European colleagues such as Riet Bons-Storm, have all contributed to a growing attention to gender within practical theology.[62] Focused empirical research into the patterns of women's and girls' faith lives has been slower to emerge, despite nearly five decades of feminist theology. This has been a particular focus of my own work, shared by colleagues Anne Phillips and Fran Porter, and by a growing number of researchers within the Symposium on the Faith Lives of Women and Girls. Thus my doctoral study of women's faith narratives sought to critique and expand existing accounts of faith development, particularly that of James Fowler.[63] At around the same time (though we did not know each other then), Fran Porter was conducting doctoral research on women's faith lives in the troubled context of Northern Ireland, highlighting the socially engaged qualities of their faith.[64] Ellen Clark-King's doctoral study, published in the same year, explored the religious experiences and theologies of working-class women in a northern British town, bringing them into creative dialogue with perspectives from feminist theology.[65] A little later, Anne Phillips' doctoral study into the faith lives of girls in a Baptist church context offers a rare example of serious study of childhood female faith.[66] Others have expanded the range of research, focusing on young adult female faith,[67] as well as the neglected lives of elderly women (mainstays of congregations yet rarely accorded serious theological reflection),[68] or considering the significance of women's practices of ritual,[69] reading,[70] silence[71] and of dieting[72] in the shaping of faith. New European research highlights the experience of women in migrant churches[73] and women who may be described as 'flexible believers'.[74] Research such as my colleague Rachel Starr's important study of domestic violence in Argentina as well as the UK expands the context of female faith lives again; and Starr's study is significant for the way in which qualitative, ethnographic research is used to challenge doctrine, in this case doctrines both of marriage and of sin.[75] Such studies illuminate the wide range of practices, both classic and contemporary, through which female faith is enacted, and demonstrate the shifting and complex relations between gender and faith, on the one hand, and between practice and belief, on the other. Moreover, changing patterns of female faith require new interpretative paradigms: a shift from what Manuela Kalsky describes as an 'either/or' to a relational, 'as well as', approach within a rhizomatic network of being.[76] We are back to the web!

I wish I had time to name and honour the whole range of research being conducted by women who belong to the Symposium, and beyond it to the richness of our research culture at Queen's, represented by student and staff colleagues here today with their varying research projects and interests. Whether in systematics, biblical or historical studies or my own field of practical theology, each of us has our own particular focus, lens and context, out of which we generate new questions, hypotheses and tentative readings. Such studies may be small in scale, highly context-specific and appropriately modest in their claims, yet together represent more than the sum of their parts. Together, such micro-analyses offer more and more adequate understandings of the richness of lived faith as it is practised by diverse groups and individuals in different contexts and situations, including the past. No one account can offer more than a glimpse of the bigger picture, yet together they build up a network of knowledge that both creates and reflects the web that connects us all and holds our diverse perspectives in relation.

My own practice as a feminist practical theologian

In the development of my own specific commitments to feminist practical theology – a development that was certainly never planned and that has proceeded piecemeal, in fragmentary fashion and with a good deal of stops and starts – I can look back and discern a number of enduring concerns and characteristics. One has been a commitment to the close scrutiny of the actuality of women's faith lives: to the ways in which women pray, preach, preside, protest and prophesy, form communities of care, create new forms of liturgy, make new theologies. This has been expressed both through a commitment to qualitative research and through an engagement in poetry as a primary means of theological analysis, critique and envisioning.[77]

It may not seem as if qualitative research and poetry have much in common with each other, but I believe they both spring from a similar passion to attend to the particularity, 'thickness' and irreducible texture of human experience, and to seek for traces of the divine within the human ordinary. The poet and ethnographer notice and observe human lives and experiences that others might consider random, odd or of little significance. They seek to capture the life in time, as a painter seeks to capture a particular scene that will not come again. As soon as it is set down, it is gone; yet by being made into something – a poem, a research paper, a lecture – it is lifted up for attention, and has the capacity to contribute to conversation and understanding, to change perceptions and habits, and thus to become part of a larger poesis.

Decades ago, Simone Weil argued that attention is at the core both of any serious study and of the life of prayer,[78] and thus she considered that academic study, pursued with diligence and concentration, was a preparation for prayer if not, itself, a means a prayer. Poetry and qualitative research have been two of the ways in which I have learnt to practise whatever skills of attention I have managed to muster. They have been, and are, primary forms of prayer, although it has taken me a while to recognize this.

Another core commitment within my own work has been the creation, very often with others, of feminist liturgy. We might think of liturgy as the place where the lived experience of seekers and believers and the normative theologies of the church come together with prayer and poetry (or could do). If the corporate, public liturgy of the church is one of the main practices that form and shape the theology and social practice of individual believers, it is a crucial testing ground for what I've been talking about in this lecture. Not only in the words of liturgy (crucial though they are), but in the visual, spatial, aural and material discourses that find expression in buildings, arrangements of bodies and space, music and visual art and symbolism, androcentrism has been the norm. For at least four decades, feminists have been subjecting the liturgical texts and practices of the churches to critical deconstruction, demonstrating the ways in which liturgy has legitimized and reinforced patriarchal patterns of dominance, as well as creating new forms of praying, presiding, preaching and performing liturgy.[79] For all this creative activity, mainstream denominations, in the UK at least, remain largely resistant to feminist reform. In recent liturgical reforms (of which there have been many), despite a plethora of new texts on offer, at most it is possible to detect a tokenistic nod in the direction of feminist prayer, for example, in occasional (and contested) use of feminine imagery for God.[80] Ruether's cry in 1985 that 'women in contemporary churches are suffering from linguistic deprivation and eucharistic famine'[81] is echoed by many today. The experimental liturgies she offered in that text – rites for critical events in women's lives largely ignored by the churches, such as rape and incest, coming out as a lesbian, the onset of menstruation and its cessation in menopause – appear as fresh and startling some thirty years later, precisely because they are still so rare. Yet where such liturgies are created and celebrated, often in small, unofficial settings, they have the capacity to repair the ravages of the broken web.

Conclusion: a celebration of tables

Talk about liturgy and Eucharist brings me back to the image of the table. There are many tables and, as my wise spiritual companion Donald Eadie opines, many hidden altars.[82] There are the tables around which students and colleagues share food and conversation, lives touching lives, both here at VU and at Queen's, where much of our theology is done – as well as the more formal tables of classrooms where we listen, learn and debate. There are tables at home and in cafes and restaurants where friends and family gather to tell stories, dissect the news, try to make sense of events happening around us both near and far. There are refectory tables in hidden monasteries, where monks and nuns eat in companionable silence, and solitary tables where scholars and poets sit, at the midnight hour or in the cold before dawn, reading and writing. There are eucharistic tables in cathedrals, churches and chapels where prayer is offered day after day, and soul food may be found. There are the small, fragile yet resilient gatherings of women, queer folks and others who have not experienced nourishment at the church's tables, making their own communities and ritual. There are tables at which there is never enough, tables which have been swept away by mudslides or floods, tables where those who do not meet the dress code are barred. There are tables in boardrooms, governments and councils where business is done, goods and land and monies exchanged, and decisions that shape all of our lives are made. All of these tables form the substance and practice with which theology has to do, even if theologians may struggle to connect them.

I end this lecture with a poem, not in the hope of gathering all the loose threads into one cohesive whole but as a way of concretizing my vision of what theology can do. A poem is, of course, no more than a fragment in time, a scattering of words on a page; yet a poem can sometimes become a sign of hope, a glimpse of wholeness, 'an act of defiance against the ever-present forces of fragmentariness in our lives'.[83] This poem speaks of 'the table of Christa', the unrecognized feminine divine who is always and everywhere in our midst seeking to break open the bread of life, strengthening those who eat it to carry on the work of making and breaking, rending and mending, in which we all share.

At the table of Christa[84]

The women do not serve
but are served

The children are not silent
but chatter

The menfolk do not dominate
but co-operate

The animals are not shussed away
but are welcomed

At the table of Christa

There is no seat of honour
for all are honoured

There is no etiquette
except the performance of grace

There is no dress code
except the garments of honesty

There is no fine cuisine
other than the bread of justice

At the table of Christa

There is no talk of betrayal
but only of healing and hopefulness

No money changes hands
but all know themselves rich in receiving

Death is in no-one's mind
but only the lust for life

No-one needs to command 'Remember'
for no-one present can ever forget

Notes

1 For the use of the metaphor of 'fragments' in recent theological discourse, see Jacques Pohier, *God in Fragments* (London: SCM Press, 1985); Caroline Walker Bynum, *Fragmentation and Redemption: Essays on Gender and the Human Body in Medieval Religion* (New York: Zone Books, 1994); Giuseppe Ruggieri and Miklós Tomka (eds.), *The Church in Fragments: Towards What Kind of Unity?* (Maryknoll, NY: Orbis, 1997); Zygmunt Bauman, *Life in Fragments: Essays in*

Postmodern Morality (Oxford: Blackwell, 1995); Enda McDonagh, *Faith in Fragments* (Blackrock, Co. Dublin: Columba Press, 1995); Teresa Berger, *Fragments of Real Presence: Liturgical Traditions in the Hands of Women* (New York: Crossoad, 2005); Duncan B. Forrester, *Theological Fragments: Explorations in Unsystematic Theology* (London: T&T Clark, 2005).

2 See, for example, Rozsika Parker, *The Subversive Stitch: Embroidery and the Making of the Feminine* (London: Women's Press, 1984), and the recent resurgence of 'craftivism' by young feminists such as Betsy Greer (ed.), *Craftivism: The Art of Craft and Activism* (Vancouver: Arsenal Pulp Press, 2014), and Sarah Corbett, *How to be a Craftivist: The Art of Gentle Protest* (London: Unbound, 2017).

3 Letty M. Russell, *Church in the Round: Feminist Interpretation of the Church* (Louisville, KY: Westminster John Knox Press, 1993). See also Rita Nakashima Brock, Claudia Camp and Serene Jones (eds.), *Setting the Table: Women in Theological Conversation* (St Louis, MO: Chalice Press, 1995); Cristina Mazzoni, *The Women in God's Kitchen: Cooking, Eating, and Spiritual Writing* (New York: Continuum, 2006); Elisabeth Gerle, 'A New Kitchen for the World – Women, Politics and Religion', *Feminist Theology* 22.1 (2013), pp. 46–57.

4 For example, chapter 8, 'In search of a round table', in Nicola Slee, *Faith and Feminism: An Introduction to Christian Feminist Theology* (London: Darton, Longman & Todd, 2003); 'Banquet', a number of graces and 'Blessing at the table', in Nicola Slee, *Praying Like a Woman* (London: SPCK, 2004); 'Mary bakes bread', 'Mary celebrates the eucharist', 'Eve and Mary in the garden', in Nicola Slee, *The Book of Mary* (London: SPCK, 2007); 'Presiding like a woman', in Nicola Slee and Stephen Burns (eds.), *Presiding Like a Woman* (London: SPCK, 2010), pp. 7–8; and chapter 3, 'The table of women', in Nicola Slee, *Seeking the Risen Christa* (London: SPCK, 2011).

5 Proverbs 9.1–6.

6 Young's commitment to serious scholarly study of early Christianity is enriched by the genres of poetry and preaching, and given sharp critical focus by her lifelong commitment to the inclusion of disabled persons in the life of the church. This is most recently exemplified in Frances Young, *God's Presence: A Contemporary Recapitulation of Early Christianity* (Cambridge: Cambridge University Press, 2013).

7 Rosie Miles, 'So here we are', in Geoffrey Duncan (ed.), *Courage to Love: An Anthology of Inclusive Worship Material* (London: Darton, Longman & Todd, 2002), pp. 78–9. See also Duncan Forrester's suggestion that '[f]ragments may be irritants (the grit in the oyster that gathers a pearl?) ... The grit stands for the awkward, probing, irritating questions that a lively theology should address to church, society and culture.' *Theological Fragments*, pp. 17, 20.

8 Forrester's *Theological Fragments* offers an apologia for a piecemeal, fragmentary practical theology that can nevertheless speak to the public square. See also Marcella Althaus-Reid, 'In the center there are no fragments: Teologiás Desencajadas (reflections on unfitting theologies)', in William F. Storrar and Andrew R. Morton (eds.), *Public Theology for the 21st Century: Essays in Honour of Duncan B. Forrester* (London: T&T Clark, 2002), pp. 365–83, for a searching analysis of how far a theology in fragments can challenge and subvert the hegemony of the 'centre'.

9 Rowan Williams, 'A Nervous Breakdown in the Body Politic', *New Statesman*, 1 May 2016, www.newstatesman.com/politics/uk/2016/05/nervous-breakdown-body-politic (accessed 8.1.20).

10 Robert D. Romanyshyn, *The Wounded Researcher: Research with Soul in Mind* (New Orleans: Spring Journal Books, 2013).

11 Gillian Rose, *The Broken Middle: Out of Our Ancient Society* (Oxford: Blackwell, 1992). See Rachel Mann's reflections on 'the broken middle' in her *Dazzling Darkness: Gender, Sexuality, Illness and God* (Glasgow: Wild Goose, 2012), pp. 131–2, and 'Presiding from the broken middle', in Slee and Burns, *Presiding Like a Woman*, pp. 133–9.

12 Nancy Eisland, *The Disabled God: Toward a Liberatory Theology of Disability* (Nashville: Abingdon Press, 1994). See also Wayne Morris, *Theology without Words: Theology in the Deaf Community* (Aldershot: Ashgate, 2008); John M. Hull, *In the Beginning There Was Darkness: A Blind Person's Conversations with the Bible* (London: SCM Press, 2010); John Swinton, *Dementia: Living in the Memories of God* (London: SCM Press, 2012); Frances Young, *Arthur's Call: A Journey of Faith in the Face of Severe Learning Disability* (London: SPCK, 2014).

13 Forrester, *Theological Fragments*, pp. 10–11.

14 Bauman, *Life in Fragments*, p. 75.

15 Kate Soper, in Bauman, *Life in Fragments*, p. 6.

16 The notion of oscillation as an aspect of practical theology methodology can be found in Mark J. Cartledge, *Practical Theology: Charismatic and Empirical Perspectives* (Milton Keynes: Paternoster, 2003).

17 The reference here is, of course, to the gospel story of the Syrophoenician woman (Mark 7.24–30) and to Elisabeth Schüssler Fiorenza's *Bread Not Stone: The Challenge of Feminist Biblical Interpretation* (Boston, MA: Beacon Press, 1984).

18 Bonnie J. Miller-McLemore, *Christian Theology in Practice: Discovering a Discipline* (Grand Rapids, MI: Eerdmans, 2012), pp. 25–45.

19 Catherine Keller, *From a Broken Web: Separation, Sexism, and Self* (Boston, MA: Beacon Press, 1986).

20 Carol Gilligan, *In a Different Voice: Psychological Theory and Women's Development* (Cambridge, MA: Harvard University Press, 1982).

21 Dorothy Dinnerstein, *The Mermaid and the Minotaur: Sexual Arrangements and Human Malaise* (New York: Harper & Row, 1976).

22 Nancy Chodorow, *The Reproduction of Mothering: Psychoanalysis and the Sociology of Gender* (Berkeley, CA: University of California Press, 1978).

23 Paul Ricœur, *Freud and Philosophy: An Essay on Interpretation* (New Haven, CT: Yale University Press, 1970).

24 See also Michael N. Jagessar's reclamation of the figure of Anancy – who takes various animal, insect and human forms, including the spider – from oral traditions in the Caribbean, to develop a 'spinning theology' and 'Anancy hermeneutics'. While Anancy is traditionally portrayed as male in Caribbean folklore and literature, in Jagessar's writings, s/he takes a multiplicity of gendered and ethnic identities. Michael N. Jagessar, 'Spinning texts – Anancy hermeneutics', in Michael N. Jagessar and Anthony G. Reddie (eds.), *Black Theology in Britain: A Reader* (London: Equinox, 2007), pp.181–6; and 'Spinning theology: Trickster, texts and theology', in Michael N. Jagessar and Anthony G. Reddie (eds.), *Postcolonial Black British Theology: New Textures and Themes* (Peterborough: Epworth, 2007), pp. 124–45.

25 Keller, *Broken Web*, p. 218.

26 Keller, *Broken Web*, p. 218.

27 Adrienne Rich, 'Natural resources', in *The Dream of a Common Language* (New York: W.W. Norton, 1993), p. 64.

28 Although feminist theologians first coined metaphors of the web before Tim

Berners-Lee's invention of the World Wide Web in 1989, contemporary feminists have not been slow to avail themselves of the networking opportunities of the internet to create new forms of feminist community, including online churches, synagogues and mosques, where women can converse and campaign as well as worship in virtual space. For a recent discussion, see Gina Messina-Dysert and Rosemary Radford Ruether (eds.), *Feminism and Religion in the 21st Century: Technology, Dialogue, and Expanding Borders* (New York: Routledge, 2014).

29 Marjorie Procter-Smith, *In Her Own Rite: Constructing Feminist Liturgical Tradition* (Nashville, TN: Abingdon Press, 1990).

30 Pamela Cooper-White, *Braided Selves: Collected Essays on Multiplicity, God, and Persons* (Eugene, OR: Cascade Books, 2011).

31 Mary Grey, *Redeeming the Dream: Feminism, Redemption and Christian Tradition* (London: SPCK, 1989).

32 Joan Alleluia Filemoni-Tofaeono and Lydia Johnson (eds.), *Reweaving the Relational Mat: A Christian Response to Violence against Women from Oceania* (London: Equinox, 2006).

33 Pamela Couture, 'Weaving the web: Pastoral care in an individualistic society', in Jeanne Stevenson-Moessner (ed.), *Through the Eyes of Women: Insights for Pastoral Care* (Minneapolis, MN: Fortress, 1996), pp. 94–106.

34 Christine M. Smith, *Weaving the Sermon: Preaching in a Feminist Perspective* (Louisville, KY: Westminster John Knox Press, 1989).

35 Helen Collins, 'Weaving a web: Developing a feminist practical theology methodology from a Charismatic perspective', in Nicola Slee, Fran Porter and Anne Phillips (eds.), *Researching Female Faith: Qualitative Research Methods* (London: Routledge, 2018), pp. 54–69.

36 Carter Heyward, *The Redemption of God: A Theology of Mutual Relation* (Lanham, MD: University Press of America, 1982); *Our Passion for Justice: Images of Power, Sexuality, and Liberation* (New York: Pilgrim Press, 1984); *Touching Our Strength: The Erotic as Power and the Love of God* (San Francisco, CA: HarperSanFrancisco, 1989).

37 Rita Nakashima Brock, *Journeys by Heart: A Christology of Erotic Power* (New York: Crossroad, 1988).

38 Grey, *Redeeming the Dream*.

39 Sallie McFague describes a model as 'a metaphor with staying power ... a metaphor that has gained sufficient scope so as to present a pattern for relatively comprehensive and coherent explanation'. In *Models of God: Theology for An Ecological, Nuclear Age* (London: SCM Press, 1988), p. 34.

40 Mukti Barton, *Rejection, Resistance and Resurrection: Speaking out on Racism in the Church* (London: Darton, Longman & Todd, 2005).

41 Keller, *From a Broken Web*, p. 223.

42 Now in the Brooklyn Museum of Art, New York, on permanent display.

43 See Judy Chicago, *The Dinner Party: A Symbol of Our Heritage* (New York: Anchor/Doubleday, 1979); Judy Chicago, *The Dinner Party: From Creation to Preservation* (New York: Merrell, 2007); Amelia Jones, *Sexual Politics: Judy Chicago's Dinner Party in Feminist Art History* (Los Angeles, CA: University of California Press, 1996); Jane F. Gerhard, *The Dinner Party: Judy Chicago and the Power of Popular Feminism, 1970–2007* (Athens, GA: University of Georgia Press, 2013).

44 Primordial Goddess, Fertile Goddess, Ishtar, Kali, Snake Goddess, Sophia, Amazon, Hatshepsut, Judith, Sappho, Aspasia, Boadaceia, Hypatia.

45 Marcella, St Bridget, Theodora, Hrosvitha, Trotula, Eleanor of Aquitaine,

Hildegarde of Bingen, Petronilla de Meath, Christine de Pisan, Isabella d'Este, Elizabeth R, Artemissia Gentileschi, Anna van Schurman.

46 Anne Hutchinson, Sacajawea, Caroline Herschel, Mary Wollstonecraft, Sojourner Truth, Susan B. Anthony, Elizabeth Blackwell, Emily Dickinson, Ethel Smyth, Margaret Sanger, Natalie Barney, Virginia Woolf, Georgia O'Keefe.

47 See, for example, Hilton Kramer, 'Art: Judy Chicago's Dinner Party Comes to Brooklyn Museum', *New York Times* 17 October 1980; and Maureen Mullarkey, 'The Dinner Party is a Church Supper: Judy Chicago at the Brooklyn Museum', at www.maureenmullarkey.com/essays/dinnerparty.html (accessed 1.9.17).

48 On the question of women's presence at the Last Supper, see the brief discussion in my *Seeking the Risen Christa*, pp. 42–3, and Dorothy A. Lee, 'Women disciples at the Last Supper', in Judi Fisher and Janet Woods (eds.), *A Place at the Table: Women at the Last Supper* (Melbourne: Melbourne Joint Board of Education, 1993).

49 Maria Harris, *Fashion Me a People: Curriculum in the Church* (Louisville, KY: Westminster John Knox Press, 1989).

50 See, for example, Dorothy C. Bass (ed.), *Practicing Our Faith: A Way of Life for a Searching People* (San Francisco, CA: Jossey-Bass, 1997); Miroslav Volf and Dorothy C. Bass (eds.), *Practicing Theology: Beliefs and Practices in Christian Life* (Grand Rapids, MI: Eerdmans, 2002); Dorothy C. Bass et al., *Christian Practical Wisdom: What It Is, Why It Matters* (Grand Rapids, MI: Eerdmans, 2016).

51 See Nancy T. Ammerman (ed.), *Everyday Religion: Observing Modern Religious Lives* (Oxford: Oxford University Press, 2007); Meredith B. McGuire, *Lived Religion: Faith and Practice in Everyday Life* (Oxford: Oxford University Press, 2008); R. Ruard Ganzevoort and Johan H. Roeland, 'Lived Religion: The Praxis of Practical Theology', *International Journal of Practical Theology* 18.1 (2014), pp. 91–101; R. Ruard Ganzevoort and Srdjan Sremac (eds.), *Lived Religion and the Politics of (In)Tolerance* (London: Palgrave Macmillan, 2017).

52 James W. Fowler, *Stages of Faith: The Psychology of Human Development and the Quest for Meaning* (New York: Harper & Row, 1981).

53 Elaine Graham, *Transforming Practice: Pastoral Theology in an Age of Uncertainty* (London: Mowbray, 1996).

54 Elaine Graham and Stephen R. Lowe, *What Makes a Good City? Public Theology and the Urban Church* (London: Darton, Longman & Todd, 2009); Elaine Graham, *Between a Rock and a Hard Place: Public Theology in a Post-Secular Age* (London: SCM Press, 2013).

55 Stephen Pattison, *Pastoral Care and Liberation Theology* (Cambridge: Cambridge University Press, 1994); *Shame: Theory, Therapy, Theology* (Cambridge: Cambridge University Press, 2000); *Seeing Things: Deepening Relations with Visual Artefacts* (London: SCM Press, 2007).

56 Heather Walton, *Imagining Theology: Women, Writing and God* (London: T&T Clark, 2007); *Literature, Theology and Feminism* (Manchester: Manchester University Press, 2007); *Writing Methods in Theological Reflection* (London: SCM Press, 2014); *Not Eden: Spiritual Life Writing for this World* (London: SCM Press, 2015).

57 Jeff Astley, *Ordinary Theology: Looking, Listening and Learning in Theology* (Aldershot: Ashgate, 2002).

58 For example, Paul Heelas, Linda Woodhead et al., *The Spiritual Revolution: Why Religion is Giving Way to Spirituality* (Oxford: Blackwell, 2005).

59 For example, Helen Cameron, Philip Richter, Douglas Davies and Frances

Ward (eds.), *Studying Local Churches: A Handbook* (London: SCM Press, 2005); Helen Cameron et al., *Talking About God in Practice: Theological Action Research and Practical Theology* (London: SCM Press, 2010); Clare Watkins and Helen Cameron, *Disclosing Church: Ecclesiology in Four Voices* (London: Routledge, 2020).

60 www.frt.vu.nl/en/research/institutes-and-centres/amsterdam-centre-for-the-study-of-lived-religion/index.aspx (accessed 31.3.20).

61 Berger, *Fragments of Real Presence*, p. 3.

62 Key texts include Elaine Graham and Margaret Halsey (eds.), *Life Cycles: Women and Pastoral Care* (London: SPCK, 1993); Riet Bons-Storm, *The Incredible Woman: Listening to Women's Silences in Pastoral Care and Counseling* (Nashville, TN: Abingdon Press, 1996); Moessner, *Through the Eyes of Women*; Carol Lakey Hess, *Caretakers Of Our Common House: Women's Development in Communities of Faith* (Nashville, TN: Abingdon Press, 1997); Bonnie J. Miller-McLemore and Brita L. Gill-Austern (eds.), *Feminist and Womanist Pastoral Theology* (Nashville, TN: Abingdon Press, 1999); Jeanne Stevenson Moessner (ed.), *In Her Own Time: Women and Developmental Issues in Pastoral Care* (Minneapolis, MN: Fortress, 2000); Zoë Bennett Moore, *Introducing Feminist Perspectives on Pastoral Theology* (Sheffield: Sheffield Academic Press, 2002).

63 Nicola Slee, *Women's Faith Development: Patterns and Processes* (Aldershot: Ashgate, 2004).

64 Fran Porter, *It Will Not Be Taken Away From Her: A Feminist Engagement with Women's Christian Experience* (London: Darton, Longman & Todd, 2004). An earlier, more substantial account of the research was published as Fran Porter, *Changing Women, Changing Worlds: Evangelical Women in Church, Community and Politics* (Belfast: Blackstaff Press, 2002).

65 Ellen Clark-King, *Theology by Heart: Women, the Church and God* (Peterborough: Epworth, 2004).

66 Anne Phillips, *The Faith of Girls: Children's Spirituality and Transition to Adulthood* (Farnham: Ashgate, 2011).

67 For example, Kim Wasey, 'Being in communion: Patterns of inclusion and exclusion in young lay women's experiences of Eucharist in the Church of England', in Nicola Slee, Fran Porter and Anne Phillips (eds.), *The Faith Lives of Women and Girls: Qualitative Research Perspectives* (Farnham: Ashgate, 2013), pp. 65–76; Ruth Perrin, 'Searching for sisters: The influence of biblical role models on young women from mainstream and Charismatic Evangelical traditions', in Slee, Porter and Phillips, *Faith Lives of Women and Girls*, pp. 111–19.

68 For example, Abby Day, *The Religious Lives of Older Laywomen: The Last Active Anglican Generation* (Oxford: Oxford University Press, 2017).

69 Jan Berry, *Ritual Making Women: Shaping Rites for Changing Lives* (London: Equinox, 2009).

70 Dawn Llewellyn, *Reading, Feminism, and Spirituality: Troubling the Waves* (London: Palgrave Macmillan, 2015).

71 Alison Woolley, 'Silent gifts: An exploration of relationality in contemporary Christian women's chosen practices of silence', in Slee, Porter and Phillips, *Faith Lives of Women and Girls*, pp. 147–59.

72 Hannah Bacon, *Feminist Theology and Contemporary Dieting Culture: Sin, Salvation and Women's Weight Loss Narratives* (London: T&T Clark, 2019).

73 For example, Alma Lanser, 'Music as Bridge: Young Women in the Immigrant Churches in the Netherlands', *Journal of the European Society of Women in Theological Research* 18 (2010), pp. 193–200. See also Mechteld Jansen and Hijme Stoffels

(eds.), *A Moving God: Immigrant Churches in the Netherlands* (Münster: Lit Verlag, 2008).

74 See Manuela Kalsky, 'Flexible Believers in the Netherlands: A Paradgim Shift toward Transreligious Multiplicity', *Open Theology* 3 (2017), pp. 345–59; also Daan F. Oostveen, 'Multiple Religious Belonging: Hermeneutical Challenges for Theology of Religions', *Open Theology* 3 (2017), pp. 38–47.

75 Rachel Starr, *Reimagining Theologies of Marriage in Contexts of Domestic Violence: When Salvation is Survival* (London: Routledge, 2018).

76 Kalsky, 'Flexible Believers', p. 345.

77 See my chapter, '(W)riting like a woman: In search of a feminist theological poetics', in Gavin D'Costa, Eleanor Nesbitt, Mark Pryce, Ruth Shelton and Nicola Slee, *Making Nothing Happen: Five Poets Explore Faith and Spirituality* (Farnham: Ashgate, 2014), pp. 9–47 and chapter 10 in this book; 'Poetry as feminist research methodology in the study of female faith', in Slee, Porter and Phillips, *Researching Female Faith*, pp. 37–53.

78 Simone Weil, 'Reflections on the right use of school studies with a view to the love of God', *Waiting on God* (Glasgow: Collins Fount, 1977), pp. 66–76, and www.hagiasophiaclassical.com/wp/wp-content/uploads/2012/10/Right-Use-of-School-Studies-Simone-Weil.pdf (accessed 1.9.17).

79 For example, Rosemary Radford Ruether, *Women-Church: Theology and Practice* (New York: Harper & Row, 1985); Procter-Smith, *In Her Own Rite*; Teresa Berger, *Women's Ways of Worship: Gender Analysis and Liturgical History* (Collegeville, MN: Liturgical Press, 1999); Janet H. Wootton, *Introducing a Practical Feminist Theology of Worship* (Sheffield: Sheffield Academic Press, 2000); Sylvia Rothschild and Sybil Sheridan (eds.), *Taking Up the Timbrel: The Challenge of Creating Ritual for Jewish Women Today* (London: SCM Press, 2000); Teresa Berger (ed.), *Dissident Daughters: Feminist Liturgies in Global Context* (Louisville: Westminster John Knox Press, 2001); Anne Elvey, Carol Hogan, Kim Power and Claire Renkin (eds.), *Reinterpreting the Eucharist: Explorations in Feminist Theology and Ethics* (London: Equinox, 2013).

80 The 1999 *Methodist Worship Book* (Peterborough: Methodist Publishing House) has one reference to 'God our Father and our Mother' in a communion service (p. 204), while *Common Worship: Services and Prayers for the Church of England* (London: Church House Publishing, 2000) similarly has one Eucharistic Prayer (G) containing the phrase 'As a mother tenderly gathers her children' (p. 201). Even more experimental and avowedly inclusive groups, such as the Greenbelt Christian Arts Festival, have been slow to embrace feminist liturgy, though I am glad to note the presence of the Red Tent at Greenbelt 2017 and 2018, a dedicated space for feminist prayer, exploration and conversation.

81 Ruether, *Women-Church*, p. 4.

82 Donald Eadie, in personal conversation.

83 Berger, *Fragments of Real Presence*, p. 15.

84 First published in Slee and Burns, *Presiding Like a Woman*, p. 178.

PART 2

A Feminist Practical Theology
of Liturgy and Prayer[1]

How to pray[2]

an empty room
asks to be sat in
for a long while

at different times of day and night
in many weathers
alone without words

perhaps hold an object in your hands
   a stone
   a cup
   a length of beads

or place something well chosen
on the floor or a window ledge
where you will look at it
for a long time

   a cup
   a vase
   a stone
   a piece of wood

without asking or telling anything
imposing your own shape on the emptiness
as lightly as possible

leave and enter
many times
without disturbing its silences

gradually over many years
a room thus entered and departed
will teach you how to furnish and dispose of
the paraphernalia of a life

Notes

1 All the pieces in this section were written and published before Ashley Cocksworth's superb introduction to the theology and practice of prayer was published. *Prayer: A Guide for the Perplexed* (London: Bloomsbury, 2018) deserves to be read and studied by all students and practitioners of prayer.

2 First published in Gavin D'Costa, Eleanor Nesbitt, Mark Pryce, Ruth Shelton and Nicola Slee, *Making Nothing Happen: Five Poets Explore Faith and Spirituality* (Farnham: Ashgate, 2014), p. 32.

Poetry, Psalmody and Prayer in Feminist Perspective

This piece was given as an address – and still has the feel of a spoken piece, which I have not attempted to smooth out – to the Modern Church Conference in July 2017, subsequently published in Modern Believing *59.3 (2018), pp. 209–17 under the title 'Getting God through Poetry and Prayer'. The topic of the conference was 'God: None, One, Three or Many?' and I was asked to speak particularly about feminist approaches to God.*

Prayer as primary and urgent

Liturgy and prayer are primary, not secondary, arenas for theology – core sites where we wrestle with the nature of God and the nature of human personhood, truth and reality. It's not as if we work out our theology first and then translate it into appropriate forms of prayer. Or, if that is what happens, it is not surprising that our prayer is lifeless and flat and has no surprises within it, and that our theology is similarly dry and lacks the infusion of spiritual life. No, liturgy and prayer are primary; they shape and form us. A melting pot of theology, they are places where we discover who God is or can be, what kind of God is sayable and prayable.

Liturgy and prayer are also urgent. We cannot wait on the theologians or philosophers to find language for us. We need to cry out to God, and to one another, daily – not only of our need for bread, but also of our hunger for truth and justice, our awareness of our complicity and half-heartedness, our longing to worship what is beyond us. As Marjorie Procter-Smith has put it, our naming of God in prayer is 'urgent and primary because liturgy is not reflection but address; an encounter is presumed'.[1] We may not know what we think or believe about God, or even that God *is*, yet we know our urgent need to pray – alone, and with others.

In my own experience, I find myself less and less sure about what I believe about the nature and reality of God – am I a realist, of the critical variety, an agnostic or a non-realist? – and find my earlier experiential sense of the presence of God more and more displaced by the sense of God's absence (although I suspect this may be partly a reflection of my absorption in a very busy working life, my lack of presence to my own life – if I cannot be present to myself, how on earth can I expect God to be?). And yet, the need and impulse to pray, to address the absent, unknown, mysterious source of my life and of all life, both in words and in large amounts of silence, alone and with others, is as strong as it has ever been. And in and around the prayer, there are unexpected glimpses of transcendence, a sense of being grasped or addressed by the Holy One, intimations of otherness, and the gifting of new insight and awareness.

Psalms, prayers and poetry

I find Walter Brueggemann's *Praying the Psalms*[2] to be enormously suggestive and helpful in understanding the primacy and urgency of prayer not only for theology but for the life of both humanity and God. Brueggemann analyses the psalms as an embodiment of authentic prayer, an expression of language working at the limits, a series of speech acts that evoke something quite new in the relation between God and humanity, God and the pray-er of these words. He shows how the psalms are profoundly dialogic texts, rooted in the relationship between God and Israel, and how this covenantal relationship is foundational and primary, even when the psalms seem to challenge it most severely. The psalms are not uttered from the settled place of equilibrium but out of profound disequilibrium and the search for new orientation. Brueggemann describes their language as 'strident, subversive and intense', born out of the rawness rather than the smoothness of life. Whether cries of lament, complaint or vengeance on enemies, or of ecstatic praise and thanksgiving for deliverance, the psalms are uttered at the limits of life. 'It is the experiences of life that lie beyond our conventional copings that make us eloquent and passionate and drive us to address ourselves to the Holy One.'[3]

Many of us will recognize how our own most authentic prayer is born out of such urgency and need. Feminist liturgy, like the liturgies of other groups seeking liberation and empowerment, emerged in the late 1960s and 70s out of just such limit situations: out of anger and rage at women's erasure and invisibility, out of acute pain and lament at the losses suffered not only by individual women through abuse and oppression but by entire generations of women whose history and traditions have been erased. Feminist liturgy was born out of protest and resistance, but also out of a claiming of agency and power, an assertion of the need and right to name what had never been named. A very real question for me and other feminists within the church is how we can pray now, within the confused and shifting currents of third- and fourth-wave feminism,[4] when some of that original urgency and rage has been dissipated by the achievements of feminism but also by fatigue and boredom.

Of course, we do not live our lives entirely in the liminal places of desperation or ecstasy (although some people perhaps do, something we should never forget), and we cannot always pray out of such places. We need forms of daily prayer that can serve in the ordinariness, the mundaneness and, yes, the equilibrium of settled life. But such prayer must not lose touch with the liminal, unsettled and unsettling edges of raw terror, need and intensity. Perhaps this is one reason – the main reason – why we need to pray the psalms, and why the psalms have become the bedrock for daily liturgical prayer in the churches. It is also a way of praying faithfully with those who do live on the edges. As Brueggemann suggests, the challenge for those of us praying the liminal prayers of the psalms who are not, ourselves, inhabiting the liminal places, is to pray them in such a way that we do not evacuate them of their rawness and rough edges. He envisages something quite extraordinary happening in the liminal spaces reflected in and created by praying the psalms and the countless other such prayers that the psalms have generated down the generations: a genuine, reciprocal encounter in which both God and humanity are changed by the exchange. In the psalms, God is summoned to respond to the urgency of Israel's situation – one of oppression and near-annihilation – through the force of complaint and lament. The character of God here, Brueggemann suggests, is 'supple and open, exposed to risk and placed in jeopardy',[5] just as the one who prays in the limit situation is also exposed to risk and jeopardy.

Perhaps the best way I can describe how this function of prayer happens in my life is by analogy with what happens when words are given in the writing of a poem. What prompts one to write in the first place is mysterious and often arises unbidden, although poetry like prayer is a discipline, a craft as well as something given. What often feels like something sacred, miraculous, gracious and gratuitous is the way that the poem unfolds new knowing that, before the writing of the poem, I did not know I knew. The poem births words and images that, themselves, birth knowledge, awareness, insight – a glimpse into the depths of things.

I often say that my poems know far more than I do, that it can take my brain and body years to catch up with the knowing of the poem: perhaps because such knowing comes out of the subconscious, similar to the knowledge that is birthed in dreams. And both are similar to the knowing – which may often be as much of an unknowing – that is birthed in genuine liturgy and prayer.

Praying within and around the Lord's Prayer

How do we pray – genuinely pray – the prayer central to all Christian traditions, prayed by Christians around the globe today, one of the few liturgical texts we hold in common: the Lord's Prayer? How do we pray this prayer, in public as well as private, in ways that do not reinforce what

Gail Ramshaw calls 'the myth of the crown', which feminists see as imbuing the prayer and much else in Christian tradition?[6] Depicting the divine in metaphors and language of powerful males – in the case of the Lord's Prayer, in both fatherhood and kingdom imagery – reinforces male power and implicitly places women, children and other marginalized people at the base of a hierarchical, patriarchal, monarchical pyramid.

I have found myself, almost by accident, writing a sequence of prayers responding to and wrestling with the Lord's Prayer. They are not intended, mostly, for public prayer, although one or two of them might be suitable for the public assembly. Rather, they are dialogues, laments, cries to the Father-Mother, Abba-Amma God of Jesus from my own life and context and situation. They all begin with the address 'Abba Amma' or one or other of these two parental forms. Many of them are working with my own specific inheritance of my relationship to my own human parents: it is impossible to pray the Lord's Prayer without drawing deeply on our own relationships with our parents, whether knowingly or not.[7]

In addressing God as 'Abba Amma', I'm also drawing on the early desert tradition of the abbas and ammas who left the cities in protest at their corruption and sought remote desert places to live out lives of solitariness and asceticism, yet in community. The desert fathers and mothers laid the foundations for the monastic tradition, which has sourced and fuelled Christian prayer for centuries, and shaped public liturgical prayer profoundly. This tradition itself – the desert tradition and monasticism – is by no means unproblematic for a feminist, enshrining what can be experienced as dangerous and dualistic theologies of the body, sexuality and femininity itself. So in praying to the 'Abba Amma' God of the desert fathers and mothers, I am wrestling with this inheritance as well as honouring and blessing it.

Here I present a couple of my 'reworkings' (I do not call them 'versions') of the Lord's Prayer – not so much as an example of what can be prayed in public, but more as an expression of the search for authentic prayer about which I have been talking. No one version of this, or any, prayer is likely to be adequate for public or even private use: no one prayer is complete, or perfect. In the praying of it, it may well become redundant. But every prayer we make, however inadequate, is an opening, an invitation, a summons to the divine and to our own best selves; a voting with our lips and our lives for wholeness and justice and mercy and forgiveness which we know we desperately need. It creates a space within which what we pray for can become more of a reality – if only marginally – than it was before.

The first reworking is perhaps the closest I have come to a version, or paraphrase, of the Lord's Prayer. It keeps fairly close to the structure of the original, but reworks words and phrases in more contemporary terms. Classic religious terms that are most problematic to feminists – father, kingdom, power, glory – are avoided and replaced by other images – abba, amma, feeding and banquet imagery.

Abba, amma: source from whom I came.
I reverence your name.
Your child indeed,
I pray you to meet my need
from your bountiful store:
neither less nor more.
I confess my greed, the way I feed
my desires which then inflate my need,
blotting out care of the self and awareness of the other –
my sister, father, mother, brother.
Out of the largesse of your grace,
give us all a place
at your overflowing table.
Feed us, that we may become able
to quieten our own hungers,
attend to others, both near ones and strangers.
May we so linger in love
at your banquet – no hurry to move –
until we are filled with your joy
rising within and between us – pure, unalloyed.

The next reworking addresses the prayer to 'amma' only, and draws obviously on maternal imagery: the birthing from the womb, the gaze between mother and infant that establishes the maternal relationship, the sense of belonging to the family of siblings born from the same womb, and the way in which maternal love is often unseen and 'disregarded'.

Amma
born from your womb
I gaze at you
your image mirrored in me
Of your beholding there is no end
you hold my life in the hollow of your hand
I return it to you
from where it is given back to me
all that is yours in me
released, set free
shared with those you've given me
to love and forgive
and hurt and learn to love again
until, pardoned and freed
we learn to let go our need
to be needed, noticed, applauded
In your disregarded, unrewarded life

poured out again and again, time without end
we'll find our way home
back to the origin and source of all we've become
children of one mother
sister to all and brother.

In the third reworking to be presented here, I work with the desert tradition
of the abbas and ammas to explore my experience of the absence of God,
which is at one and the same time a searing deprivation and an attraction
into the otherness of the divine, and into the nothingness of the prayer
encounter. Images are drawn from the spacious emptiness and remoteness
of the desert, uniting imagery from the psalms and Song of Songs with the
writings of the desert saints.

Abba, Amma,
You are the one who has gone a long way from me.
You left the city with its passageways and thoroughfares
towards the secret spaces of the desert crevices.
Abba, Amma,
I hunger for your presence as a pelican in the wilderness.
I have paced the dark streets of my memories
searching for the signs of your kindness.
You have taken yourself away from me.
Only the lingering scent of your fragrance is suspended
in the air, as the moon, a huge pale orb –
luminous with an absence
more terrible than the presence
of an army of lovers.

These are only three of a growing sequence of responses to the Lord's
Prayer. I hope each one is authentic in itself, but they also work together,
speaking to each other and offering a theological conversation on prayer as
well as a range of prayer offerings. They take different forms and moods,
enfleshing the prayer relationship with the Abba-Amma of Jesus in diverse
ways. I hope they might encourage others to experiment with their own
reworkings of the Lord's Prayer.

In authentic prayer, something new is birthed and enacted, something –
or perhaps we should say, someone – that we did not and could not know
before or outside prayer. Like the new knowing of a poem, this is soul-food
that nourishes us deeply and we receive it from the hand of God, even the
God we hardly believe in or know. We are changed by this encounter:
enlivened, comforted, strengthened, our cynicism or despair eased, our
fatigue consoled. We discover again that God is beyond our comprehen-
sion yet graspable, knowable, haveable or gettable in the only way we can

know and have and get it – in the present moment, in the lived reality of prayer.

Notes

1 Marjorie Procter-Smith, *In Her Own Rite: Constructing Feminist Liturgical Tradition* (Nashville, TN: Abingdon Press, 1990), p. 88.

2 Walter Brueggemann, *Praying the Psalms: Engaging Scripture and the Life of the Spirit* (Eugene, OR: Cascade, 2007).

3 Brueggemann, *Praying the Psalms*, p. 6.

4 The first wave of feminism is identified with the struggle for women's suffrage in the nineteenth and early twentieth century; second-wave feminism refers to the emergence of modern, radical feminist critique of family, society and religion from the 1960s onwards; third-wave feminism, developing from the 1990s onwards, refers to the engagement with diversity within feminism. Some now speak of a 'fourth wave', characterized by the use of new technologies by young(er) women to further feminist causes.

5 Brueggemann, *Praying the Psalms*, p. xvi.

6 Gail Ramshaw, *God Beyond Gender* (Minneapolis, MN: Fortress, 1995), p. 59.

7 The prayers that follow appear, with many others, in *Abba, Amma: Improvisations on the Lord's Prayer* (Norwich: Canterbury Press, forthcoming).

3

How Many Ways are there of Praying?

This is the more or less verbatim text of a talk I gave to an SCM conference on prayer, at Nottingham University in February 2011. It was one of those occasions that gave me the opportunity to think through my actual practice of prayer and my understanding of how prayer is part of my life, in a way that was illuminating and helpful for me – and I hope may have been for others. The theme of integration of life that I come to at the end of the talk is picked up by the following chapter in a way that problematizes it rather more. A case of saying one thing in one talk/article and complexifying it in another!

Prayer as traditioned discipline

I am waking to the voice of Sue McGregor on the *Today* programme. It's cold outside, dimly light behind the curtains. I force myself up, throw on my dressing gown, pad into the bathroom. Downstairs, I put on the kettle, feed the cats, make a large mug of tea; I light the dozen or so candles in and around the grate and settle down to say my morning office. Or I should say, 'sing my morning office', because I do largely sing it, using plainchant I've learnt over the years.

I use a variation of the Franciscan daily office, leavened with some of the Malling hymns, bits and pieces of Jim Cotter, Janet Morley and anything else that comes to hand. When I get to the intercessions at the end of the office, I do an informal kind of Ignatian examen, reflecting back on the past 24 hours and praying for the individuals, situations and issues I've been engaged with. I also have several lists of people and places I pray for – the USPG prayer list, which keeps me in touch with Anglican churches around the world, the Birmingham diocesan prayer diary, and my own personal list. Once the office is over, I sit in silence for five, ten, fifteen, maybe twenty minutes, repeating some short phrase from the morning's psalm that seems to speak to me, as a way of anchoring me in the silence.

I blow the candles out, make breakfast, move into my day. Later on, in the evening, I may do a shorter, simple evening or night office, though I'm a bit more erratic about that.

Here is one way of beginning to answer the question, 'What does prayer mean to me, and how do I do it?' It's a quintessentially Anglican response, and what I do each morning isn't hugely different from what thousands of Anglican clergy, religious and lay folk do, day in, day out, in churches, monasteries, homes, hospitals and universities around the world. And that's part of its power and point, of course – that what I'm doing on my own every morning in Stirchley is part of something much vaster, more ancient and enduring than my modest efforts at prayer, and both holds me and connects me in my praying to the whole Christian community, living and departed, in time and in eternity.

The Anglican pattern of daily offices, whether said alone or in community, is a shorn-down version of the ancient monastic offices, still to be found in monasteries and religious communities around the world. It's a tradition that I am deeply grateful for and it has taught me much about prayer. It affirms rhythm and order, regularity, connection to the cycle of the seasons; it is deeply scriptural, drawing heavily on the Bible for its content; it is rooted in a profound awareness of community, it goes on whether I am doing it or not, and if for some reason I am too late out of bed to say the office I am comforted to know that many others will have prayed it near me in Birmingham as well as in other places of the world.

So I want to say this tradition of prayer is holy and good. But I also want to say it is problematic. It's problematic, I think, less for what it affirms than for what it excludes and denies. For, of course, it is a model that assumes a condition of life that is not open to many, based as it is on the historical experience of an elite caste of mostly male, celibate priests and the few honorary women – nuns, single women – who could share their lifestyle. I have the freedom and luxury to maintain this kind of prayer life because I am sufficiently well off to enjoy solitude and space on a regular basis (I'm not sharing a room or house with 11 other people), I am childless and live a relatively patterned life; I don't work night shifts or have small children to feed and get off to school in the morning.

And probably most of you don't, either, at the moment. But that doesn't mean we shouldn't be aware of the limitations of this approach to prayer.

Prayer in and through daily life

So let's start again.

I'm pitching into my day, immersing myself in the task, whatever the task is, trying to give myself as wholeheartedly to it as I can. Perhaps I'm listening to a middle-aged woman who has come to see me for spiritual accompaniment. She is talking about her grief and anger at the loss of her job, the way she's been treated by her boss, her bewilderment and confusion and how that is impacting on all the family. I'm trying to listen out for what she's saying and what she's not saying, keeping as close as I can to the pattern of her pain and her search to make sense of it, trying to open up a safe space for her to pour herself into, a space in which – we both believe – God is actively present to hear, to comfort, to save. At the end of this session, we will spend a few moments in prayer, but it's not just those moments that are the prayer, it's the whole meeting and listening and endeavouring to hold before the person who has come the reality of the presence and love of God in her life, and in our shared conversation.

Or I'm teaching, with some of my colleagues, a class of MA students at Queen's, on a Wednesday evening. We're thinking about contextual theology and what it means to read the Bible from markedly different contexts. It's a lively, eager, diverse group of gifted and experienced learners from different countries and Christian traditions who have come together to be trained for leadership. I'm trying to offer my own partial, provisional knowledge, speaking truthfully about what it is I know and have learnt, sharing such scholarship and wisdom of others as I've had the time and privilege to imbibe. I'm holding the space, encouraging students to listen carefully and respectfully to each other, to speak out their questions, insights and confusions, to enquire diligently of and with one another, as well as of me and of the particular subject matter (subject that matters, as my old friend Maria Harris used to describe it[1]) we're dealing with. We, too, a group of Christian learners and teachers, will end the evening with a short act of worship; but again, I want to say the whole enterprise of what we are about is akin to prayer, is preparation for prayer, or is a fruit of prayer, if not directly prayer itself. Simone Weil compares the quality of disciplined attention that characterizes prayer with the intentional, studied attention we bring to learning, arguing that in engaging wholeheartedly in study, we learn the capacity to attend to the other with all our heart, mind and will, which is the essence of prayer.[2] So reading a difficult book with our full attention, giving it time and serious consideration, or wrestling in a lecture with a difficult idea that we can't fully comprehend, refusing to choose the easy options in modules or courses (something Adrienne Rich said was particularly important for women students),[3] drafting and redrafting an essay until we feel as satisfied with it as we can – all of these are self-offerings that school us in the offering of prayer.

And if that sounds a bit cerebral, I don't want to leave the body out of this account, for we pray with our bodies as well as our minds and hearts, and our bodies, treated aright, will help us to pray. Far from needing to be curbed, denied or repressed, our bodies, if we listen to them and gently love them, can I think teach us how to pray. For the body never lies, storing within itself memories of all that has happened to us, holding our grief as well as our ecstasy, the repository of all our most basic as well as our most profound longings, hungers and desires. Our bodies, given a chance, will teach us how to practise stillness, how to centre ourselves, how to listen out for the basic rhythm of our lives. Other traditions have often been far better than 'poor little talkative Christianity' at harnessing the wisdom of the body, but there have always been those in our tradition, too, who have known that the body is not the enemy of prayer but its friend.

So, in the middle of a day, or in the middle of working on something like this talk, when I'm getting tired and my mind is faltering, if I've got enough wisdom, I'll stop what I'm doing, down tools, and go for a walk – ten minutes out through the working-class estate where we live in Stirchley to the local shop or post office, or out along the canal and tree-lined roads of plush Edgbaston, if I'm at Queen's. My feet slap along the pavement, the psalm mantra may repeat in my mind, my breathing will quicken, my body relax and pick up a new energy, my stale mind let go and walk itself into new creativity. If I stay at my computer, stuck in my head, I'll just grind myself down into exhaustion and the writing is likely to go badly. If I can get up and get moving, preferably outside, in the fresh air, my body will walk its way into freedom and new life.

Prayer at liminal moments of life

So far, so good. There's the prayer we learn from the particular ecclesial and theological traditions that have nurtured us – in my case, Anglicanism, monasticism, in particular the Benedictine and Franciscan traditions, but also liberation, feminist and queer theologies, and a whole lot more besides. One of the great things about the era we live in is that there's a much greater awareness of the huge wealth of spiritual wisdom and riches from many different Christian traditions, let alone other religious and spiritual traditions we can draw from.

Then there's the prayer we learn and practise in our everyday lives, in and through our work, our relationships, our encounters with others, our daily patterns of walking, eating, cooking, resting and sleeping – all of which can be forms of implicit prayer, training or preparation for prayer, or the outworking, the expression of what we learn in more formal prayer practices.

But there is more to prayer than the learnt disciplines of prayer and the prayer that is woven into the everyday. There is also the prayer of agony and of ecstasy, the liminal times in our lives when something out of the ordinary – whether wonderful or terrible – disrupts the quotidian, and pitches us into another realm, far outside our normal range of feeling, thinking, acting, living – and of praying. These are the times that test our prayer – times when we learn what our lives are really made of, and what it is that endures when much is stripped away. These are also times that form our prayer – times of grace as well as testing, when we learn what it is to live from the depths, and when we discover resources of courage, hope and love that we did not know we had in us – and perhaps, in truth, we did not have in us, but have been given to us when we most needed them.

So let me speak of love breaking out into this middle-aged woman's life at a time and in a way least expected, and also of the unexpected wounding and testing of love that came in the aftermath of making my vowed commitment to my partner – and of the prayer learned through such experience. And let me do so in the language of poetry – a language that is perhaps most capable of giving form and expression to those experiences that push at the edges of ordinary discourse.

Here's a poem entitled 'Charis' (the Greek word for 'grace'), which I wrote when newly in love with my partner Rosie. It describes, in the sacramental language of religious rites, the erotic encounter of lovers:

> You touched my flesh
> with infinitely tender embrace:
> the touch of charis,
> the caress of grace,
> the chrism of bliss.
>
> You sought my face
> with your lips,
> came closer than breathing
> to give me the kiss of peace.
> No one loved me like this.
>
> You opened my body
> like rain parting leaves,
> like the blessing of oil
> on a dying man's brow.
> You blessed, broke and offered
> the bread of your body.
> You ate of my flesh,
> you drank of my juice.
> You forsook every other
> and cleaved unto me.
> We are flesh of one flesh.
> We are forged of one will.
> We are still,
> in the heart,
> in the bone,
> in the dark,
> in the tongueless,
> wondering place
> where two are made one.
> We are gift,
> we are grace,

we are the face of love.
We are one, we are one.[4]

Lovers of God have drawn on the experience and language of erotic desire for millennia to express and evoke their devotion to God. And human lovers, of all beliefs and none, have long sensed that to touch the human beloved in authentic embrace – in tenderness, trust and radical openness – is also, somehow, to touch sacred reality. Lovers, when they are making love, are hardly thinking of God or of prayer (and it would seem an offence to the human beloved if they were – rather like fantasizing about making love with someone else when you are in the arms of your partner); yet it is surely not blasphemous to say that, when we experience profound bodily union with another, we are given a foretaste of the heavenly banquet and we know for an instant something of the intensity of divine love and longing for the universe. Sex isn't necessarily prayer, but surely the experience of bodily love is one of the places where human beings learn what it is, at one and the same time, to transcend the ego in reaching out to the other, and to receive the self as the gift of the other. Perhaps in making love we learn, in a limited way, something of the free, mutual exchange at the heart of the life of the Trinity, and we are invited into that depth of loving exchange.

But to love another person, and God in that person, and that person in God, is also to open the self to vulnerability and the potential for pain. The free gift of the self to another, and the openness to receive the life of the other into one's own heart and body, means that one is unprotected from the wounding of love. Every love affair is a paschal journey into suffering, loss and death at some level, and most of us know something of that, even if we haven't actually had to lose a human partner. In and through this human paschal process, we are drawn, if we will, to enter more deeply into the paschal process of the life of God – the loving and losing that are at the heart of God's giving to the world in and through Jesus.

There's a long Passiontide sequence in my book *Seeking the Risen Christa*,[5] which I wrote after a lengthy period when Rosie became very seriously ill only two weeks after we had celebrated our civil partnership. She went in for what should have been a routine operation, only to get into serious complications due to a tear in her ureter, leading to a leakage of urine into her abdomen that was not picked up for some time by the medics, despite endless trips to the hospital when it was clear that she was not recovering from surgery but was, in fact, getting steadily worse. Eventually, several months after the original surgery, she was moved to the care of the urology ward and operated on to mend the tear – a delicate procedure, but one that allowed her finally to start recovering. But not before she had experienced a great deal of physical pain and anxiety, and I had become increasingly alarmed at her rapid physical deterioration.

The poem sequence uses the framework of the gospel passion narrative of Jesus' journey from Last Supper to the agony in the garden, his betrayal, crucifixion and death to chart something of our own journey from the carefree delight and ecstasy of our eucharistic banquet as we made our tryst in the company of many guests, through the confusion and agony of Rosie's physical pain, and my own frequent journeys to visit her in hospital where I washed her body in gestures reminiscent of Jesus' footwashing, and traipsed up and down the hospital corridors day after day, and watched and waited by her bedside as the women in the gospel narratives watched and waited beside the dying body of Jesus.

During the long saga of Rosie's illness, I didn't have sufficient spare creative energy or perspective to write anything so formed as this poem sequence eventually became. I did, however, pray intensely and continuously, out of my weakness and fear, not I think primarily for Rosie to be healed, not precisely for anything in particular, just for mercy to keep on doing what had to be done (carrying on with work, keeping the house in a semblance of order, answering the phone and responding to friends and family) and for being what I needed to be with and for Rosie. Although some people said to me, 'Don't try to pray, we'll pray for you', I experienced an intense craving to pray, just as I had an intense craving for small daily doses of beauty (half an hour in the local art gallery or botanical gardens) to offset the ugliness of the hospital and, I suppose, the precariousness of Rosie's condition. I discovered I could only take limited amounts of being in the hospital by her side; I was far less heroic than my own fantasies about myself, and my need to pray was one of the ways in which I protected and restored my ravaged, frightened self. I'm intensely grateful for all the years of saying my prayers that, at that critical moment in my life, I could fall back on to and collapse into. I discovered that the pattern held, that I was somehow held – *we* were held – in the everlasting arms. Such knowledge didn't guarantee any particular outcome, but I knew that, whatever the outcome, the reality of divine presence and care was constant.

The heady experience of falling in love, leading over time to the celebration of our vows, followed in quick succession by Rosie's illness and the all-too-quick testing of my vows, became the site where I had to make my own paschal journey. The sequence of poems placed my own experience of passion, in all its senses, next to the passion of Jesus, and was its own form of praying, as my writing often is (and is for many theologians and poets – I do not wish to claim anything unique).

Prayer as locus of integration

There are many aspects of prayer I haven't spoken about – the prayer of anger and protest, of wrestling with God, the prayer of boredom and distraction, the prayer in which the absence of God is far more real than divine presence. All of these have been and are included in my experience of prayer. I've discovered that, in trying to think and speak about prayer, one is, in fact, trying to speak and think about the whole of one's life – and in one talk, it's not possible to say everything!

Whatever else prayer may be, it is the workshop in which we sift and filter the whole of our lives and try to become present to God in the whole of life, in as intentional, attentive way as we can manage. However we do or don't do it, prayer is a way of being as real before the face of God, and of ourselves, as we can muster – and of offering all that we are to God for healing, renewal, transformation. Prayer therefore, is a place of integration, of bringing together all the many threads of our lives, which can seem terribly fragmented and disjointed, and of weaving them into a unity. That isn't something we do ourselves, fundamentally, but it's a work prayer does in us and through us – and something that only becomes apparent over a long stretch of time, as we look back and recognize how there has been a constant thread weaving its way in and out of our lives, even when we didn't think we were consciously praying. Perhaps, by the time we reach our life's end, we will be able to say 'everything was prayer', which is another way of saying, 'God was present to act and save in all things', nothing was outside the love and saving power of God. In the end, it is God who is at work praying in us, and God is faithful to God's own loving purposes – so, while we may feel that we fail in our prayer and are pretty useless at it, the Spirit of God is to be trusted in her mysterious work in our hearts and our lives.

Notes

1 More formally expressed in her wonderful *Teaching as Religious Imagination: An Essay in the Theology of Teaching* (San Francisco, CA: Harper & Row, 1987, p. 167), where she defines teaching as 'the incarnation of subject matter in ways that lead to the revelation of subject matter'.

2 Simone Weil, 'Reflections on the right use of school studies with a view to the love of God', *Waiting on God* (Glasgow: Collins Fount, 1977).

3 Adrienne Rich, 'Claiming an education' and 'Taking women students seriously', in *On Lies, Secrets and Silence: Selected Prose 1966–1978* (London: Virago, 1980), pp. 231–5, 237–45.

4 Originally published in Geoffrey Duncan (ed.), *Courage to Love: An Anthology of Inclusive Worship Material* (London: Darton, Longman & Todd, 2002), pp. 185–6, and subsequently in Nicola Slee, *Praying Like a Woman* (London: SPCK, 2004), p. 110.

5 'Eucharist', 'Betrayal', in Nicola Slee, *Seeking the Risen Christa* (London: SPCK, 2011), p. 61.

4

God-language in Public and Private Prayer: A Place for Integrating Gender, Sexuality and Faith

This article began life as a workshop offered at the Embodied Ministry Conference, July 2014, at Ripon College, Cuddesdon, and was subsequently published in Theology and Sexuality 20.3 (2014), pp. 225–37.

Introduction

Whatever else defines the work of the church and the work of theological education, prayer is at the heart of it. Whatever else Christians do when they gather together, they pray. This is true, in a more concentrated and intense way, in institutions of theological formation. Prayer, in its public form as liturgy, is one of five ecclesial forms identified by Maria Harris[1] in her model of church (based on the description of the early church in Acts 2), which, along with didache (teaching), kerygma (proclamation), koinonia (community) and diakonia (ministry/service), make up the curriculum of the church – the forms in and through which the church learns to become what it is, the body of Christ. While recognizing the importance of the other four forms in shaping what the church practises and performs in relation to gender and sexuality, in what follows I seek to work towards some insights into how prayer may be a site of integrating gender, sexuality and faith for those who pray. In doing so, I seek to problematize and scrutinize the notion of integration as well as bringing to bear a hermeneutic of suspicion upon notions or practices of prayer that reinforce the dominant hetero-patriarchy.[2] After considering the relationship between images of God, prayer and the sense of self in the pray-er, I go on to explore the particular ways in which prayer may be a site of integration of the erotic, the obstacles to such integration and the role of images and metaphors in the work of prayer. I argue for prayer that engages with a multiplicity of embodied, erotic and queer images of God (and particularly Christ), as necessary to the complex work of personal and political integration with which prayer is charged as well as gesturing towards the fullness and mystery of God who both inhabits and transcends the limitations of metaphorical discourse about the divine.

The relation between prayer, God-image, gender and sexuality

There is no simple one-to-one correspondence between prayer and life, the images of God employed in prayer and the psychological maturity of the pray-er(s), any more than it is possible to predicate a direct and uni-lateral relationship between dominant images of God in society and the sociological patterning of gender in that religion or culture. For Christians, prayer is a mystery in which the primary activity is the work of the Spirit in the life of believer. If Christians believe (and the majority probably do) that prayer effects good in the life of the one who prays and also in the wider world, this is a secondary good. The primary good is the activity of prayer itself, although even to describe it as 'an activity' may be a betrayal of the conviction that prayer is first and foremost God's activity in the life of the believer, not the converse. Nevertheless, from its human side, prayer can be described as a form and means of attention, a means of bringing as much disciplined attention of which one is capable to one's own life in all its myriad commitments and distractions, to the complex, changing life of the world in which one is set, to the lives of others with whom one is connected both far and near, living and dead, and to God present in each of these.

Even if one holds that the work of prayer is gratuitous, for its own sake and not for any good that it may obtain, this does not mean that prayer does not, actually, bear fruit – for good or for ill – in the lives of those who pray and in the corporate body. 'The symbol of God functions', as Elizabeth Johnson expresses it;[3] the terms and images of our prayer are profoundly formative not only of thought but also of desire, will and action. Speaking of images of Jesus, Robert Beckford names them ideological constructions which 'function as systems of meaning interpreting life'.[4] The formative power of images of God may be more powerful in language addressed *to* the divine than that used *about* the divine, for in prayer the critical consciousness may be less to the fore, and the powerfully subconscious shaping of desire, imagination and motivation may be all the more pervasive than in more conceptual discourse.

Johnson distinguishes between the psychological, sociological and theo-logical functioning of the God-symbol. The God-image has profound psychological impact on individuals and communities: where God is spoken of only in male terms, men come to believe themselves to be closer to the divine, more entitled to represent the divine and speak on behalf of God, while women are regarded (and regard themselves) as less in the image of God, less worthy of divine service. This is supported by Jann Aldrege-Clanton's study of the relationship between gender concepts of God and the self-concept of women, in which she found that the exclusive use of masculine God images correlated with women's feelings of unworthiness, whereas women who conceived of God as androgynous or transcendent of gender were more creative, assertive, aspirational and had higher levels of self-esteem.[5] Where God is imaged largely in terms of (male) potency, power and control, and humanity imaged in contrasting terms of weakness and vulnerability, this may have destructive consequences for male sexuality, as theologians such as James Nelson and others have explored and as Clanton's findings confirm, in which men who conceived of God in exclusively masculine terms tended to be rigid, conservative and conventional, scoring more lowly on both change and autonomy scales.[6]

Religious symbols function not only at the personal level, but also at the social. They legitimate ways of relating between persons, ways of holding power, ways of structuring society. Feminists have suggested that the patriarchal image of God as father has legitimated male headship in families and societies, and this is supported by Cartledge's study of UK theology students, where he found a positive association between the image of God as Father, the belief that a man is the head of the house and the idea that the best kind of leadership is top-down. Conversely, belief in the ordination of women was associated with the image of God as mother, with alternative names for the Trinity and with gender-ambivalent images of God.[7] Cartledge concludes that 'there is an association between gender-specific language for God and social roles and values'.[8] Exclusive or uncritically dominant images of God also function theologically, idolizing certain understandings of God and limiting the scope of divine self-disclosure. This is what McFague names as *idolatry*,[9] where we come to identify our language for God with Godself, usurping divine freedom and transcendence. Cartledge's research also found a connection between gender-specific language for God, social roles and values and theological models of the Trinity. For example, he found a correspondence between what he describes as the Orthodox-exclusivist model of the Trinity, figurative patriarchy (God as father) and social patriarchy (a man as the head of the household, rejection of the ordination of women).[10]

To put it simply, it matters how we talk about and to God, in public worship and in personal prayer; how we depict or narrate or gesture towards God in verbal, visual, spatial and physical discourse.[11] Prayer is a fundamental ecclesial practice which both forms and reflects the thinking and behaviour of the church as well as the life of the individual believer. One of the reasons why the relationship between prayer and the psychological well-being of the individual is not a straightforward one is because this relationship is always working within the wider dynamics of ecclesial and social reality, which may contradict, as well as confirm, the experiences and longings of the individual. Our prayer is never some merely private affair any more than our love-making. When we pray, we pray as part of the wider body, inhabiting and experiencing as well as expressing its struggles, wounds, conflicts and alienation. Can prayer do what the church resolutely refuses to do? Where there is a refusal to acknowledge the realities of people's complex and shifting gendered and sexual lives, and the changing ways in which gender and sexuality are enacted in society, is it possible for prayer to be a site of integration and healing of the wounded erotic?

The notion of integration

To speak of personal integration or wholeness – a language often employed by pastors and preachers – as the goal of the life of faith also needs to be submitted to a hermeneutic of suspicion. If divorced from wider socio-political discourse, the focus on psychological wholeness can engender escapist, pietistic and dualistic thinking and practice in the church. Even if integration is understood in a wider, communitarian and political setting, is it a useful or illuminating concept? At a time when a number of discourses – queer and post-colonial theology in particular – point up radical fissures and contradictions in personal and ecclesial identities (not simply as problematic, but as potentially enlivening), language of integration may assume a singular, essentialized self rather than invite us to recognize and work with the instability and multiplicity of gendered and sexual identities with which we have to do. 'Wholeness' is, at any rate, an impossible ideal, either in personal or in communal life: it implies perfection, completion, the fulfilment of the trajectory of a person's life and faith. Integration as a goal may smack of complacency, a too comfortable residency in the structures of injustice that characterize the world. Christian faith surely requires the pilgrim to inhabit a posture of tension, contradiction and disequilibrium towards the world, as Jesus and the prophets did in their time. Some of the most creative and politically active individuals are far from integrated, out of whose lived contradictions, wounds and painful irresolution enormous energy and passion are born.

Nevertheless, the notion of integration may still be useful in the current context in which churches and religious discourse frequently function as sites of sexual dishonesty and alienation, if the notion of integration is understood in a sufficiently dynamic and eschatological sense. Rather than moving towards the goal of some fixed, unchanging, settled identity, we may rather imagine human identity as a constantly changing and shifting eschatological process of embodied becoming, mirroring the eschatological becoming of a God whose name is no name but 'I will be what I will be' (Exodus 3.14). I wish to affirm the significance of prayer as one site (among others) in which both individuals and groups may wrestle honestly with their own lived, bodily, gendered and sexual histories and experiences and seek to bring them into consonance with faith. As Susannah Cornwall has suggested:

> Where sexuality cannot be successfully integrated into one's psyche, this may lead to spiritual alienation and a sense that one is 'hiding' from one-

self and from the divine. Inclusive sexuality therefore means not holding that one's sex life may be separated from one's spiritual and emotional life – and that dividing self from self generally does not have good psychological consequences.[12]

If prayer is the outworking of our relationship with self, other and God, it requires an honesty and transparency about the reality of our lives, including our sexuality, in all their alienated, fragmented, diffuse and confused states, as well as what is joyous and ecstatic.

It is precisely the work of prayer to confront, wrestle with and hold all that is unacknowledged, unhealed, unredeemed and unreconciled – both in the life of the individual and in the wider life of the body politic and ecclesial. Prayer operates as a crucible or workshop out of which a more authentic theology and practice can emerge. Prayer may be a site of working towards a greater reality – my own, that of the ecclesial body from and within which I pray, and even God's. If prayer is a genuine interchange between God and the pray-er, in which the Spirit is active and working, should we not expect God to be changed by prayer? If God is in mutual cooperative relationship with the world and with persons who seek to live in truthful, loving relationship to God, then it is not only the person praying who may be changed by prayer or even the wider corporate praying body, but, in ways we cannot comprehend, God too is moved and changed by our prayer. If we think of prayer as an ongoing process of wrestling and working with the intractable clay of our bodily yearnings and passions, Christians affirm that we do not wrestle alone. We are joined in our night-time struggles, at the liminal places of our lives, by the mysterious stranger/wrestler/lover whom we may experience as both attacking and embracing us in a fierce passion that will not let us go (Genesis 32.22–32). While the biblical account emphasizes the impact on Jacob of his encounter with the stranger – having striven and prevailed with God, he goes away blessed and limping – we may also suppose that the stranger is not unaffected by the encounter. If, as Sarah Coakley has suggested,[13] our prayer is a genuine participation in the Trinitarian life of God (in which our sexuality plays a full part), it is not simply some passive absorption into the dynamic interchange of energy and love between the three persons which leaves God unchanged, but a genuine participation in that perichoresis in which the life of the Godhead is open and vulnerable to human passion and pain. As Rublev's famous icon of the Trinity imagines a space at the table for the one gazing on and praying the icon, so the Trinitarian embrace presupposes the presence and engagement of the whole of creation within the love of God, without which the divine life is incomplete. The relational God of whom Christians speak both seeks our connection and consents to be shaped by it.

Prayer as a site of integration of the wounded and joyous erotic

Audre Lorde's classic essay, 'The uses of the erotic', offers an understanding of the erotic that has been highly influential in much theological writing about sexuality. For Lorde, the erotic (a broader category than the sexual) is 'a considered source of power and information within our lives', 'the nurturer or nursemaid of all our deepest knowledge', the essential bridge between the spiritual and the political.[14] For Lorde, the erotic 'provid[es] the power which comes from sharing deeply any pursuit with another person'; is the ground of 'the open and fearless underlining of my capacity for joy'; is a force that resists powerlessness, resignation, despair, self-effacement, depression and self-denial; and is 'the energy to pursue genuine change within our world'.[15] It is for these reasons that the erotic, when affirmed and embraced, can become the site of integration – not simply within the life of the individual but within the dynamics of the body politic. The erotic that drives towards connection in the celebration of bodily joy and union is the same force that drives towards connection between persons and societies that are divided or alienated.

In the work of Carter Heyward, Lorde's notion of the erotic is taken up into a theological vision of right relationship, extended to every sphere, from intimate personal relationship to political structures, relationships between humanity and the earth, and the humanity–divine connection. For Heyward, God cannot be more adequately described than in precisely such terms, as the power of mutual connection and touch:

Without our touching, there is no God.
Without our relation there is no God.
Without our crying, our raging, our yearning, there is no God.
For in the beginning is the relation, and in the relation is the power that creates the world through us, and with us, and by us, you and I, you and we, and none of us alone.[16]

For Heyward, 'God *is* our power in mutual relation and is not merely "in" our power',[17] so that 'through *us*, the Spirit roars and spins and whispers and cries'.[18] The erotic is fundamental to this drive to connect:

Our sexuality is our desire to participate in making love, making justice, in the world; our drive toward one another; our movement in love; our expression of our sense of being bonded together in life and death. Sexuality is expressed not only between lovers in personal relationship, but also in the work of an artist who loves her painting or her poetry, a father who loves his children, a revolutionary who loves her people.[19]

While affirming prayer as a site (not the only one) for working towards greater consonance between gender, sexuality and faith, it is important to recognize the obstacles to such integration, both in the wounded erotic that is the condition of individual and corporate sexuality, and in the dominance of hetero-patriarchal prayer that reinforces dualistic and body-denying thought and practice.

Our capacity for authentic erotic connection is wounded, not simply by the hurts and damage we have received in our personal lives but more broadly by the body-denying, sexuality-fearing and misogynistic dualism of hetero-patriarchy, reinforced by a culture of lies and deception within the church which refuses to speak truthfully about the realities of people's sexual lives. Emilie M. Townes asserts the need for black women to 'begin with the wounds' in their search for empowerment, at the same time as recognizing both the protective and the damaging potential of wounds:

> We can, if we must, begin with the wounds
>> those scars ... that are our mothers', daughters', sisters'
>> thick and hard so no one can ever pass through to hurt us again
> the folds of those old wounds, that have in some cases maimed us
>> with the lies, secrets, and silences we are told about other women
>> that we are told about ourselves
> those wounds mark us, but they do not need to define us.[20]

Our prayer and liturgy cannot be authentic if they do not name the realities of our wounds, at the same time as resisting a pathological attachment to suffering and an unhealthy eroticization of pain. Yet it is difficult to be honest about our gendered and sexual lives if our language for and about God is already predicated in terms that exclude the erotic from the spiritual realm, that express a binary and oppositional understanding of reality and of God's relationship to the world and to human bodies, and that construct gender in unchanging and classically patriarchal ways. It is important to recognize the ways in which we have learnt forms of prayer that alienate, disconnect, oppress and disempower, reinforcing the patriarchal mind/body, male/female, God/world split. It is not only our own wounded erotic and the dividedness and dishonesty of the church with which we must wrestle in prayer, but the very forms and practices of prayer itself, many of which reflect and reinscribe the gendered and sexual binaries we seek to undo. 'The master's tools will never dismantle the master's house,' as Lorde's famous dictum has it.[21]

Feminist critiques of prayer seek to expose the master's tools and offer new ones more adequate to the task. Attention has been paid not only to the language and texts of prayer (important though that this) but also to Procter-Smith's other forms of discourse: physical, visual and spatial. Thus feminists have proposed praying with eyes open rather than shut,[22] as a way of affirming the goodness of the created world (rather than regarding it as a distraction from God), and also to call attention to the need of women and girls to be alert in a church and world that are frequently unsafe and where their bodies and minds are at risk. Similarly, the adoption of alert, attentive, awake and resistant postures for prayer expresses a mutuality between God and the pray-er rather than kneeling, bowing or prostrating (particularly since, in corporate prayer, the individual is often bowing or kneeling towards a male priest or minister).[23] Feminists emphasize prayer that honours and cherishes as well as disciplines the body, prayer that connects the sexual, sacred and political body, both in the language and imagery employed and in the ways the bodies are respected and engaged in liturgy.[24] Womanist experience and discourse have something powerful to contribute here, where, according to Townes, the splits between private and public, personal and communal, of which white feminism speaks, have not been black women's reality. Townes writes powerfully of her own body awareness growing within 'a witness of women

who knew violation
enjoyed sex
moved with dignity
and shook from religious ecstasy.[25]

As such, womanist experience and discourse may offer resources for the kinds of integration of the personal and political, the spiritual and the sexual, of which I am thinking.

Feminist prayer values horizontal rather than hierarchical relations, generally preferring the circle over the traditional cruciform shape of churches;[26] it may be more appropriate to bow to other worshippers in the assembly than to the altar, as the authentic expression of the 'body of Christ', for example. Visual symbolism that affirms the inclusion of all members of the body of Christ in relationships of co-dependence and mutuality are sought, over and against dominating, infantilizing, coercive or violent imagery.[27] Questions are raised about many of the dominant visual symbols of God, Christ and the Trinity in churches and the liturgy, including the cross, which may reinforce rather than challenge violence against those who are powerless.[28] And, of course, considerable attention has been paid to the language of prayer, applying insights from wider feminist discussion of religious language and God imagery to the practice of prayer; this has included critique and rejection of the dominance of exclusive male language for God and all imagery and language of domination, the retrieval of biblical and traditional female God-language (Sophia, Wisdom, maternal and midwifery images and so on) and new forms of Trinitarian language, as well as reworkings of classic liturgical texts such as the Lord's Prayer, the creeds, confessions and litanies and so on.[29]

While much feminist liturgy focuses specifically on women's embodied experiences and seeks to claim liturgical space for women, others have recognized the significance of feminist liturgical critique in exposing broader dynamics of power and authority that do not only concern women. Similar critique and reclamation of prayer and liturgy have been advanced by queer and post-colonial critics,[30] although queer and post-colonial liturgy are at early stages of development.

Prayer in and through the embodied, erotic and queer image

Sallie McFague suggests that images and metaphors form the building blocks of theology and are thus crucial for shaping both thought and experience. Her analysis is helpful in considering how both verbal and visual discourses operate together within Christian thought, liturgy and prayer, and is useful as a bridge between the wider discussion of prayer as a site of integration of gender and sexuality with faith and the specific focus on praying in and through images (where 'image' encompasses verbal as well as visual and three-dimensional representations).

McFague sees theology as consisting of a network of interrelated images, metaphors, concepts and theories or theologies that together form the way in which reality is described. While systematic theology tends to operate at the level of highest abstraction, with concepts and theories, much of the activity of faith (such as liturgy, prayer, Bible reading and study) operates at the more concrete level of image and metaphor. Images and metaphors are the building blocks for more sustained models, concepts and theories.

In her thinking, the wellspring of Christian discourse and theology is the humble metaphor and image out of which the larger system of interlocking models and concepts emerge and on which they are dependent. If this is so, then the language used in worship and prayer, including hymnody and preaching, is powerfully formative of theology and action. Far from being 'just a matter of language', the metaphors and images employed to evoke the divine and our relationship to the sacred are constitutive of that reality. There is no thinking about or relating to God without them. This is not to deny the crucial role of the apophatic in Christian tradition[31] – the ascetic detachment from images and the unsaying or negation of language – but it is to insist that apophatic and kataphatic are mutually interdependent and cannot exist in isolation from each other.

From scripture onwards, Christian discourse has employed sexual and erotic imagery to evoke and explore the divine–human relationship. Erotic desire for the beloved, quest for the beloved, the agonies as well as the ecstasies of sexual desire, are engaged to evoke the passion and longing of God for humanity and humanity for God. Mystics and theologians throughout the ages developed and multiplied the erotic imagery of the scriptures, so that the language of sexual desire and union became a standard means of expressing love mysticism in personal prayer.

The hetero-patriarchal presuppositions of much sexual and gendered discourse for the divine–human relationship are, of course, far from unproblematic. Much Christian sexual imagery presumes that God is the dominant, male lover in pursuit of the female, often faithless and promiscuous, beloved, thus positioning the church/believer in a passive and sinful posture. Moreover, much biblical imagery of the erotic divine–human relationship is violent and punitive; even recognizing the linguistic excess of sexual metaphors that employ hyperbole and violence to express the emotional intensity and passion of the sexual encounter, this language is dangerous in a hetero-patriarchal church where women, children, LGBTQI+ persons and others are already at risk.[32] Where erotic imagery and metaphor are drawn on in Christian worship and hymnody, rather than simply ignored or denied, these hetero-patriarchal and coercive assumptions are often simply reinforced.

Yet Christian discourse is far more varied and queer than the dominant hetero-patriarchal model suggests. The Song of Songs gives unparalleled expression to the sexual desire and agency of the woman, as well as the male lover, offering a positive image of the black female lover that runs counter to dominant white, as well as male, discourse and imagery. Jesus' favouring of the metaphor of 'friend', coupled with his intimate friendships with both women and men, highlight mutuality and co-dependence in the divine–human relationship and offer gender-equivalent avenues for prayer and relationship to the divine. Janet Martin Soskice calls attention to 'the play of gendered imagery' in much classic theology and spirituality, in which both male and female images are used with 'rhetorical excess', both affirming the image of God in male and female and, at the same time, problematizing any straightforward identification between sexed gender and God. In the Syriac *Odes of Solomon,* for example, both Spirit and Father are feminized while retaining 'He' language:

A cup of milk was offered to me
And I drank it with the sweetness of the Lord's kindness.
The Son is the cup,
And He who was milked is the Father,
And she who milked Him is the Holy Spirit.[33]

Similarly, Julian of Norwich says of Jesus, 'He is our true Mother', developing a rich maternal understanding of Christ while never abandoning the male gendered referent. She thus brings together in creative tension male and female gendered language, not only to speak *of* Jesus but to address Christ. This is not dissimilar to the way in which, in scripture, feminine imagery for God is often juxtaposed with male imagery, so that both qualify and expand as well as critique each other. For example, in Genesis 49, Jacob's blessing for Joseph incorporates the blessings of God the 'father', the 'Almighty' with the 'blessings of the breasts and of the womb', combining and juxtaposing paternal and maternal imagery. In Isaiah 42, the image of God as a fighting soldier, a warrior (verse 13) is followed by the image of God as a birthing woman, crying out in labour (verse 14) – two very differently gendered experiences of physical *extremis* and danger. In the parables of Jesus, albeit there are only four that focus explicitly on female experience or imagery, these four appear to be coupled with similar parables rooted in the male world (the parable of the lost coin paralleling the parable of the lost sheep; the parable of the woman mixing leaven paralleling that of the mustard seed; the parable of the widow and unjust judge paralleling that of the friend at midnight, and the parable of the ten bridesmaids paralleling that of the wedding feast) – as if Jesus was deliberately employing differently gendered settings and images of God to speak to women and men respectively. Commentators have highlighted the queer gender relations underlying the metaphor of the church (posited as female) as the (male) body of Christ.[34] These examples not only demonstrate a multiplicity of gendered images for God in scripture, but also challenge any literalist reading of God-imagery and implicitly suggest the limitations of any one image of God.

Christian tradition, as Paul Murray writes, 'exists between the necessary use and the necessary unsettling of all images, understandings and concepts of God',[35] and prayer as well as theology sits at this place of creative tension between the cataphatic and apophatic. If practices of prayer require attentiveness, exchange, openness to repetition as well as novelty, as I have attempted to argue, then they echo the broader tensions of continuity/discontinuity, repetition-and-novelty that already exists in the tradition and that is played out in the rhythms of liturgical life, where the formality and givenness of texts and traditions is constantly renewed and transformed by the spontaneity and specificity of each new performance (and where texts and traditions themselves are open to constant revision).

Rather than providing a place of retreat from such tensions, prayer is precisely a place where questions of sex, sexuality and gender (as well as everything else to do with our bodiliness) can be understood as both concrete and irreducible. One reason why we need specific images to inform and focus our prayer – particularly, perhaps, images of Christ (including female and gender queer ones) – is to insist on the embodied specificity of divine self-revelation, even as we recognize the way in which that revelation transcends any and every embodiment of it. Thus we may hold that gender and sexuality, along with other markers of identity, are both irreducible and non-ultimate, less significant than our primary identities grounded in God but ineluctably interwoven into our humanity in ways that cannot be unravelled – at least, this side of the eschaton. Just as we cannot unmake our histories without unmaking who we are, we cannot transcend our embodied particularity without ceasing to be who we are. Our own marked, irreducible, particular human bodies with their utterly unique histories and scars *are* who we are, not merely some expression of a prior identity. It is out of these particular bodies that we live and pray, desire and hunger, bleed and weep, grow and change. This is why we need a bodily God and why we need the body of Christ to take/change shape in a multiplicity of sexed, gendered, ethnic and disabled forms. For many of us, the route to our own socio-political sexual wholeness as well as to deeper encounter with the divine, lies in and through gendered and erotic images of God – from Beckford's appropriation of Robert Lentz's Maasai warrior Christ showing his penis[36] to Kwok Pui-Lan's celebration of a multiplicity of gendered images of Jesus as the corn mother, feminine Shakti, theological transvestite, bi/Christ,[37] to my own work in search of a risen Christa.[38] Each of these Christological images destabilizes heteronormativity as well as a variety of other power dynamics, by performing gender, ethnicity and sexuality in a range of queer ways, rendering prayer and liturgy queer not merely at its margins but at its centre.

Notes

1 Maria Harris, *Fashion Me a People: Curriculum in the Church* (Louisville, KY: Westminster John Knox Press, 1989).

2 For a critique of the heteronormativity of much Christian liturgy, see Siobhan Garrigan, 'Queer Worship', *Theology and Sexuality* 15.2 (2009), pp. 211–30.

3 Elizabeth Johnson, *She Who Is: The Mystery of God in Feminist Theological Discourse* (New York: Crossroad, 1992), p. 5.

4 Robert Beckford, 'Does Jesus have a Penis? Black Male Sexual Representation and Christology', *Theology and Sexuality* 5 (1996), p. 11.

5 Jann Aldredge Clanton, *In Whose Image? God and Gender* (London: SCM Press, 1991), pp. 66–80.

6 James Nelson, *The Intimate Connection: Male Sexuality, Masculine Spirituality* (London: SPCK, 1992); Mark Pryce, *Finding a Voice: Men, Women and the Community of the Church* (London: SCM Press, 1996); Clanton, *In Whose Image?*, p. 86.

7 Mark J. Cartledge, 'God, Gender and Social Roles: A Study in Relation to Empirical-Theological Models of the Trinity', *Journal of Empirical Theology* 22 (2009), p. 133.

8 Cartledge, 'God, Gender and Social Roles', p. 136.

9 Sallie McFague, *Metaphorical Theology: Models of God in Religious Language* (London: SCM Press, 1982), pp. 4–5.

10 Cartledge, 'God, Gender and Social Roles', p. 137.

11 Marjorie Procter-Smith identifies these forms of liturgical discourse in *In Her Own Rite: Constructing Feminist Liturgical Tradition* (Nashville, TN: Abingdon Press, 1990), pp. 59–84.

12 Susannah Cornwall, *Sexuality: The Inclusive Church Resource* (London: Darton, Longman & Todd, 2014), pp. 99–100.

13 Sarah Coakley, *God, Sexuality, and the Self: An Essay 'On the Trinity'* (Cambridge: Cambridge University Press, 2013).

14 Audre Lorde, 'Uses of the erotic: The erotic as power', in James B. Nelson and Sandra P Longfellow (eds.), *Sexuality and the Sacred: Sources for Theological Reflection* (London: Mowbray, 1994), pp. 75–9.

15 Lorde, 'Uses of the erotic', pp. 76, 77, 78.

16 Carter Heyward, *The Redemption of God: A Theology of Mutual Relation* (Lanham, MD: University Press of America, 1982), p. 172.

17 Carter Heyward, *Touching our Strength: The Erotic as Power and the Love of God* (San Francisco, CA: HarperSanFrancisco, 1989), p. 61.

18 Carter Heyward, *Saving Jesus from Those Who are Right* (Minneapolis, MN: Fortress, 1999), pp. 69, 70.

19 Carter Heyward, *Our Passion for Justice: Images of Power, Sexuality, and Liberation* (New York: Pilgrim Press, 1984), p. 86.

20 Emilie M. Townes, 'A Womanist Perspective on Spirituality in Leadership', *Theological Education* 37 (2001), p. 85.

21 Audre Lorde, 'The master's tools will never dismantle the master's house', in *Sister Outsider: Essays and Speeches* (Berkeley, CA: Crossing Press, 1984), pp. 110–14.

22 Marjorie Procter-Smith, *Praying with Our Eyes Open: Engendering Feminist Liturgical Prayer* (Nashville, TN: Abingdon Press, 1995).

23 See Janet R. Walton, *Feminist Liturgy: A Matter for Justice* (Collegeville, MN: Liturgical Press, 2000), p. 38, though note Sarah Coakley's advocacy of the 'kneeling work' of slaying patriarchy that feminists alone can do, in *God, Sexuality, and the Self*, p. 327. Against a certain consensus in feminist liturgy, Coakley argues for a feminist Trinitarian reclamation of kenotic vulnerability in contemplative prayer.

24 See, for example, Stephanie Paulsell, *Honoring the Body: Meditations on a Christian Practice* (San Francisco: Jossey-Bass, 2002) and many of the rites in Rosemary Radford Ruether's classic *Women-Church: Theology and Practice* (New York: Harper & Row, 1985), which address the bodily realities of women's lives ignored in mainstream liturgy (for example, incest, rape, burglary, abortion, miscarriage, stillbirth, coming out as a lesbian, and so on).

25 Townes, 'Womanist Perspective', p. 98.

26 See Teresa Berger, *Women's Ways of Worship: Gender Analysis and Liturgical History* (Collegeville, MN: Liturgical Press, 1999), p. 128.

27 Procter-Smith, *In Her Own Rite*, pp. 71–81.

28 Procter-Smith, *Praying With Our Eyes Open*, pp. 100ff.

29 See, for example, Gail Ramshaw, *God Beyond Gender: Feminist Christian God-Language* (Minneapolis, MN: Fortress, 1995), and Ruth C. Duck and Patricia Wilson-Kastner, *Praising God: The Trinity in Christian Worship* (Louisville, KY: Westminster John Knox Press, 1999).

30 See Garrigan, 'Queer worship'; and Michael N. Jagessar and Stephen Burns, *Christian Worship: Postcolonial Perspectives* (Abingdon: Equinox, 2011).

31 For a helpful overview, see Edward Howells, 'Apophatic spirituality', in Philip Sheldrake (ed.), *The New SCM Dictionary of Christian Spirituality* (London: SCM Press, 2005), pp. 117–19.

32 See, for example, Renita J. Weems, *Battered Love: Marriage, Sex, and Vio-*

lence in the Hebrew Prophets (Minneapolis, MN: Fortress, 1995); Carol J. Adams and Marie M. Fortune (eds.) *Violence against Women and Children: A Christian Theological Sourcebook* (New York: Continuum, 1998).

33 Janet Martin Soskice, 'Trinity and feminism', in Susan Frank Parsons (ed.), *The Cambridge Companion to Feminist Theology* (Cambridge: Cambridge University Press, 2002), p. 144.

34 For example, Natalie K. Watson, *Introducing Feminist Ecclesiology* (Sheffield: Sheffield Academic Press, 2002), pp. 42–4.

35 Paul D. Murray, 'God, Images of', in Sheldrake, *New SCM Dictionary*, p. 326.

36 Beckford, 'Does Jesus have a Penis?'

37 Kwok Pui-Lan, *Postcolonial Imagination and Feminist Theology* (London: SCM Press, 2005), pp. 168–85.

38 Nicola Slee, *Seeking the Risen Christa* (London: SPCK, 2011).

5

Riting the Body: Making and Reclaiming Liturgical Space

This piece began life as a paper presented to the International Academy of Practical Theology in April 2017 at Oslo University. Substantial parts of it will appear in my essay 'Prayer, gender and the body' in the T&T Clark Companion to Christian Prayer, *edited by Ashley Cocksworth and John C. McDowell. The theme of the IAPT conference was 'Reforming: space, body, and politics', which prompted the desire to write about liturgical space in some detail.*

Introduction

Space is a feminist issue. The ownership and control of land, seas, rivers, cities, public as well as domestic spaces, parliaments, armies, law courts, universities, schools, hospitals and, of course, religious buildings, remains very largely in the hands of men in even the most liberal, egalitarian countries in the world. Under patriarchy – the rule of the fathers – such male ownership is, in fact, the norm. And it ranges widely, from the most public to the most personal of spaces (both of which, of course, are political): from the vast reaches of empire to the most intimate spaces of bodies and how they may (or may not) comport themselves in the world; from national dictatorships and ownership of multinational companies to 'manspreading' and the largely female slimming industry. Under patriarchy (or kyriarchy, as Fiorenza prefers to speak of systems of mastery),[1] women and children, slaves, those of 'other' races or minority sexual status, are owned and controlled by the patriarchs. They have no right to own land or property or even a 'room of [their] own';[2] their very right to take up space in the physical world is disputed, their bodies and free movement governed and policed and, even under benign patriarchal regimes, strictly controlled. Of course, patriarchy has never been absolute and women, no less than slaves and children, have found ways of subverting its iron grip and resisting its rule, offering subtle as well as more overt forms of protest and elaborating alternative spaces within which to exercise freedom and resistance.

Social geographers Linda McDowell and Joanne Sharp offer a helpful summary of 'why space matters in the analysis and explanation of ... gendered social relations':

> Spatial relations and layout, the differences between and within places, the nature and form of the built environment, images and representations of this environment and of the 'natural' world, ways of writing about it, as well as our bodily place within it, are all part and parcel of the social constitution of gendered social relations and the structure and meaning of place. The spaces in which social practices occur affect the nature of those practices, who is 'in place', who is 'out of place' and even who is allowed to be there at all ... Physical and social boundaries reinforce each other and spatial relations act to socialize people into the acceptance of gendered power relations – they reinforce power, privileges and oppression and literally keep women in their place. But one can also 'push against oppressive boundaries' to 'invent spaces of radical openness' (hooks 1990: 145, 148) within which to challenge dominant power, taking it on from the margins.[3]

McDowell and Sharp go on to note the ways in which 'space' and 'spatiality' have become increasingly theorized, not only within feminism but in many fields of critical theory, used in both metaphorical and material ways to analyse not only spatial relations at a societal level but also the mapping and melding of individual human bodies. Interestingly, the analysis of religious and theological space is notably absent from their otherwise comprehensive reader. Yet, arguably, the ownership and arrangement of religious space has functioned – and in many societies still does – to symbolize and endorse all other societal and interpersonal configurations of space. Who controls the religious realm (God, popes, bishops, clergy, rabbis, imams) is mirrored in the control of religious spaces (temples, cathedrals, churches, synagogues and mosques), which is itself mirrored in the social and gendered arrangement of public spaces and the domestic realm. Where the Father Almighty reigns in heaven, his rule is enacted and represented by his male representatives – the 'fathers in God' who rule in his churches/temples/mosques and the 'fathers' who rule the household and the family. Analysis of religious space is therefore crucial as part of any comprehensive critical theory.

To put this another way: the ownership, control, regulation and shaping of physical, as well as psychic, intellectual and cultural space is a theological issue and, specifically, a *practical* theological issue.[4] If people of faith are formed by their embodied practices as much as, if not more than, by teaching and doctrine, and if public prayer and ritual represent one major form of such embodied practice, then paying attention to the formational aspects of space is a vital task for liturgical studies as well as for practical theology. Classical liturgical studies and even contemporary liturgics have tended to concentrate overly on liturgical *texts* as their primary data to the exclusion of other aspects of liturgy; yet, as Marjorie Procter-Smith has argued, verbal discourse is only one dimension of liturgy; and some liturgy, such as Quaker worship, may not have much of this. Even where rites follow written texts, the texts are comparable to the script of a theatrical performance, which may be more or less closely followed and will always be interpreted in terms of the specific social and cultural context. To focus only on texts is to miss the many subtle and powerful performative features of lived ritual. Procter-Smith calls attention to visual and spatial discourse alongside verbal discourses as equally significant in framing and constructing theological meaning.[5] In other words, liturgical formation is in and through ritual practice itself, in all its elements, of which words and cognitive assent may be one, relatively insignificant, element. It is necessary, too, to consider the ways in which the various forms of discourse – verbal, visual, spatial and potentially others (aural is one discourse Procter-Smith does not consider) – interact. Do they support and reinforce each other, or are they in conflict and contradiction? Words may be undone or underlined by the visual clues and dominant spatial arrangements in the liturgy. Which is not, of course, to say that words do not matter; only that they are not the whole story. Indeed, words may be of very limited interest to young children or adults with profound learning needs and even to many adults who form the body of congregations – at least in their cognitive function, in distinction from the range of other ways in which words operate (for example, the repetition of familiar words to create a deep sense of security and familiarity in ritual).

In this chapter, I propose to examine feminist liturgical developments over the past three to four decades (particularly from my knowledge of the British context) as a case study of feminist space and embodiment. I will consider how feminists have used the metaphor of space in thinking and writing about feminist liturgy and what this may indicate about its significance, before going on to chart feminist critique of liturgical space, including transgressive feminist ritual action as embodied forms of such critique. I will then examine feminist reclamation of liturgical space in a number of guises: the reclamation and celebration of domestic liturgical space and metaphors associated with the domestic; the creative making, adjustment or (if neither are possible) imagination of alternative spaces for ritual; the affirmation and reclamation of women's bodies as the fundamental spatial category for feminist liturgy and the associated reclamation of nature and earth spaces as primary settings for feminist liturgy. In all of these strategies of reclamation, certain images dominate: the image of the circle, and worshipping in the round; the affirmation of the horizontal plane and worshipping on the level; and the insistence on the primacy of human personhood and worshipping face to face. I outline the implications of these metaphors and also note some counter arguments that seek to resist a new, feminist hegemony.

Metaphors of space

Metaphors of space are ubiquitous in contemporary parlance, both in everyday speech and in academic discourse. We speak of 'personal space', 'emotional or psychic space', 'liminal' and 'marginalized' space. Identity politics of many kinds operate through a strong sense of location – whether on the margins, in the interstices or the edges, in the borderlands or the fluid spaces of hybridity. Feminists have made persistent use of metaphors of space to critique women's exclusion from power and material spaces and to claim their own agency and location – literally and metaphorically to expand their horizons. Images of confinement – the Victorian 'angel in the house', the sick and enfeebled woman forced to 'rest' (for example, in Charlotte Perkins Gilman's famous story, 'The Yellow Wallpaper'), Maya Angelou's 'caged bird' which still sings, the madwoman in the attic in Charlotte Brontë's *Jane Eyre* – express women's sense of imprisonment under patriarchy. These contrast with metaphors of travel, expansion and movement in feminist writings and film, from Margaret Atwood's *Surfacing* to Virginia Woolf's *The Waves*, from *Thelma and Louise*'s drive across America in the ultimate feminist road movie to Cheryl Strayed's solo trek into the American wilderness portrayed in her memoir and associated film *Wild*; each of these is expressive of the feminist quest for freedom and, not merely a *room* so much as a *country* of one's own.

At the same time, metaphors of space have been used to critique male 'colonization' of space, for example in the contemporary neologism 'manspreading' to refer to a man sitting (usually in public transport) with his legs spread, thereby taking up more than one seat and leaving little room for others to sit, or 'manslamming' to refer to the way that men 'slam into' people as they move around public spaces with little social awareness of their impact on others.[6] Third and fourth wave feminists use social media platforms to record such experiences and speak of the ways in which girls and women are socialized to be small and neat, to take up little space in the world, while boys and men are socialized to assume that physical, psychological, political and intellectual space belong to them and to take up as much of it as they want.[7]

The metaphor of space recurs, too, in feminist liturgical writings and reflections. A feminist Christian women's group meeting in London during the 1990s convened by Hannah Ward and Jennifer Wild called itself 'Womenspace', indicative of the felt need for a women-only space for women to speak, share, study and reflect. The same name is used by an Australian feminist collective that offers 'a sacred space for women to connect', one of whose aims is 'to celebrate women's spirituality through rituals congruent with their lived experience'.[8] Several centres supporting women victims of domestic violence also take the same name, offering a safe and therapeutic space for women for whom the domestic space is far from safe.[9] Monica Furlong, writing of the setting up and development of the St Hilda Community – an experimental, feminist liturgical community of women and men meeting in London in the 1980s and 90s – uses a spatial metaphor to express the sense of creativity and expansiveness operative within the community, particularly in the early days. '[O]ur feet seemed to be set, as it says in the Psalms, in a large room, a larger room than we had begun with.'[10] She is certainly not speaking of the physical space in which the St Hilda Community began: the small, round, domed chapel of St Benet's in Queen Mary College. Rather, she refers to the sense of psychic and spiritual spaciousness among a group of worshippers who, after campaigning for years for women's ordination, had decided they would wait no longer to experience women's eucharistic ministry and had taken steps to create their own liturgical community as a prophetic counterpart to the mainstream denominations.

Feminist critique of patriarchal liturgical space

Feminist metaphors of space can be seen as both enacted in feminist liturgical practice and arising out of that practice. This takes critical, dissenting forms as well as creative, innovative forms. As with feminist theology more widely, feminist liturgical writing and practice have tended to be funded by radical protest and critique as the first movement in a deconstruction of patriarchal tradition and space, before an alternative can be imagined and created; or, sometimes, as the alternative is envisaged so the necessity to critique the malestream is provoked.[11]

Feminist liturgists protest and rebel against male ownership of religious space and the exclusion of women from significant presence and active ministry within that space. Feminists have critiqued the hierarchical, phallic and dominating architecture of church buildings which enshrine the will to power and the subjection of all who are excluded from the small clerical caste who own power. Enormous buildings that dominate towns and cityscapes, costing millions to build and maintain, with high towers thrusting up into the skyline, are hardly subtle symbols of male potency, pride and will to control. Inside these vast edifices, architectural space reflects and dictates theology: high altars blocked off from the main body of the congregation in the nave, to which access is strictly controlled (and from which women may be excluded), literally and symbolically map out the persons, objects and actions that are deemed sacred and those that are not. Similarly, huge pulpits jutting out from the chancel elevate the preacher 'six feet above contradiction' and enact a visual and spatial hierarchy that even a child can read. The placing of altar and pulpit are only two of the most obvious of spatial symbols that encode gendered and hierarchical social relations. Other clues are given by noting who may move about the building freely and who may not: laity in many churches are limited to the main body of the church and may only move out of their pews at certain, defined points in the liturgy, while clergy and vergers and other robed officers may move about as they wish, commanding the space. Equally significant is whose voices are permitted to fill the space: who speaks – preaches, leads prayers, offers notices and so on – as well as who sings (a fierce battle to allow girls and women to join Anglican cathedral choirs has taken many years to take effect) and who does not. 'Buildings', as Winston Churchill is purported to have said, 'always win.'[12]

Feminists have enacted a range of strategies to critique the patriarchal dominance of liturgical space and to reclaim these spaces and their own ritual agency. Some have walked out and called others to come with them, perhaps most famously exemplified in Mary Daly's Exodus from the Harvard Memorial Church in 1971, when invited as the first woman preacher in Harvard's 366-year history, followed by about 50 members of the congregation leaving with her as a symbolic enactment of their Exodus from patriarchy.[13] Some have invaded and reclaimed male space: a particularly powerful example of this is Pussy Riot's performance in the sanctuary of the Russian Orthodox Cathedral of Christ the Saviour in Moscow, February 2012, as a means of protesting the Orthodox Church's support of Putin's policies.[14] Others have created their own alternative feminist spaces in neglected, marginal or uncelebrated sites; when the St Hilda Community was evicted by the Bishop of London from the chapel where the community had been gathering for a couple of years, we decided to hold the celebration of the Eucharist in the car park at St Benet's chapel, a dramatic enactment of our eviction into a liminal wilderness on the edges of the church that would not welcome us.[15] These and other physical enactments embody feminist protest, resistance and rejection of patriarchy, as well as the insistence on women claiming their own spaces for ritual, self-definition and worship.

Feminist reclamation of liturgical space

Pussy Riot's invasion of the sacred space of the Orthodox cathedral is but a dramatic instance of a wider phenomenon in feminist liturgy: the reclamation of liturgical space by and for women. Women do not want to be the passive objects of worship, recipients of male-led, male-designed and male-written liturgy, but the active subjects of their own ritual. This includes the insistence by women of claiming their own spaces for ritual. Here I note four widespread manifestations of this feminist reclamation.

Domestic liturgical space

Women have, from time immemorial, prayed, reflected on the scriptures and made their own rituals in the home. Teresa Berger notes that, in Christian tradition, 'the earliest ecclesial and therefore liturgical space was women's space'. The extended household, a realm organized by women, 'was home to Christian communities for well over two hundred years'. Women often functioned as heads of these house churches, alongside men or in their own right.[16] It was only later, when Christianity was adopted as the religion of the Roman Empire, gatherings became too big to be held in homes and orders of ministry became more formalized, that liturgy was pushed out of its domestic setting and women were robbed of their leadership roles. Jewish tradition has tended to maintain a stronger sense of women's roles as leaders of ritual in the home, from ancient to modern times. Particularly, though not exclusively in the Sabbath rite, women and children have a core role in leading the weekly entry into the sacred space of Sabbath. Similarly, Passover is a home-based festival gathered around the table in which women and children play key roles.[17]

In Christian liturgy, many feminists argue, women's domestic and bodily experience has been stolen from them and re-appropriated by a male clerical elite as their own possession to be performed in the public space and liturgy of the church. Women's birth-giving through blood and water, accompanied by the washing and care of the newborn infant, have been re-appropriated in baptism, just as the basic work of preparing food and feeding the community, which women have done from ancient times, has been stolen from them and transformed into Eucharist – from which women themselves have then been excluded as celebrants and even, at times, from receiving the sacred food.

Nevertheless, the home remains a vital centre of feminist ritual and prayer, and much feminist liturgy takes place there, celebrating and affirming women's bodily presence and everyday lives within the domestic realm. Jan Berry's ethnographic study of women's rituals created by British women to mark significant transitions in their lives notes that the majority of women favoured domestic space as the setting for their rituals. They offered a range of reasons for this, from the practical (ease of access, low or no cost) to the social and psychological (the safety of the space and its integral connection to the women's identity, a strong desire to practise hospitality and inclusion) and the theological (the holiness and intimacy of the home as a space of divine encounter).[18]

Feminist communities gather in women's homes and gardens, around the table for shared food and reflection, using symbols drawn from the everyday lives of women and from the natural world (candles, flowers, colourful cloths, water, sand, stones and so on). The home itself is affirmed as a sacred place by simple ritual practices, many of them ancient, such as the setting up of home shrines in a corner of a room,[19] the lighting of candles on a windowsill or grate, the offering of blessings throughout the day for daily routines such as rising, washing, dressing, 'smooring' the floor[20] and so on. Women's ancient traditions of storytelling, folk art, song and dance – communal, anonymous and passed on from generation to generation, much of which has been home-based – continue to be employed and adapted in contemporary feminist liturgy. Scriptures may be read but will invariably be interpreted in and through women's own concrete, lived experience, often with alternative sacred texts (poems, manifestos, stories) brought to bear alongside them. Simple chants, folksongs and contemporary sacred songs may be sung.[21] These actions can, of course, take place in a variety of locations, not only within the home, but they have their roots in women's daily singing, storytelling, moving and dwelling within the home. And even if such acts can be performed anywhere, the creation of ritual in the home resists the sacred/secular binary that feminists see as a core characteristic of dualistic patriarchy.

Letty Russell's proposal of a 'roundtable theology'[22] to undergird the ecclesiology of Womenchurch is one theological outworking of this reclamation of domestic space. Russell takes the concrete images of the 'round table', the 'kitchen table' and the 'welcome table' as metaphors for a vibrant, inclusive, justice-seeking ecclesiology. But these are not only metaphors; they are rooted in everyday practice in ordinary homes, neighbourhoods and churches, where adults and children gather round kitchen and other tables for 'table talk', shared food and inclusive table hospitality which seeks to bring the marginalized and outsiders to God's table. The kitchen table, in particular, is an image

> far removed from the 'tables' that are lists of church order, in which persons are ranked according to position. Instead, its emphasis is on the daily work of women who care for homes and families, preparing the dough for the future of their children and sometimes breaking the bread not only at home but in the assembled church community.[23]

While the home is affirmed as a primary locus of feminist prayer and ritual, at the same time feminist liturgy does not ignore the fact that the home may be a far from safe space for many women. Recognizing that the home is a primary scene of male control and domestic violence, home-based liturgies may also be rites of lament and mourning, healing and exorcism.[24]

Imagining new liturgical spaces

While the home is a primary place for female prayer and ritual, it is not in itself sufficient. Homes may not be large enough, or suitably equipped, for the kinds of liturgical gatherings women and feminist men long to create. And, of course, the home remains inscribed in patriarchal imagination as the realm of the private and the personal, and can therefore easily be ignored and marginalized by liturgical scholarship. Feminists desire their own public places of ritual and worship, designed and built by them for their own needs, gatherings and flourishing. Where women are excluded from mainstream churches, synagogues or temples, or exclude themselves, they look to the creation – or, if creation is not possible, the imagination – of alternative feminist spaces.

Ruether offered one of the earliest such blueprints of feminist liturgical space in her still classic text, *Women-Church: Theology and Practice*,[25] a primer of the Womenchurch[26] movement, which sets out the basic theological underpinning of the movement and offered a range of radical liturgies for use in feminist liturgical communities. Recognizing that 'most Women-Church groups will gather in each other's houses', Ruether envisaged the shaping of a building suitable for the various needs of feminist communities. This included space for liturgies 'that is both centering and elevating': 'a round room able to hold as many as 150 people, but comfortable with only a dozen or so'. A flexible space with no immovable furniture, oriented to catch the light at the winter and summer solstices, 'it would have a dome of light in the center of the ceiling and panels of colored glass in rainbow hues around this center, standing for the plurality and unity of all good things in creation'. 'Under the celebration center there would be a round crypt', 'used particularly for rites connected with birth and death'. Connected to the celebration centre would be 'a kitchen to cook collective meals', 'a conversation circle for study and discussion gatherings', an indoor garden containing a hot tub, cool plunge, saunas and so on. The whole should be 'set in some area of pleasant meadows and woods', with 'several small cottages scattered about ... where women could stay for several days to meditate, read, and write. A circular outdoor meadow area for outdoor celebrations ... would also be desirable.'[27]

While many feminist liturgical communities continue to meet in borrowed public spaces – churches, synagogues, schools or halls – some have been able to resource their own, purpose-built, feminist-inspired gathering spaces. The Sophia ecumenical feminist spiritual community in Adelaide, Australia, created in 1991 from the legacy of a community of Holy Cross Dominican Sisters, houses a complex of rooms that support the wide range of activities of the community: social, educational, therapeutic and liturgical. Nestled in the shade of an enormous fig tree, the building is a purpose-built spiral shape, with mud-coloured walls that speak of the earthiness of the surroundings and its spirituality. It contains a library, offices, large and small meeting rooms; outside is a spiral garden with running water.[28]

Other feminist liturgical communities have bought or rented property, which, while not purpose-built, nevertheless embodies the 'space of our own' that women aspire to. For example, the Australian community, Womenspace, has had a variety of homes and now resides in a colonial style building in Sandgate, Brisbane, where the high-ceilinged, light-filled rooms are available for rent. Retreat centres with a particular focus on women's spirituality, such as Holy Rood House in Thirsk, England, offer other examples of spaces that have been adapted, if not designed, to be safe, welcoming and inclusive places for women to find refuge and solace, seek healing, gather for shared meals, conversation, study and ritual.[29] Like Ruether's imagined gathering of Womenchurch, these feminist liturgical/spiritual communities enshrine in their architectural space, as well as their practices, many fundamental feminist metaphors and principles, to which I turn below.

A more recent development in feminist liturgical innovation is the use of the internet and social media platforms as alternative *virtual* spaces for feminist discussion, theologizing and even ritual-making.[30] A number of feminists see the internet, social media and virtual space as providing an alternative feminist community that is largely women-led, free from constraint and policing by men, and crosses diverse ethnic, social, religious and cultural boundaries. The analysis of such virtual spaces, particularly as sites of liturgical action, is beyond the scope of this paper, but should be noted as a significant development that requires scholarly attention.

The *(female) body as the fundamental liturgical spatial category*

Patriarchy enshrines a fundamental fear and hatred of female flesh, which must be strictly controlled and policed. This is enshrined in theologies of original sin (in which the original woman, Eve, is to blame for bringing sin into the world), understandings of materiality and sexuality (associated in particular with the feminine and projected on to women) and in liturgical practices in which women are excluded from the most sacred liturgical sites, offices and rituals. Men, queer folk, differently abled as well as black and Asian people also suffer alienation from their bodies and a fear and hatred of physicality as a result of this binary dualism, and many join with feminists in reclaiming the basic goodness and holiness of the body. A core assertion of feminist theology and liturgy, then, is the reclamation of the (female) body as good, sacred, life-giving and free.

Feminist liturgies enact this core conviction in a wide range of ritual practices. Many feminist liturgies focus on neglected rites of passage and bodily experiences that have been completely ignored in mainstream liturgy. Turning again to Ruether's *Women-Church*, there are liturgies here for menarche and menopause, rites for healing from an abortion, from domestic abuse and other kinds of violence, as well as celebrations for lesbian partnerships, the birth of a child and so on. Women's life-giving bodies and blood are honoured in feminist Eucharists in contrast to mainstream eucharistic liturgies which focus on the exclusive holiness of Jesus' body and blood in violent death.[31]

In simple yet powerful ways, women refuse to adopt bodily postures that are perceived as controlling or demeaning, or demanding a passivity that is dangerous to women in a patriarchal world and church order. For example, women refuse to pray with eyes closed, but insist on 'praying with eyes open', both as an affirmation of the beauty of the world and the other people around them and on the insistence that women need to keep eyes open to be alert to threat or danger. Most feminist liturgies do not adopt postures of kneeling or prostration which reinforce women's subservience and male dominance, choosing rather to stand or sit on the level with others. As Janet Walton asserts, 'we do not kneel down to pray' because kneeling is associated with submission.[32] Marcella Althaus-Reid points out the parallel between kneeling in the liturgy and kneeling before another for sex,[33] and this is a particularly demeaning posture for women who have been forced to have sex on their knees. While I would caution against any imposition of particular feminist postures (which would seem to be an aping of patriarchal domination and control), there are cogent reasons for avoiding such postures as bowing, kneeling and closing of eyes. Perhaps the crucial factor here is power and choice; for those with the power to choose, any bodily posture may be expressive of agency and personhood. But women have not, traditionally, held such power – and still, in many places in the world, do not. When all are free to choose to kneel or prostrate themselves without fear or danger, then perhaps it will be appropriate for any to make such a choice. There is also a world of difference between kneeling freely in a sacred space in honour of the earth or of other worshippers, and kneeling down at the feet of a priest or minister to receive blessing. It is difficult to see how this second form of kneeling could ever be an act of mutuality (unless it were reciprocated with the actors in reverse position, as sometimes happens in church).

Feminist liturgies also celebrate movement in a variety of processions, dance and ritual walking (such as the labyrinth) as a way of refusing the passivity and control of the female body. They might include anointing the body with oil or water, gentle touch which is passed between participants, and walking or dancing processions. Such practices challenge misogynistic thinking and practice and envisage a new world order in which the bodies of all will be honoured, protected and nourished, and earth's resources more equitably shared.

The affirmation of the body in feminist liturgies is not only about justice and care, but also about pleasure and delight. The senses are celebrated as the gateway to the divine; food and drink, colour and texture and the things of the earth are relished. Eyes are kept open not least to take in all the beauty and bounty of God's good earth. Touch, taste, smell and hearing all play a part in the liturgy and convey a sense of delight. In rejection of patriarchal fear and control of the senses and of pleasure itself, feminist liturgy affirms the goodness of bodily pleasure and feminist liturgies often involve a cornucopia of sensual experience.

The *reclamation of nature and earth spaces*

Feminists have long seen the close connection between oppression and colonization of women's bodies and the colonization, rape and mutilation of 'mother earth', or Gaia. Alongside the reclamation of female flesh as sacred, feminist liturgy affirms the natural realm as holy. A number of feminist theologians speak of the earth as the body of God, the fundamental sacrament of existence. Feminist liturgies affirm and honour the seasons, the elements and the vital connections between human well-being and the care and preservation of the cosmos. Conversely, feminist liturgies lament and mourn the destruction of habitats and species and the breakdown of human awareness of our dependence upon, and connection with, other living creatures.

Feminist liturgies affirm the vital connection to the natural realm not only in what they say but also in the symbols they employ and the spaces in which ritual is celebrated. Symbols from the natural world abound: Berger notes the 'intense predilection for symbols' in feminist liturgies, and lists many drawn from nature, as well as women's domestic lives: 'rose-scented water, freshly baked bread, milk and honey, fragrant oil, burning incense, flowers, candles, branches, ashes, earth, grain, bulbs, straw, wine, fruit – yes, even apples'.[34]

An outdoor setting is frequently favoured for feminist liturgies, access and weather permitting. Neo-pagan, Goddess, wiccan, Celtic and other influences mix with feminist strands to create many variations on this theme. Not only at threshold times, such as solstices, but in every season, feminist liturgies affirm the natural cycles of the earth and situate rituals in open spaces (commons, moorlands, fields), in woods and by rivers and wells (which are, of course, frequently ancient sites of pilgrimage and ritual). Participants may be encouraged to stand barefoot on the earth in order to feel their connection to the earth and to experience a groundedness in matter; to breathe deeply the fresh air; to listen to natural sounds of wind, birdsong and animal movements; to smell the fresh aromas of earth, plants, herbs and flowers – all as manifestations of the divine.

Some specific physical sites may be regarded as symbolic of female morphology and therefore as peculiarly appropriate for feminist liturgy. Stone circles, mounds and burial chambers, caves and wells, for example, may be regarded as symbolic of women's dark, internal spaces running with life-giving water: nurturing, circular and womb-like, inviting descent into the depths, in contrast to church buildings which are totemic and phallic in shape and design. On a trip to Crete a number of years ago, I experienced the extraordinary power of a cave dedicated to St Sophia, which had a small chapel nestling in the dark, wet rock covered with icons of Sophia with her three daughters, Faith, Hope and Charity. In a hot and dry climate, the dark, cool and wet cave offered shelter and relief from the remorseless light and heat. Stepping into this space conjured a sense of profound psychic journey and resonated with my own sense of the hiddenness of much feminine spirituality as well as my own interior bodily spaces. Without wishing to endorse any kind of crude biological essentialism, we may nevertheless note how vastly different the experience of inhabiting different kinds of physical space may be and affirm what such spaces may or may not suggest about the nature of the divine (female, dark, hidden, interior, a place of mysterious fecundity in contrast to male, light-filled, dominating the skyline, and so on).

Some core feminist liturgical metaphors

I turn finally to three key metaphors which represent widely shared commitments and characteristics of feminist liturgical practice across a great diversity of contexts, traditions and beliefs.[35] Most feminist liturgies conform to these characteristics. Nevertheless, they are not imposed and they do not represent a new feminist hegemony that cannot be challenged. In offering these metaphors, I suggest reasons for their power and popularity but also, from time to time, offer counter-images or practices.

In the round

Circles are the norm in feminist liturgical writing and practice. Classic texts, such as Ruether's *Women-Church* and Letty Russell's *Church in the Round*, offer a robust rationale for the centrality of the circle in feminist spiritual communities. Russell makes 'round' the key image in her imaginative explication of a church inspired by feminism, particularly in her offering of the image of the 'round table' around which church gathers. The masters' tables, long and rectangular, with their hierarchical arrangements, need to be overturned in place of the round kitchen table where all gather to eat and share and where there is no single locus of power.[36] In such 'kitchen table solidarity', a community of hospitality is formed, in which leadership is exercised 'in the round', in a dispersed, fluid manner. While Ruether has less to say about the circle, her description of the imaginary Womenchurch building is completely dominated by circles: all the spaces, inside and out, are circular, or egg-shaped (a variation on the circle) and the architectural sketch included makes this very clear.[37]

Circles symbolize mutuality and reciprocity, the dynamic flow of energy around and between persons who make up the circle. In a circle, everyone can see everyone else and there are no 'special' places. There is space for everyone – a circle can expand or contract as required – and, at the same time, there is always space within a circle, symbolizing the hospitable space of God and the church. Letty Russell reads the symbol of the 'round table' as one speaking of hospitality, sharing and dialogue, but also pointing proleptically towards the 'sign of the coming unity of humanity'.[38] Suzanne Fageol suggests, 'The circle is a symbol of containment – the womb, the vessel – which includes and births the divine in us.'[39] Circles are important, in short, because of what they suggest, in Russell's word, about 'communalization'. They are part of a critique of clericalism and an insistence on the full participation of all in liturgy as in the entire life of the church. This principle is reflected, to a degree, in post-Vatican II liturgical architecture in which the gathering in the round dominates, reflecting the new emphasis on the church as the whole people of God, although practice has not always lived up to the lead of architectural renewal. The Metropolitan Cathedral of Christ the King in Liverpool, a dramatic building designed in the shape of a crown, is a telling example of this tension between affirming the collegiality of the gathered people of God and continuing to venerate a monarchical God who upholds patriarchal power.[40]

A variety of practices within the ecclesial gathering enact the principle of communilization. One way is for processions in the liturgy to involve all rather than merely a few (usually ordained) persons. The church of St Gregory of Nyssa, San Francisco, famous for its vibrant and inclusive architectural space as well as its dancing liturgy, exemplifies this practice in its regular Sunday liturgy.[41] Richard Giles also advocates the passing of a stole to each vocal/focal leader as the liturgy proceeds, rather than being the sole possession of the preacher, on the grounds that the stole is not a symbol of ordination but a symbol of ministry.[42] The St Hilda Community practised mutual absolution around the circle, with each person signing the person next to them with the sign of the cross and declaring forgiveness, as well as passing the elements of bread and wine around the circle.[43] Circle dances are powerful symbols of gathering, sharing and moving together in the power of the Spirit. 'Circle principles' are now widely used in many gatherings, organizations and communities inspired by egalitarianism, consensus-based decision-making and feminist visions of mutual ministry and empowerment.[44]

On the level

As Janet Walton asserts, feminist liturgy depicts and enacts equality, and this is obvious in the symbol of the circle. Another feature of the circle is that all are on the same level as each other. The horizontal plane takes precedence over the vertical. No one is elevated above another, no one looks down on another and no one is diminished within the circle. Where liturgy is not on the level, it not only elevates the leaders but excludes; this is obvious to anyone with impaired mobility who wishes to get around a church building. How many church buildings have disabled access to altar-space? What does that assume and say, to and about, what 'ministry' is assumed to mean for persons with disabilities?

Being on a level is a symbol not only of equal access but also of equal right to speak and equal authority. In the circle, all are listened to with equal respect and all are heard into speech. None is given special privilege to speak to, or on behalf of, others. Feminists are empowered within the circle to talk back to the tradition, to 'level with' all that they experience as discriminatory or patronizing, to challenge and critique taken-for-granted assumptions about ministry, leadership and power. Within the conversation circle and around the kitchen table, diversity is the norm. Inclusion does not imply sameness but respect for difference and an attentiveness to the lived experience and wisdom of each one.

Theologically, the primacy of the horizontal over the vertical axis suggests a strong emphasis on divine immanence rather than transcendence. The divine manifests within, rather than above or beyond, the gathered community, in solidarity with human community rather than standing in judgement or opposition to it. While some have strongly condemned this feature of architectural modernism,[45] it concurs with feminist theologies that prefer to speak of God in mutual, relational terms (Friend, Companion, Lover, Beloved and so on) rather than hierarchical ones (Lord, Father, King, Judge). This raises the question about the place of transcendence within feminist liturgical expression and whether (as I believe) it is possible for immanence and transcendence to co-exist. One clue to this may lie in liturgical architectural spaces which, while in the round, nevertheless manage to gesture towards divine transcendence through use of vertical space. For example, the large modern cement chapel at Malling Abbey, which is home to a community of enclosed Benedictine nuns, is a huge ark-like space in which the nuns sing the daily office and celebrate the Eucharist in the round, with a vast, empty space above in which the play of light and rain and sound evokes a sense of transcendence within the immanence of the community's life.

Face to face

Being in the round and on the level implies being face to face, and the priority of the personal over the institutional. This is a politics and a theology of encounter, in which the human gaze and touch are emblematic of the divine–human encounter. In a circle, everyone has a place next to another and all are joined through the circle, sometimes by touch but more frequently by sight, which can take in all the other participants within the circle. Unlike in the traditional cross-shaped church in which laity are in rows separated from each other and looking up ahead to the clergy whose gaze confronts them (or whose backs are turned away from them in east-facing presidency), feminist liturgies insist on the fully embodied, face-to-face gaze and encounter.

Thus Sarah Coakley's advocacy of east-facing presidency as a model of reformed gender relations[46] is hardly in line with most feminist trajectories of thinking. The 'etiquette' required of the president (if indeed there is one – and in many feminist liturgies, such holding of the liturgy as happens is generally dispersed[47]) requires a subtle shaping and holding of the circle, not standing at the 'head', still less with back turned.[48] The image of the round table needs to be seen not only in terms of having no head/front but also to imply equal distance from 'holy things'. No one gets to be 'more sacramental' than anyone else. The ritual needs to embody this, as and before it is put into words.

Whether the 'face-to-face' relation that dominates in feminist ecclesiology implies a symmetrical relationship or allows for degrees of difference and, indeed, imbalances of power and access, is a question that cannot be discussed here, but I would suggest that, while 'face-to-face' relation implies mutuality of engagement within a non-hierarchical circle of ministry, it does not necessitate symmetry or sameness. It is possible to engage 'face to face' with those who are utterly unlike me and who may possess greater or lesser degrees of power, access, responsibility and so on. Many different kinds of relationship are possible within the face-to-face encounter, and it is precisely in encountering the other in all their strangeness, challenge and difference as a brother or sister with whom I am intimately joined in the circle and the gaze, that I may meet the divine Other face to face.

Conclusion

Feminist liturgical practice in a variety of settings, cultures and traditions around the globe offers a lively and richly illustrative case study of how persons and communities marginalized and pushed out from main/male-stream find their own ways to resist and refuse that marginalization and, from the margins and neglected sites of their lives, reclaim space, agency and power. These embodied practices are evolving and developing all the time, and doubtless there are many more that have not been included here. Together, they represent a kind of 'defecting in place'[49] that is spirited, resilient, optimistic and defiant, and give the lie to the myth of hegemonic space that discourses of power tend to assume.

Notes

1 Elizabeth Schüssler Fiorenza, *Jesus: Miriam's Child, Sophia's Prophet* (London, SCM Press, 1995), p. 14.

2 Virginia Woolf, *A Room of One's Own* (London: Penguin, 2002).

3 Linda McDowell and Joanne P. Sharp (eds.), *Space, Gender, Knowledge: Feminist Readings* (Abingdon: Routledge, 2nd edn, 2016), p. 2. The reference to bell hooks is to her article, 'choosing the margin as a space of radical openness' in *Yearning: Race, Gender and Cultural Politics* (London: Routledge, 2015).

4 Sigurd Bergmann notes the 'spatial turn' in theology, in 'Theology in Its Spatial Turn: Space, Place and Built Environments Challenging and Changing the Images of God', *Religion Compass* 1.3 (2007), pp. 353–79.

5 Marjorie Procter-Smith, *In Her Own Rite: Constructing Feminist Liturgical Tradition* (Nashville, TN: Abingdon Press, 1990), pp. 59–84.

6 See, for example, 'From Manspreading to Mansplaining: 6 ways men dominate the spaces around them', at http://everydayfeminism.com/2015/09/6-ways-men-dominate-space/ (accessed 10.4.17).

7 See Lisa Isherwood, *The Fat Jesus* (London: Darton, Longman & Todd, 2008) for an analysis and critique of the American slimming industry, undergirded by Evangelical finance and preaching, that encourages girls and young women to slim as a religious practice.

8 www.womenspace.org.au/?page_id=280 (accessed 10.4.17).

9 See http://womenspaceinc.org and www.selfinjurysupport.org.uk/group/women space-leeds/ (both accessed 10.4.17).

10 Monica Furlong, 'Introduction: A "non-sexist" community', in The St Hilda Community, *Women Included: A Book of Services and Prayers* (London: SPCK, 1991), p. 9.

11 Thus, the creation of the St Hilda Community in London developed out of the despair and anger felt by a group of Anglican women when the General Synod failed to pass a modest measure that would have allowed women lawfully ordained abroad to preside at the Eucharist in the UK.

12 This may be an apocryphal attribution, as I have not been able to find the reference!

13 See Daly's account in *Outercourse: The Be-Dazzling Voyage* (London: Women's Press, 1993), pp. 137–40.

14 See https://en.wikipedia.org/wiki/Pussy_Riot for an overview of the band's career and a brief description of the performance in the cathedral. For a fuller discussion and analysis, see the special issue of *Religion & Gender* 4.2 (2014), devoted to Pussy Riot's punk protest in the cathedral.

15 Furlong, 'Introduction', pp. 12–13.

16 Teresa Berger, *Women's Ways of Worship: Gender Analysis and Liturgical History* (Collegeville, MN: Liturgical Press, 1999), p. 33.

17 For examples of contemporary Jewish feminist home-based ritual, see, for example, Sylvia Rothschild and Sybil Sheridan, *Taking Up the Timbrel: The Challenge of Creating Ritual for Jewish Women Today* (London: SCM Press, 2000).

18 Jan Berry, *Ritual Making Women: Shaping Rites for Changing Lives* (London: Equinox, 2009), pp. 105–10.

19 See Kay Turner, *Beautiful Necessity: The Art and Meaning of Women's Altars* (New York: Thames & Hudson, 1999) for an account of women's altars around the world. Susan J. White's *A History of Women in Christian Worship* (London: SPCK, 2003) pays attention to the significance of the Christian home as a primary space for women's liturgical ministry.

20 The *Carmina Gadelica*, a collection of blessings, charms and runes from the highlands and islands of Scotland, contains many such examples. See Alexander Carmichael, *Carmina Gadelica: Hymns and Incantations from the Gaelic* (Edinburgh: Floris Books, 1992).

21 See June Boyce-Tillman, *In Tune with Heaven or Not: Women in Christian Liturgical Music* (Oxford: Peter Lang, 2014) for a full discussion of the significance of women's music-making in Christian tradition.

22 Letty M. Russell, *Church in the Round: Feminist Interpretation of the Church* (Louisville, KY: Westminster John Knox Press, 1993).

23 Russell, *Church in the Round*, pp. 75–6.

24 See Rosemary Radford Ruether, *Women-Church: Theology and Practice* (New York: Harper & Row, 1985), chapter 8, for examples, and Marjorie Procter-Smith, *Praying with Our Eyes Open: Engendering Feminist Liturgical Prayer* (Nashville, TN: Abingdon Press, 1995), chapter 2, for a broader discussion of the importance of 'the prayer of refusal' in feminist liturgy.

25 Ruether, *Women-Church*.

26 While 'Womenchurch' is a widely used term in the USA to denote alternative feminist liturgical communities, it is not so widely used in the UK and mainland Europe.

27 Ruether, *Women-Church*, pp. 146–7.

28 See www.sophia.org.au (accessed 11.4.17).

29 See www.holyroodhouse.org.uk (accessed 13.4.17).

30 See, for example, Gina Messina-Dysert and Rosemary Radford Ruether (eds.), *Feminism and Religion in the 21st Century: Technology, Dialogue, and Expanding Borders* (New York and Abingdon: Routledge Taylor & Francis, 2015).

31 See Procter-Smith, *Praying with our Eyes Open*, chapter 6, for a variety of feminist eucharistic rites.

32 Janet R. Walton, *Feminist Liturgy: A Matter of Justice* (Collegeville, MN: Liturgical Press, 2000).

33 Marcella Althaus-Reid, *The Queer God* (London: Routledge Taylor & Francis, 2003), pp. 10–11, 18.

34 Berger, *Women's Ways of Worship*, p. 126.

35 I owe these metaphors to Stephen Burns, as well as many other insights in this chapter.

36 See Chuck Lathrop's poem, 'In search of a roundtable', in *A Gentle Presence* (Washington, DC: Appalachian Documentation, 1977), p. 5, and available at a number of places online.

37 Ruether, *Women-Church*, p. 148.

38 Russell, *Church in the Round*, p. 17.

39 Suzanne Fageol, 'Celebrating Experience', in St Hilda Community, *Women Included*, p. 22.

40 See www.liverpoolmetrocathedral.org.uk.

41 See www.saintgregorys.org (accessed 13.4.17).

42 Richard Giles, *Creating Uncommon Worship* (Norwich: Canterbury Press, 2004), p. 75.

43 St Hilda Community, *Women Included*, pp. 20, 60.

44 See, for example, www.millionthcircle.org and www.circlesolutionsnetwork.com/circle-principles/ (accessed 11.4.17).

45 See, for example, Moyra Doorly, *No Place for God: The Denial of the Transcendent in Modern Church Architecture* (San Francisco, CA: Ignatius Press, 2007).

46 Sarah Coakley, 'The Woman at the Altar: Cosmological Disturbance or Gender Subversion?', *Anglican Theological Review* 86.1 (2004), pp. 75–93.

47 See Nicola Slee and Stephen Burns (eds.), *Presiding Like a Woman* (London: SPCK, 2010) for further discussion of the scope and potential of feminist understandings of 'presiding'.

48 Though it should be noted that Coakley is not alone in arguing for a reconsideration of eastward-facing eucharistic presidency. See Stephen R. Shaver, 'O Oriens: Reassessing Eastward Eucharist Celebration for Renewed Liturgy', *Anglican Theological Review* 94.3 (2012), pp. 451–73.

49 Miriam Therese Winter, *Defecting in Place: Women Taking Responsibility for Their Own Spiritual Lives* (New York: Crossroad, 1994).

PART 3

A Feminist Practical Spirituality

Body and soul

after Jane Kenyon

Water speaks to the pitcher: hold me
Pitcher says to water: spill me

Plate begs of the prisoner: eat me
Prisoner asks of the plate: fill me

Horse whispers to its rider: release me
Rider urges the stallion: carry me

Moon sings to the ocean: mirror me
Ocean moans to the moon: pull me

Fruit talks to the sun: ripen me
Sun smiles on the fruit: draw me

Blossom pressed in the book: preserve me
Book receiving the blossom: pattern me

Heart contracting with joy: consume me
Joy expanding the heart: receive me

Death overcoming the lover: embrace me
Love overcoming death: embrace me

6

A Spirituality of Multiple Overwhelmings

I have been a long-time member of BIAPT – the British and Irish Association of Practical Theology – and participated in many of its annual conferences as well as other events. I was invited to give a keynote lecture at the 2016 conference, which took place in Limerick, Ireland, under the overall theme of 'Wrestling with Angels? Practical Theology as Spiritual Practice'. The conference took place just after the referendum vote in the UK, on 23 June 2016, to ask the electorate whether the country should remain a member of, or leave, the European Union. This left many of us at the conference in a state of confusion and perplexity, and I wanted to speak into this reality, as well as to name some of my own issues about living with a variety of 'overwhelmings'. This essay forms the substance of my address, and was originally published in 2017 in Practical Theology *10.1, pp. 20–32.*

Introduction

I wish to engage in an extended theological reflection on the metaphor of 'multiple overwhelmings', which I believe can speak powerfully to the context of our contemporary church and world. This is an exercise in 'metaphorical theology',[1] grounded in the conviction that metaphors are not mere ornaments to thought but essentially meaning-making, cognitive at core. Metaphors connect what, in a more linear or analytic approach, may appear disconnected, bringing together two different frames of reference in a way that sparks novel insight. One metaphor cannot do everything, of course, and such is the case for this one, but it seems to me a potent metaphor for our time. In particular, I wish to reflect theologically on our situatedness and practice as practical theologians amid such 'multiple overwhelmings', and to consider the nature of a spirituality that is both shaped by the condition of multiple overwhelmings and is adequate to respond to it.

This is not an original metaphor. I am borrowing it from Professor David Ford who, in *The Shape of Living*, named the situation of 'multiple overwhelmings' as the essential context and condition of our contemporary world and of human life in the twenty-first century.[2]

Multiple overwhelmings in Ford's *Shape of Living*

Ford speaks of the common human experience of being overwhelmed, not merely as an occasional occurrence but as something that defines our humanity. Rather than perceive it as an aberration or a problem to be solved, he invites us to consider being multiply overwhelmed as normative, constitutive of selfhood and, for religious people, faith. 'Coping with multiple overwhelmings, both good and bad' is 'the most important thing in our lives', he asserts.[3] Asking a group of colleagues and acquaintances the question, 'What do you find most overwhelming?', Ford received a variety of responses: 'Information and knowledge overload; financial and job insecurity; responsibilities; overeating; pain; despair; beauty; confusion; inadequacy; poverty, generosity; gratitude.' He continues:

> Human history is shaped by many overwhelmings. There are some continuous strands – sex, money, power, violence, knowledge, pleasure, responsibility. There are the huge events – a war, a massacre, a stock market collapse, an AIDS epidemic, the birth of a new nation, public events which affect millions and change the course of groups and nations. Or there are more personal events – falling in love; the birth of a child; divorce; serious illness; finding or losing a job; bereavement.[4]

The experience of being overwhelmed, whether positive or negative, is of being caught up, carried along or bowled over, by some event, force or person, over which one has no control. Overwhelming can be terrifying, life-threatening, a force of destruction; but it can also be marvellous, wonderful, uplifting and transformative. Feelings of being overwhelmed are a common symptom of anxiety, manifesting in physical symptoms such as rapid heartbeat, laboured breathing, chest pains, nausea, light-headedness or dizziness, as well as mental stress and distress. Yet we also speak of being overwhelmed by music or art or natural beauty, by the love of God or of friends. It is a pervasive, totalizing experience which affects every aspect of body, mind, emotions and consciousness. There is a sense of enormity, of existential dread, awe or wonder – not of any particular thing, but of the nature and force of existence itself – which can be paralysing or energizing, terrifying or joyful.

Philosophers and theologians have named and analysed the experience of overwhelming in a variety of ways, from Kierkegaard's existential dread or angst that a man feels on standing on the edge of a precipice and peering into the abyss,[5] to Tillich's anxiety that underlies the threat of non-being and is the pervasive condition of modern man.[6] More recently, a variety of feminist practical theologians have spoken of contemporary forms of overwhelming such as Chopp's trauma situations of extreme agony or ecstasy which require a 'poetics of witness';[7] Bons-Storms' 'unstories' of women whose pastors would not believe or legitimate their testimonies of abuse;[8] my own work on women's apophatic faithing,[9] a paradoxical, negative form of expressing faith through what cannot be articulated, professed or owned.

Ford suggests three imperatives necessary to a positive response to multiple overwhelmings. First, there is the imperative to 'name it', to bring into language that which is fearful, inchoate and beyond understanding or control, and thereby give it some solidity, shape and objectivity. This is the work of theology, poetry and prayer. As Ford suggests, 'Poetry at its best has wrestled with the great overwhelmings, and out of that engagement has shaped a language through which we too can respond.'[10]

After naming comes the further work of describing the experience of multiple overwhelmings, narrating the texture and timbre, the very weather of the experience, so to speak, to story it from the inside. This is the work of fiction, film, social science and the arts, as well as of prayer and liturgy. The scriptures provide many descriptions of multiple overwhelmings: from the archetypal myth of the flood in Genesis to Job's cataclysmic overwhelming by catastrophe; from the psalmists' laments of being overwhelmed by sorrow, pain and sin to the prophets' awareness of being besieged and engulfed by a fire within them which they cannot resist; from the overwhelming experiences of Israel in slavery, exodus and exile to Christ's overwhelming by temptation, Gethsemane agony and dereliction on the cross; from the brooding of the Spirit over the waters of chaos to the Pentecostal outpouring in flame, wind and tongues. The Bible provides an entire lexicon for articulating the many diverse aspects of the profound shaping of our lives by multiple overwhelmings. I will return to some of these scriptural themes later.

Ford's third imperative is to 'attend to the shape of living', avoiding the temptation of either drowning in the overwhelming or fiddling with some of the details in the endeavour to 'stretch our minds, hearts and imaginations in trying to find and invent shapes of living'.[11] Both paying attention and giving shape to experience are classic metaphors for the work of spirituality, and I will return to the work of attention later.

Speaking personally: an exercise in autoethnography

In what follows, I want to attend to some of my own 'multiple overwhelmings' in a modest exercise of autoethnography. These are, of course, particular to my own life, context and commitments and cannot be generalized. Yet some of my personal overwhelmings may be shared more widely and, even if they are not, my attempt at description may encourage readers in an exercise of mapping out their own. In their multiplicity and interconnectedness, if not in their specific detail, the ecology of my overwhelmings may be typical of the kinds of overwhelmings in which we all participate, and out of which we live. For, as Ford emphasizes, it is the *multiplicity* of our experiences of being overwhelmed that forms an essential part of their challenge. 'The various forms of overwhelming are all parts of a whole. To deal with one part separately without taking account of the rest throws all the dynamics out of balance.'[12]

Personal and domestic overwhelmings

Compared with many people I know, my own domestic context appears rather simple. I live with my partner and two cats in an unremarkable neighbourhood a few miles from my place of work. I do not have children, though I come from a large and somewhat dispersed family. I am comfortably well off. My health is reasonable for a woman of my age. For all the relative straightforwardness of my personal circumstances, I frequently feel overwhelmed by all there is to handle and do in daily life. The sheer amount of *stuff* that pours into the house in the form of emails, magazines, circulars, books, work files is a constant challenge, as is trying to maintain some semblance of order and space in the living environment. The daily work of cooking, cleaning and gardening can ground my life in ways for which I am grateful, but it only takes a minor crisis – the car or fridge packing up, a leak in the roof – to precipitate anxiety and stress. Outside of maintaining the core relationships of immediate family and work colleagues, there never seems sufficient time to be in touch with, let alone see, close friends. I make lists of all there is to do, in a vain attempt at control and order. At times, quite regularly, it is all too much to contemplate or manage. Working on this paper to deliver at the BIAPT conference, I experience overwhelming feelings of dread and anxiety, physical pain, writing blocks and insomnia.

Professional overwhelmings

Perhaps one reason for the sense of personal and domestic overwhelming I have confessed to, is the growing level of professional pressure I observe in my own working life – and that of many colleagues and friends – as I look back over the past few decades. It is now almost 20 years since I first arrived at the theological education institution where I work and, year on year, I have witnessed the increasing pressures and expectations on both staff and students alike. Of course, this has gone hand in hand with my own professional development and increased levels of responsibility within the institution. Someone who stays in one institution for many years and is halfway competent at their job is likely to accrue increasing amounts of work. At the same time, the institution itself has massively diversified and become a much more complex organization than it was when I first arrived. In an era of austerity, declining church membership and the increasing bureaucratization of higher education, theological colleges and courses feel the pinch from both directions (church and higher education) and have to do more and more with less and less in order to survive in a highly competitive market. This is a form of professional overwhelming that is pervasive in the public and voluntary sector and will be very well known to most readers of this journal.

Political overwhelmings

I have been preparing this paper at a time of massive political upheaval in the (so-called) United Kingdom[13] that seems to demand metaphors of excess (though this is still a matter of degree in comparison with the kind of wholesale political and social devastation in countries such as Syria or Haiti). The result of the Referendum on leaving the European Union seemed to take the country's political leaders by surprise and catapulted both major political parties into their own crises of leadership. More concerning, the result has exposed and exacerbated profound divisions in British society between the financially secure, middle-class Europhile establishment on the one hand and, on the other, disaffected low-earners and the unemployed who are pushed to the very edges of society, whose voices have largely been ignored by mainstream politics. Race relations may well have been put back decades by the Referendum, not to speak of the impact on the delicate relations between Northern Ireland and the Republic. Perhaps we will look back on the events of this time as the point at which the European project envisaged by the founders of the EU began to unravel. This is a political overwhelming the like of which I have not seen in my lifetime, which is likely to change the face not only of Europe itself but of international relations.

Historical overwhelmings

At precisely the point when Britons voted by a narrow majority to exit the European Union, war veterans, politicians, members of the royal family, church leaders and media commentators were gathering on French and English soil to mark the centenary of one of the bloodiest wars in history, the Battle of the Somme. Standing on French soil drenched in the mingled blood of English, Irish, Scottish, Welsh, French and German soldiers, the millions of war dead have been honoured. However many times one hears the numbers – 57,470 casualties in the British army on the first day of the battle of the Somme, more than 1 million men wounded or killed in the five months of the battle – or see the images of blasted trees, the lice-infested dugouts, the piles of rotting corpses, it is impossible for someone who has never experienced war at close quarters, such as myself, to grasp the enormity of this terrible historical overwhelming. The horror of it is made all the more poignant by the sweet loveliness of the French countryside, the poppy-waving fields that have grown over the slain bodies of Europe's youth.

Socio-cultural overwhelmings

Thinking back to a Europe on the cusp of the twentieth century brings to awareness the huge gulf that separates that world from ours one hundred years later. We could speak of any number of multiple overwhelmings that have characterized those hundred years, whether of the forces of globalization that have both expanded and shrunk our sense of the global community or of giddying scientific and technological advances that have inaugurated the era of the cyborg and the World Wide Web, proliferating exponentially both knowledge itself and our access to it. We could think of massive shifts in the gravity of power away from the 'old' centres of European civilization to the new cultures of Asia and the Americas, or of worldwide liberation movements of women, ethnic and sexual minorities, which have begun to challenge and disrupt entrenched systems of power even as gender, racial and sexual slavery mutate into ever new forms. Conflicts in the Middle East and Africa, pressures on the economies of those countries, as well as in Eastern Europe, coupled with the ease of access to images and stories of unimagined wealth and opportunity in Western Europe, have produced the pressures of migration that have played their part in the result of the UK Referendum. It is impossible to employ the metaphor of 'overwhelming' without calling to mind images of unseaworthy boats stuffed with human cargo, bodies afloat or washed up on European shores and the desperate need that drives so many to take deadly risks to traverse the perilous deeps.

Cosmic/ecological overwhelmings

Nor can we only refer to personal, interpersonal, social and political change in this exercise of bringing to awareness the multiple overwhelmings within which our lives are set. This century and the last one have seen the most far-reaching ecological and cosmic overwhelmings that threaten to overturn life on this planet or at the very least wipe out whole species and ecosystems that will drastically change the nature of planetary existence.

Spiritual responses to overwhelming

By definition, it is not possible to choose whether or not we will be overwhelmed. Yet there is always some degree of choice in how we respond to the experience. It is possible to identify more or less helpful, theologically authentic, psychologically and spiritually adequate responses to the experience of being multiply overwhelmed: those which in some way or other refuse the challenge of being pervasively shaped by our experiences of overwhelming, and those which submit to that challenge at the same time as endeavouring to shape appropriate ways of living within the reality of the overwhelming. What follows is not intended as a comprehensive account of possible spiritual responses, but an indicative assemblage of postures that may be more or less functional, more or less authentic means of responding to the mass challenge of multiple overwhelmings. There is not space here to spell these out in any detail, but my hope is that in naming such postures, however briefly, readers may recognize their own habitual responses and be encouraged to choose those that are appropriate and life-giving.

Inadequate, but common responses

Denial via masking, faking and smiling

There's a poster found in a variety of forms on the internet of a woman smiling excessively with the caption, 'I smile to hide how completely overwhelmed I am'. This might stand for any number of postures of faking and hiding in denial from the reality of being overwhelmed, far more common a posture – both in the church and in the professional arena – than we might care to admit. Stevie Smith's popular poem, 'Not waving but drowning',[14] offers a chilling parable of what happens to one who spends a lifetime smiling and waving when they are in fact drowning.

Escapism via addictions of various sorts

Denial may lead to escapism, the attempt to blot out the fear and dread of being overwhelmed by a variety of drugs – from alcohol, shopping and overwork to overeating and excessive consumption of one kind or another, including religion and spirituality as forms of escapism, of which we can detect many versions in contemporary culture. This response is a paradoxical one – escaping the overwhelmings by retreating into a compensatory overwhelming, trying to overwhelm the overwhelmings by an all-absorbing, totalizing habit, which may succeed in blotting out the more profound overwhelmings, at least temporarily, but only at the cost of feeding and multiplying a hunger that is out of control.

Anger, aggression and violence

In this response, the fear of being overwhelmed is projected on to others who can be conveniently blamed as the 'cause' of the overwhelming. We may then experience our own potency (which is threatened by the reality of being overwhelmed) through the capacity to wound and inflict hurt and damage on others. 'Look how powerful I am if I can make you bleed!' For the duration of the time in which I am engaged in attack – whether verbally, emotionally or physically – I can deflect attention away from my own pain and vulnerability, and find satisfaction in the process of othering, at the same time rejecting the right of the other to share a common space. I defend my own uncertain ground by attacking those I perceive as threats to it.

Reductionism

This is the attempt to reduce the complexity of the situation of multiple overwhelmings to a one-dimensional depiction of reality and to offer simple solutions that will save us from the need to think critically and hold the tension and mess of being multiply overwhelmed. This is the response of fundamentalism of various sorts (including many forms of so-called New Age spirituality), which offer simplistic responses to suffering and conflict: 'If you only believe strongly and unquestioningly enough (whether in Jesus, crystals, psychotherapy, UKIP or a particular diet), you will be saved from danger, complexity, illness, confusion, job insecurity or the devil' – take your pick.

Omnicompetence

An alternative to seeking to reduce the overwhelmings is to endeavour to expand our own power in responding to them. This stance represents the idolatry of seeking to master and control the forces that overwhelm by over-extending the ego in an effort to coerce what is overwhelming. This may look very like, or mutate into, a form of addiction in its own right, as the habitual response to ever-growing demands is to take them on board, expanding the hours of work, numbers of projects, emails, relationships, and so on, that one seeks to accommodate. It is a particularly contemporary form of hubris which over-extends the self and does not recognize the need to live within limits.

Despair, passivity, shrinking in on the self

This posture can be seen as the opposite to the over-extension and aggrandizement of the self, as the overwhelmed self experiences its own impotency and shrinks in upon itself, fearful and despairing of being able to act meaningfully within a situation of multiple overwhelming. Such a stance may manifest in depression, paralysis, mental and physical health symptoms and a loss of appetite or energy. It is another form of refusal to meet the demands of the situation, perhaps an inversion of anger, a form of aggression turned in upon the self rather than externalized on to others.

Any or all of these dysfunctional responses to being overwhelmed may and often do combine. One form of dysfunctional response feeds off another, exacerbating the stress and inadequacy of the lived relation to complexity. I may work longer and longer hours, refusing to rest, in an effort to cope with all that threatens to overwhelm me; at the same time, experiencing despair and anger, retreating in addictions of various kinds and lashing out at others who are easy targets for my own frustration and impotence.

Metaphors that might shape more helpful responses

I do not want to offer specific spiritual practices as an antidote to these dysfunctional responses to the condition of multiple overwhelming, so much as a few metaphors that might shape more helpful responses. I offer three: immersion, holding or bearing the tension, and attention.

Immersion

Rather than resisting or fighting the forces of overwhelming, it may be that we are required to accede to the overwhelming and consent to it, giving oneself up to the reality. It may be that the divine invitation, fearful and overwhelming as it is, is to swim or dive deeper into the ocean, to walk out unprotected in the storm, to submerge in the flood.[15]

This is a response of consent to being overwhelmed, in the belief and trust that the ultimate reality, the ground of all being, is God and that God is present and at work in the overwhelming. Such a response is grounded in the conviction that the experience of being multiply overwhelmed is, despite all appearances to the contrary, an essentially creative, rather than a destructive or death-dealing, process. The experience of being overwhelmed is an invitation to greater and fuller life, rather than the crushing of life; it is, at least potentially, a process of birthing, although it may manifest as a form of death. The obvious liturgical symbol that may help here is that of baptism, in which the disciple is called to immerse in the waters of death with Christ in order that she may rise to a new reality, a new person in Christ. The metaphor of baptism itself draws on the primary human experience of birth, which entails being pushed out of the safe, dark waters of the womb through the constriction of the birth canal, into the overwhelming of life outside the mother's womb. To the newborn infant as well as to the mother, this process of labour is experienced as one of profound loss, akin to death; giving birth is still one of the most dangerous of human endeavours and is, for that very reason, a powerful analogy for religious conversion.

Non-metaphorically, 'immersion' can stand for the embrace of an appropriately 'this-worldly' spirituality. Our default model of holiness or spirituality still tends to be one of withdrawal, 'involving long periods of quiet, focused reflection, dark churches, and dignified liturgies', as Janet Martin Soskice describes it in her essay 'Love and attention'.

> In its higher reaches it involves time spent in contemplative prayer, retreats, and sometimes the painful wrestlings with God portrayed by John Donne or George Herbert. Above all, it involves solitude and collectedness. It does not involve looking after small children.[16]

As this last comment makes clear, this default model of holiness, predicated on the lonely, detached, rational and controlling Enlightenment male self, disenfranchises many people, especially women. Soskice herself, along with others such as Margaret Hebblethwaite,[17] offers an alternative model of engaged, embodied spirituality that is practised in 'the management of ordinary life and the realm of necessity'.[18] Through attention to the minute particularities of caring, feeding and cleaning, for instance, Soskice argues that parents learn and practise essential spiritual disciplines of self-mastery, patient humility and disinterested love, in the process being bodily as well as spiritually changed. Rather than try to escape the overwhelming demands of parenting, the mother or father of a newborn infant immerses willingly in the task, both losing and finding themselves in attending to the overwhelming reality.

Feeling/bearing/holding the tension

Immersion within the forces of overwhelming implies this second stance or posture, as we experience and bear within ourselves the extraordinary buffeting, tension and constriction of being in the place where the forces of overwhelming meet and mingle. Rather than collapsing the tension or trying to resolve the confusion in favour of one overwhelming or simple solution, a spiritually mature response to multiple overwhelmings requires one to hold the space at the intersection of the forces of overwhelming, to reside in the place of greatest tension in the conviction that, out of this place of intersection, a new reality may be envisaged and birthed. Continuing the birth imagery, this is the work of labour which requires enormous concentration and suffering in the interests of new life; it requires a willingness to reside, at least for a time, within the birth canal where the forces of life and death converge.

Other images for this work of holding, feeling and bearing the tension at the convergence of the forces of overwhelming may be offered. The myth of the flood provides the image of the ark, which offers a place of respite and refuge from the forces of overwhelming, a place where life is protected and born aloft on the abyss. David Whyte speaks of 'the ability to rediscover a simple dwelling at the center of a complex world'.[19] Those who work in therapeutic settings, such as counsellors, therapists and chaplains, will recognize the significance of the work of creating a safe space in which experiences of overwhelming can be examined, explored and entered into at one remove, and choices can be made with the support of the therapist, counsellor or soul-friend. Teaching may also operate with a similar agenda of creating safe space for the exploration and analysis of fearful, threatening and overwhelming ideas from sources that are difficult and strange to the student. Writing and research may be another form of space-making, of stepping back from the immediacy of felt and lived experience to refract the experience in words and analysis, patterns on the page.

Attention

At its simplest, being multiply overwhelmed requires a response of concentrated, disciplined and focused *attention*, within which one makes choices about what is possible. Rather than seek to respond to the totality of all that demands our care and attention, we seek to discern the 'one thing necessary' – the next task or person or hour's endeavour (which might be to rest, to sleep or to play, as much as to work). We narrow the focus to something specific within the overwhelming, practising the discipline of patient particularity within a fundamental attitude of trust and respect for the ecology of God's providence. This is not an exercise of reductionism or naive simplification of complexity, though it might look deceptively like it. It is, perhaps, counter-intuitive to a logic that would suggest we need to encompass all of the multiple strands of what faces us in our complex situations of overwhelming; part of the spiritual wisdom required in our overly driven world is to discern what needs to be resisted and left to one side (if only temporarily) in order to focus on the essential.

The model of spiritual practice as a form of attention has been developed by many writers, from Weil's classic essay on 'the right use of school studies with a view to the love of God'[20] to Murdoch's *Sovereignty of Good*[21] and Soskice's essay to which I have already referred. (Is it incidental that these are all women?) Weil argues that prayer consists of a disciplined and focused attention towards God, and that the discipline of attention can be learnt and practised through the focused work of study, whether the subject of the study is religious or something entirely secular such as algebra. The pure, disinterested application of attention in intellectual thinking prepares the soul for the love of neighbour and of God. The agnostic philosopher

Murdoch defines attention as 'a just and loving gaze directed upon an individual reality', and regards it as 'the characteristic and proper mark of the active moral agent'.[22] Following Weil, she describes prayer as 'simply an attention to God which is a form of love'.[23] Soskice develops the account of attention in a close analysis of the formative work of parenting which she regards as an instance of embodied, self-emptying and spiritual practice.

Elizabeth Jennings' poem, 'Night Sister',[24] offers an example of such focused, disciplined and embodied attention in the compassionate care of a nurse in a psychiatric hospital ward. Rather than be overwhelmed or hardened by the mixed anguish, helplessness and suffering of her patients, the nurse goes about her work quietly and patiently, giving attention to each one in turn and so easing their pain and communicating to them a sense of their profound worth and value. At home behind the 'locked doors' of the ward, able to hear without fear the 'sudden shouts and tears' of the patients, the nurse has 'a memory for everyone' and meets each one in their distress.

Such a response of practised attention is held within a wider ecology of the ecclesial body. It becomes possible for me to focus down on the person in front of me and, for a time, ignore or forget the dozens or hundreds of others I should be concerned about, because I am not the only agent of love or care within God's kin-dom[25] and I can trust God's economy to supply the rest. If I imagine, erroneously, that everything depends upon me, that I cannot put my pen or my ladle or my head down for a moment without things starting to unravel (and I do, often enough, behave as if I believe this), it becomes impossible for me to choose particularity and limitation. If I believe and trust that I am part of the body, no less worthy of care and respect than any other part and no less capable of contributing to the whole, then I can accept my own limitations and offer what I can gladly and willingly, knowing that it does not have to be either perfect or comprehensive.

Coda: a theology of overwhelming

'The wisest way to cope', Ford suggests, 'is not to try to avoid being overwhelmed, and certainly not to expect to be in control of everything; rather it is to live amidst the overwhelmings in a way that lets one of them be the overwhelming that shapes the others. That is the "home" or "school" in which the practicalities of coping can be learnt.'[26] For people of faith, the primary overwhelming that shapes and schools all the others is, of course, God, the Holy One, depth and ground of being, source and goal of all things. It is in allowing ourselves to be overwhelmed by God, caught up in the unpredictable, uncontrollable, gratuitous excess of God that the other overwhelmings find their shape and mitigate their demands. The various traditions of spirituality, both historical and contemporary, teach disciplines and practices that are intended to enable the reality of God to be the primary ground and telos of all our other desires, needs and overwhelmings. The spiritual practices of prayer, worship, scriptural reading and reflection, Eucharist, fasting, tithing, pastoral care, social justice and community life, are all intended to orient individuals and communities towards the one overwhelming reality of God and to shape our personal and common life so that it accords with the being and purposes of God.

We might think of the Judeo-Christian tradition and its peoples as those formed by the divine overwhelming, as those who learn to live faithfully within such overwhelming. Creation itself may be thought of as an overwhelming overflow of the generative being of the Making One, whose excess of love and life results in the magnificent uniqueness and splendour of the cosmos – formed, as scientists describe it, through millennia of overwhelming compressions and outpourings that are staggering to the human mind. The history of the Israelites is of a people formed, purged and irrevocably marked by a series of overwhelming episodes: flood, captivity, slavery, exodus, exile, the destruction of the Temple, and wave after wave of persecution culminating in the near-annihilation of the Nazi Holocaust. Christians are inheritors of this history even as they have contributed some of its most brutal and shameful assaults.

The story of Jesus, too, might be read as a sequence of overwhelmings, beginning with the overshadowing of Mary by the Spirit which leads to the birth of the liberating prophet whose visionary preaching, signs and wonders, as well as his relationships with people, testify to God's compassionate and generous love for the least and the lost. The 'success' of Jesus' mission and ministry appears to be crushed by the defeat of the cross, as Jesus occupies the place of the curse and becomes the scapegoat for the venom of the religious establishment and the ruling empire. Yet death could not annihilate the life that erupted from the empty tomb, a force conjured out of Jesus' willingness to go to that place of ultimate overwhelming and annihilation and absorb its worst intentions, thereby transforming them.

And then comes Pentecost, the theological epitome of divine overwhelming in the outpouring of the Spirit upon frightened disciples in disarray. The Spirit comes in wind, fire, tongues, signs and wonders – symbols of anarchic excess and overflow, of the confounding of rationality – to energize and empower a new community drawn from every social class and nation in the known world. In this overwhelming, distinctions between slave and free, Jew and Gentile, male and female, young and old are overcome, yet without obliterating distinctiveness or particularity. There is a radical democratization of power, an overcoming of the binary dualism of 'othering' upon which all racial, gender, sexual and other distinctions are based, a creation of communion that is not threatened by difference.

In the history of Christianity it has often been noted that there is a repeated pattern of hardening and solidification of the free movement of the Spirit which follows each fresh outpouring: the attempt to fix and systematize doctrines, structures and practices. Yet again and again, the Spirit overwhelms efforts to control and circumscribe, inspiring new prophetic, liberationist and subversive movements of various kinds. Even where these are ruthlessly suppressed and the price is paid in martyrs' blood, the overwhelming overflow of the Spirit can never be quashed.

There is much more that could be said about a theology of overwhelming and, in particular, there are profound questions to be asked about the model of God that underlies such a theology. Is God over and above the process of overwhelming, sending it, mastering it, using it to shape – whether in grace or in judgement – the creation and humanity? Or is God more intrinsically part of the very process of overwhelming, caught up in the huge forces of creation and subject to them in not dissimilar ways to our own inescapable involvement in what sweeps over us? Process theologians and ecofeminist theologians, among others, invite us to consider this more risky, immanent and vulnerable image of a God who permits Godself to be caught up within the overwhelming. Within such a vision, the Spirit of God is the dynamic, erotic energy of connectedness, the go-between working within and between the multiple overwhelmings to create life, make love and pursue justice. Caught up within the perichoretic divine life, the whole of creation and human beings in particular are offered myriad opportunities to participate in that work of holding, bearing and channelling the forces that can lead to justice, love and truth.

Notes

1 Sallie McFague, *Metaphorical Theology* (London: SCM Press, 1982).

2 David F. Ford, *The Shape of Living* (London: Fount, 1997).

3 Ford, *Shape of Living*, p. xiv.

4 Ford, *Shape of Living*, pp. xix–xx.

5 Søren Kierkegaard, *The Concept of Anxiety* (Princeton, NJ: Princeton University Press, 1980).

6 Paul Tillich, *The Courage to Be* (New Haven, CT: Yale University Press, 1952). The use of the male pronoun in referring to Kierkegaard and Tillich is deliberate, as both historically accurate and gesturing towards the androcentrism of thought present in these writers.

7 Rebecca Chopp, *Saving Work: Feminist Practices of Theological Education.* (Louisville, KY: Westminster John Knox Press, 1995).

8 Riet Bons-Storm, *The Incredible Woman* (Nashville, TN: Abingdon Press, 1996).

9 Nicola Slee, 'Apophatic Faithing in Women's Spirituality', *British Journal of Theological Education* 11.2 (2001), pp. 23–7.

10 Ford, *Shape of Living*, p. xvi.

11 Ford, *Shape of Living*, p. xvii.

12 Ford, *Shape of Living*, p. xvi.

13 And, subsequently, by similar political forces at work in the USA.

14 Stevie Smith, 'Not waving but drowning' (1953), www.bbc.co.uk/arts/poetry/outloud/smith.shtml (accessed 13.10.16).

15 See my poem, 'Edge', in Nicola Slee, *Praying Like a Woman* (London: SPCK, 2004), p. 46.

16 Janet Martin Soskice, 'Love and attention', in *The Kindness of God: Metaphor, Gender, and Religious Language* (Oxford: Oxford University Press, 2007), pp. 12–13.

17 Margaret Hebblethwaite, *Motherhood and God* (London: Geoffrey Chapman, 1993).

18 Soskice, 'Love and attention', p. 23.

19 David Whyte, *The Heart Aroused: Poetry and the Preservation of the Soul in Corporate America* (New York: Doubleday, 1994), p. 213.

20 Simone Weil, 'Reflections on the right use of school studies with a view to the love of God', *Waiting on God* (Glasgow: Collins Fount, 1977).

21 Iris Murdoch, *Sovereignty of Good* (London: Routledge & Kegan Paul, 1970).

22 Murdoch, *Sovereignty of Good*, p. 34.

23 Murdoch, *Sovereignty of Good*, p. 55.

24 Elizabeth Jennings, 'Night sister', in *New Collected Poems*, ed. M. Schmidt (Manchester: Carcanet Press, (1962) 2002), p. 74.

25 A term proposed by Ada Maria Isasi-Diaz as an alternative to 'kingdom', in *En la Lucha: In the Struggle* (Minneapolis, MN: Fortress, 2004), p. 53.

26 Ford, *Shape of Living*, p. xxv.

7

The Landscape of the Gap:
Charting a Cartography

This address was given to the annual Continuing the Journey conference in April 2012, at the Swanwick Convention Centre, Derbyshire. Continuing the Journey is an association that brings together those 'wanting to explore the margins and the common ground between counselling, pastoral care, therapeutic or psychological work, and also spirituality, theology and faith issues.'[1] The theme of the whole conference was 'Mind the gap'.

Beginnings

There are openings in our lives
of which we know nothing.[2]

***

A gap in the hedge offers a view,
a glimpse into another world:
a wider sense of horizon, sky, fields and woods.
A gap in the fence lets in rain, wind, next door's dog.
It's a nuisance, something to be fixed, batoned over.
I look down the garden
and the broken line of fence
offends my neat eye.

There are gaps to be mended and gaps to be enjoyed.

***

A space on the page or canvas –
the wide margin around a poem,
lovely lines dancing in the uncrowded plane of the painting –
a place to pause, to ponder.
Don't rush on to the next line, next stanza.
Slow down, read slowly,
mind the gaps.
Appreciate what the artist has left out

so that your eye may focus.
What is not said in a poem
speaks as powerfully as the chosen words.
The way a poem is set out on a page
creates room for the reader.
An invitation to enter otherness.

***

A lull in conversation in which words settle,
thoughts take up their own space.
In the momentary silences, we pay attention to the quality of the encounter,
the felt presence in the room:
of fullness, perhaps, or awkwardness,
a space in which to move towards something not yet birthed.
The gap of gestation.

***

On the stage at Symphony Hall,
Tasmin Little is playing Beethoven's Violin Concerto,
the orchestra pausing around her,
conductor's baton stilled.
She sways on the platform,
making such sounds as will slay me or raise me,
I can't tell which.
At the end of phrases are merciful little stops of silence,
relief for mind and body
pitched past normal endurance.
At the end of each movement,
a longer pause for coughs, fidgets, shuffles,
as we ready ourselves for the next bout of concentration.
On the final note
some two thousand listeners catch their breath as one,
caught in a timeless moment of profound gratitude
before the eruption of thunderous applause.
It's a second or two which could change the direction
of a person's life.

***

Every night, the pattern of daily consciousness is broken, rinsed, resolved
by six, seven, eight hours of sleep.
We sink down into that somnolent unconsciousness,
the nightly practice of death.
'I don't like', God says in Charles Péguy's great meditation on sleep,
'the man who doesn't sleep.'

God praises his daughter Night:
'Among all others I glorify you and among all others you glorify me
And you are my honour and my glory,
For you obtain sometimes the most difficult thing in the world,
The surrender of man ...
Just to relax, his poor tired limbs on a restful bed.
Just to relax, his aching heart on a restful bed.
For his head, above all, to be still. It goes on far too long, that head of
    his. And he calls it work when his head goes on like that.
And his thoughts, no, or what he calls his thoughts.
For his ideas to be still and no longer shake about in his head like seeds in
    a pumpkin.
Like a rattle made from an empty pumpkin.
When one sees what they are, the things he calls his ideas.
Poor creature.'[3]

Moving on

For many years, as a writer, I struggled to come to terms with all the gaps and interruptions that seemed to beset the writing process. The distractions from the empty page. The procrastinations, hundred and one reasons I could find for avoiding my desk. The wanderings out into the garden to play with the cat, to weed a flowerbed, to see what had grown overnight. I regarded all this as a failure of nerve or concentration, castigated myself for my idleness. When did I wake up to the realization that these are not distractions *from* the work, something apart from the 'real thing', but an absolutely necessary part of the work, the gaps, pauses, breathing spaces that are intrinsic to it, which ask to be loved and respected?

These days, if I'm stuck in the flow of ideas on the page or the words seem to be flat and tired, instead of forcing myself to sit there and battle on, nine times out of ten I'll stop, turn the computer off and go out into the fresh air, immerse in the body for a while. I'll weed or hang out the washing or, best of all, go for a good, brisk stroll to the local park. There is something about the rhythm of walking that unlocks the mind's deadlock, gets things moving again – quite literally. Maybe, just maybe, there is the tenth occasion when it becomes necessary to face the resistance head-on and engage the struggle. But not often.

* * *

During a long period when I was ill with Chronic Fatigue Syndrome, my friend Jo Ind sent me the eleventh saying from the Taoist classic, the *Tao Te Ching*:

> Thirty spokes share the wheel's hub;
> It is the center hole that makes it useful.
> Shape clay into a vessel;
> It is the space within that makes it useful.
> Cut doors and windows for a room;
> It is the holes which make it useful.
> Therefore profit comes from what is there;
> Usefulness from what is not there.[4]

This piece of ancient wisdom spoke to me very powerfully of the spiritual significance of emptiness, at a time when my own capacity to act meaningfully in the world was drastically reduced. It helped me to regard the hours I was spending lying on a bed day after day not as useless wastes of time but as their own mysterious gift, even if I didn't have much sense at that time quite what the gift was. Looking back now, I can see that the flourishing of my writing and the development of a rich freelance life of lecturing and speaking gradually emerged out of that time of stripping down, of illness, joblessness and homelessness. However, I don't want to say that the 'value' of that experience of emptiness is only gauged by such measurable achievement. A far more intangible gift to me during this time was the birth of a new and mysterious sense of God – a God who did not heal me or rescue me from substantial loss, a God who in some senses seemed powerless, at least in the kind of ways I might have wanted him to act (and I think at this stage, he probably *was* still a 'he'!); a God rather who intimately befriended me in the vast spaces of my life, a God known not in light but in darkness, in uncertainty and unknowing, whose absence became a new form of compelling presence to me.

I wrote my poem 'Hole' in response to the saying from the *Tao Te Ching*, and out of this time in my life. The poem explores the paradoxical difficulty that I – and I think many of us – experience in keeping the gaps, the pauses, the empty spaces where they need to be: at the centre of things. It was one thing for me to preserve the spaces when my body wouldn't permit me to do much at all; quite another to keep the emptiness there when I began to recover and pick up the normal duties of life again. I want to say that it is precisely this commitment – to preserve the emptiness at the heart of things, to keep a profound space for presence and attention – that is the vocation of the contemplative, the Christian vocation to prayer. It is the task of prayer not to become yet one more activity in a busy life but to guard the interstices, to pray into and out of the gaps.

Hole

keeping the hole
where it should be
so that the spokes
don't buckle

keeping nothing
right there
at the centre
preserving the tension

keeping what is not
in place
so that what is
may not displace it

keeping the O
round and yawning
and empty
refusing to fill it

letting the heart lurch
and the body quiver
and the tongue stumble
on its own hopelessness

letting the throat
constrict in wordlessness

letting the formlessness be

permitting the unmaking
of thoughts and lines and words
and the grasp of and the hold on things
over and over to slip

permitting the unmaking of soul

ah this keeps the doctors running
and the poets writing
and the singers silent
and the madwomen for long hours staring[5]

Different kinds of gap

So, a gap can be a pause, an intake or out-take of breath; a space on the page or at the centre of a jug or a jar; a silence within and around music; an attentiveness to what is not expressed but is profoundly present between friends or lovers or between the soul and God. A gap may be a threshold, a transition, a movement from one place or state to another – or a longing to move from one state or place to another and not being able to, being caught in the in-between place.

The gap isn't always or perhaps often comfortable. It may take a lifetime to learn the balance and rhythm of incorporating the gaps into the flow and dance of our days – not least because that balance itself is likely to be constantly shifting and changing. It's not as if we can learn it once and expect it to hold for the rest of our lives. And while we're seeking to learn that balance, the gap may be awkward, jagged, painful, dangerous – which is precisely why we need to be mindful of it, pay it careful and respectful attention.

Transitions are very often bumpy, rarely simple or quick, as we move from one place or state of life or belief system to another – something I hardly need tell a room full of counsellors and therapists! There has to be a necessary undoing, dismantling, what my poem calls 'the unmaking of soul', before a new pattern or configuration can be found. I try to conjure something of what the transitional space feels like in the two poems I just read – not explaining it (how could I?) but evoking the visceral experience of the gap – in which 'the heart lurch(es)', 'the body quiver(s), the tongue stumble(s) on its own hopelessness', 'the throat constrict(s) in wordless-ness', and we feel 'the grasp of and the hold on things' 'over and over' to slip.

This gap can be a terrifying and lonely place, with a profound sense of loss and bereavement as one reality that has served a person (or perhaps a group) for a long time suddenly or gradually breaks down, and we are cast into limbo, for a longer or shorter time, desperately seeking a new, more adequate configuration. Old certainties are gone, old friendships and relationships may no longer function as once they did, including the rela-tionship with God; the very ones we have habitually turned to in times of crisis no longer seem able to come with us in the way we want them to. The language and means of expression we formerly called upon to articulate our sense of self and faith appear to have died on us or self-destructed, and we don't yet have a new language to name things with. As Adrienne Rich puts it in one of her sonnets: 'The rules break like a thermometer … the maps they gave us were out of date/ by years.'[6]

This is the gap as abyss, 'the great dark that surrounds us/ the vast "O" that beckons us/ the fearsome awe that threatens us/ … the descent to the deeps'.[7] This is the gap as desert, as void, as raging ocean, as wild and featureless landscape that seems to offer no milestone and where the pilgrim can very easily get lost. Christian tradition speaks of this spiritual experience in terms of the 'via negativa', the apophatic way, in which the soul is drawn away from light and certainty and has to learn to walk by faith rather than sight; in which any certainties we once held are replaced by the sense of paradox, mystery, contradiction, and God's presence may be occluded by a sense of divine absence. It becomes more and more difficult to name God or what we believe positively; we are only able to stutter 'not this, not that'.

In and of itself, this is a demanding and fearful place to be, but it is made massively more so by the fact that very many people are not prepared for such an experience of faith. Many, perhaps most, churches do not offer guidance or teaching to support spiritual seekers who find themselves in this desert country. Many, perhaps most, churches trade in certainty, absolute clarity and uniformity of belief, regarding any vestige of doubt as evidence of failure or collapse of faith rather than as a challenge to grow into a more mature and secure faith which can accommodate ambivalence, uncertainty and the unresolved mess and chaos of life.

Yet precisely because I believe this experience of being plunged into the place of the gap is necessary on the journey towards spiritual maturity, it is, of course, extremely common. I meet it all the time, as I imagine you do – in women and men whose early, cheerful or simplistic forms of faith no longer work for them and who are seeking something different; in those who feel disenfranchised, excluded, pushed out by a church that does not speak to them or for them – yet who can't somehow give up on faith or find it won't give up on them. Or perhaps they *have* left, outwardly, yet still have a deep sense of loss and longing for what the church once offered them. I think the boundary between 'belonging' and 'not belonging', or between 'believing' and 'not believing', is so much more blurred, confused, permeable than we often give it credit for. Very many of us feel that we both belong and don't belong to the institution of the church (and probably to a whole lot of other institutions too); that we do believe in some form of Christianity, yet can't believe what others seem to expect of Christian doctrinal assent. I resonate with Alice Oswald, the poet, when she says:

I don't like the facile distinction that is made between belief and non-belief. Those who don't believe are normally talking about a god they've invented; and for the rest of us, it doesn't feel like a question of belief, more like a slow process of experiencing what the terms really mean. There's a greater distance between the beginning and end of that process than there is between belief and non-belief.[8]

Whether it's women who feel themselves pushed to the edge of a patriarchal church, or black and Asian Christians struggling to live in a post-colonial, recovering racist church, or lesbian and gay Christians who feel there is no place for them in a church that is utterly compromised in its sexual morality; whether it's Fowler Stage Four and Five types trying to survive in a church that operates primarily at the conformist Stage Three, or mystic contemplatives looking for a place of belonging in an overwhelmingly activist church – there are very many of us who identify with the liminal edges of Christian belief and belonging, even though it is perhaps part of the reality of this edge that it feels a very lonely place and we may not be aware of the vast community of edge-dwellers with whom we share much in common. Perhaps this community itself is rather hidden and necessarily dispersed, existing largely in the invisible space between the gaps of most groups and organizations offered by the church – it doesn't have an obvious manifesto or agenda, it can't say exactly what its purpose is or who it's for. But it's none the less real for all that, and my experience is that I recognize fellow pilgrims when I come across them in chance encounters or in books, poems, films and artwork that seems to speak to me of a landscape I recognize – and occasionally in groups that exist for those who, in different ways, feel excluded from the centre.

The gap as wound

For all these, and other, reasons, then, the gap is a place of tension: tension between the person I am now, the person I once was who has disappeared on me, and the person I long to be. Between the place I once lived, the place I live now, and the place I am looking for beyond the horizon. It is therefore a place of longing, of desire, of sometimes painful awareness of what is unfulfilled or unresolved in our lives. A major temptation in the place of the gap is to collapse the tension, to try to fall back into the comfort of the place or state we've left behind or to seek a too-quick, false resolution. There's plenty of false religion and false therapy offering a quick fix, a way out of living the tensions and the questions. Staying with, living within the place of unknowing without seeking premature resolution requires courage, persistence and support. This, it seems to me, is the work of prayer and of spiritual accompaniment – to offer a secure holding environment in which the person is accepted and affirmed in the reality of their painful contradictions, in which they are able to be real about their shifting sense of who they are and what they do – or don't – believe, and in which there is nevertheless the promise of the faithfulness of God who calls us into greater life and deeper truth. But the invitation into greater fullness of life and of truth comes not by bypassing the gap but precisely by traversing it, by entering more fully into it. It may well be necessary for the tension and the contradictions and desire to *increase*, to build up to some kind of breaking point, in order that a birthing into a new place becomes possible. Yet this is the work of the Spirit who acts as a midwife to support and encourage the believer who is giving birth to a new self, a new form of faith.

For the gap is also the wound in the side of Christ, which is the womb out of which the individual and the church are birthed. Christ's wounds aren't some embarrassing sign of defeat or failure, but the very fertile space out of which the new life of the church is born. In John's Gospel, the soldier pierces the side of the dead Jesus on the cross, and water and blood flow out – the same liquids that attend a birth. We are meant to think back to Jesus' saying in John 3 that anyone who wants to enter the kingdom must be 'born again'. And disciples are invited to put their fingers into that fleshy wound – a shocking and disturbing invitation to enter into the most intimate place in Christ's body. The medieval church held the wounds of Christ in high honour and if you've ever seen prayer scrolls with images of Christ's wounds, you may have been shocked, as I was when I saw some at the *Seeing Salvation* exhibition in 2000,[9] at just how graphically sexual the depictions of the wounds are. They looked remarkably like vaginas to me; and if I was puzzled and discomfited by that overt sexual representation then, now it seems to be absolutely fitting. For the wound in the side of Christ is the birth canal out of which believers are born.

The landscape of the gap

I've described the landscape of the place of the gap in terms of desert, void, abyss and sea – a fearsome and dangerous place where the landmarks have disappeared and survival is at threat. But I want to say that the place of the gap is also a landscape of intense beauty, if we can but see it. A few years ago, on an Irish holiday, I spent some time in the Burren, a huge plateau of limestone and shale that covers over 100 square miles of north-west Clare. The unique topography of the Burren has come back to me as I've been working on this address. Here's how the *Rough Guide to Ireland* describes it:

> Bleak and grey, the northern reaches of the Burren can come as a shock to anyone who associates Ireland with all things lush and verdant. It's an extraordinary landscape of stark rock, fading to lower green fields, and above all the sky and the ocean. Its cliffs and terraces lean towards the sea in huge steps of wind-pocked pumice. Bone white in sunshine, in the rain the rock becomes darkened and metallic, the cliffs and canyons blurred by mists. A harsh place, barely capable of sustaining human habitation, it was aptly summed up in the words of Cromwell's surveyor Ludlow: 'savage land, yielding neither water enough to drown a man, nor a tree to hang him, nor soil enough to bury'.[10]

You have to come in close to the topography of the Burren to discover its unique beauty. What I remember most about my time there, apart from the wild, windswept beauty of the landscape, is the somewhat precarious experience of walking on top of some of the limestone pavementing and what I witnessed there. Split by parallel grooves known as grykes, it is a dangerous, uneven surface of fissures and cracks; a terrain that can easily lead to a twisted ankle or a fall and that requires a great deal of care to negotiate. Yet it is infinitely worth the effort and the risk for the extraordinary beauty that is hidden within these clefts of rock. The wet, protected, dark spaces of the grykes create a unique and fertile ecology in which plants and wild flowers thrive – rare Arctic, Alpine and Mediterranean plants grow side by side. You won't find this mixture of flora anywhere else in Europe. No one knows exactly how these plants came to be here, nor why they remain, yet here they are: intense, vivid colour, delicacy of petal and fern, exquisite miniatures growing up out of the jagged fissures of rock.

Scripture speaks of the 'cleft of the rock' as a place of divine protection and encounter, a place of spiritual insight and treasure at the same time as it is a place of hiddenness and darkness. In Exodus 33, God hides Moses in a gap in the rock while God passes by; it is too much even for Moses to receive the full revelation of God's being, but in the cleft of the rock he may experience God's passing in a way that does not harm him. In the Song of Songs, the beloved is imaged as a bird hiding in the cleft of a rock whose face the lover longs to see, whose voice the lover longs to hear. The psalms are full of references to the 'hiding place' in the rock which is a place of protection from the storms and ravages of life. So the gap can be a place of intimate encounter and of beauty within the harsh landscape of alienation and struggle.

I'm going to finish with a poem by Kathy Galloway, entitled 'The Crack'.[11] Some of you may know it. It's an extraordinary poem which gives us something of the tension and the jagged discomfort of living in the place of the gap, but also affirms the gap as a place of growth, fertility and beauty. The way the poem is set out on the page is very important – it makes a long jagged crack on the page, starting off with a single narrow fissure which, at a certain point, breaks into two columns, the two sides of the crack which do not fit neatly together. The poem speaks about standing on either side of the crack, holding and loving both sides together – and out of 'that crucial agonizing coupling' something extraordinary is born. It's not a poem that resolves the tensions or ties up all the ends neatly, but it is a poem that may teach us something about how to 'trust the crack'.

The Crack

There is a
crack
jagged and
long and
very deep.
The crack
is bleeding
having been torn
a howl
comes from its
heart
how to get back
together
with the proper fit
in right
relationship

the sides will not dovetail	neatly into place
too much of the edges	having crumbled away
nor can they	be forced together
without killing the fragile	flowers that cling to them
the crack	is permanent
one must, however, stand	on either side
as if it were not there	(although it is)
(knowing it is)	within the good
loving the other	in its absence
whichever side it is	embracing it
without that	crucial, agonizing coupling
there is	only
the barren landscape of despair	the blackened territory of madness

trust the crack
it wants to be
a wild luxuriant valley
with waterfalls
a river running through
and on either side
fertile   fruitful
lands.

Notes

1 See www.continuingthejourney.com.

2 Jane Hirshfield, 'The Envoy', *Each Happiness Ringed by Lions: Selected Poems* (Tarset: Bloodaxe, 2005), p. 15.

3 Extracts from Charles Péguy's meditation on night, in Elizabeth Goudge, *A Book of Faith* (London: Hodder & Stoughton, 1976), pp. 295–8.

4 Lao Tsu, *Tao Te Ching: A New Translation* by Gia-Fu Feng and Jane English (London: Wildwood House Ltd, 1973), Eleven (pages unnumbered).

5 Nicola Slee, 'Hole', in *Praying Like a Woman* (London: SPCK, 2004), p. 45.

6 Adrienne Rich, 'Twenty-One Love Poems', XIII, in *The Dream of a Common Language: Poems 1974–1977* (New York and London: W. W. Norton, 1993), p. 31.

7 Nicola Slee, 'In praise of', in *Praying Like a Woman*, p. 44.

8 Alice Oswald, in Clare Brown and Don Paterson (eds.), *Don't Ask Me What I Mean: Poets in Their Own Words* (London: Picador, 2003), pp. 107–8.

9 For examples of such images and discussion of their significance, see Gabriele Finaldi, *The Image of Christ* (London: National Gallery, 2000), chapter 5, and particularly pp. 160–7.

10 *The Rough Guide to Ireland* (Rough Guides, 2003), pp. 439–40.

11 Kathy Galloway, 'The Crack', in *The Dream of Learning Our True Name* (Glasgow: Wild Goose Publications, 2004), p. 42.

8

The Work of Standing, the Joy of Dancing: A Spirituality to Sustain the Long Haul

This is the oldest piece in this collection, a keynote lecture given to what was then the Lesbian and Gay Christian Movement AGM in London, in April 2008 (LGCM amalgamated with Changing Attitude in 2017 and became OneBodyOneFaith). It may seem strange to include an address from more than ten years ago on same-sex relations and the church, when this is one of the areas of social life that has changed most dramatically during that time. The Civil Partnership Act 2004 enabled same-sex couples to form civil unions with essentially the same rights and responsibilities as civil marriage. This was followed in 2013 by the Marriage (Same Sex Couples) Act, which legalized same-sex marriage in England and Wales. There has been a widespread liberalization of attitudes towards same-sex unions in that period, although the churches remain divided on this issue. I have chosen to include this essay not only because I believe it may still speak into the reality of many LGBTQI+ people seeking full inclusion within the churches, but also because I believe the metaphor of standing is applicable to a range of theological and political situations beyond the one I had in mind at the time.[1]

Introduction

Nelson Mandela has written memorably of his 'long walk to freedom'.[2] For those of us committed to the full inclusion of lesbian, gay, bisexual and transgendered persons (LGBTQI+) within the churches, it seems to be a similarly long haul. While civil society – at least in Europe and other parts of the western world – has taken major steps to affirm the legal and civil standing of those who are LGBTQI+ and to celebrate their place in public life, the church (I speak as an Anglican) seems racked with indecision, hostility, anxiety and compromise. LGBTQI+s are made to feel that we are a 'problem', an embarrassment, a hindrance to the kingdom, a running sore that needs to be healed, or even an evil that requires exorcism – instead of the joyous, diverse, wounded but still singing children of God that we are.

How do we resource ourselves for the long haul? In the time that is available to me, I want to explore the nature of a mature and liberative spirituality that will resource us for the long haul, and to see if I can identify some of the essential marks of such a spirituality.

Sources for a spirituality of standing

As I have pondered this question, I have found myself drawn towards the metaphor of 'standing'. We might want to speak, with Mandela, of walking towards freedom – to consider ourselves on the move – but the reality for me feels frequently otherwise. At the very least, there is a huge tension between the immense strides that have been made in civil society in the past few years (represented by new legal rights and protections but not limited to that) and a sense of paralysis, stalemate and standstill within the church where, if anything, we might feel that we have moved backwards into greater invisibility, fear and a certain hardening of the status quo (represented in the Anglican Communion by reactions to the appointment of Gene Robinson as Bishop of New Hampshire, the Canadian church's authorization of rites to bless same-sex unions, the Jeffrey John debacle, the Windsor Report and, more recently, the so-called 'listening process'). I frequently feel that I inhabit dual universes, worlds that occasionally collide but mostly do not touch. There is one world in which it is utterly unremarkable and even potentially boring to be gay, lesbian, bi or trans, in which we know our lives and others know them to be much the same as anyone else's, with their mix of humdrum ups and downs and occasional moments of glory. (And, actually, LGBTQI+ Christians are no more or less orthodox or radical, faithful or faithless than our heterosexual brothers and sisters.) Then there's another world in which our sexual identities are a constantly spotlit stigma – or, and often at the same time, an unmentionable taboo, rather like cancer was some decades ago, something people dread even to mention in case they might get infected by it. I frequently fail to recognize myself or my gay and lesbian sisters and brothers in official church pronouncements or reports, where our ordinary, extraordinary lives – offered to the church in all their halting brokenness and beautiful unremarkability – are never received as the profound gift of grace that they are. We stand in that place of tension between worlds, straddling parallel universes, longing to move on and to move our churches on into the freedoms we enjoy and begin to take for granted in the secular world, yet unable (for the most part) simply to walk out and away from those churches we both love and hate, churches that are to us sites of frustration, wounding and oppression at the same time as they have been and continue to be sites of grace, privilege and communion in the love of God and the life of the Spirit.

I speak of 'the work of standing', then, because it does, indeed, require immense effort to stand and keep standing in this place of tension and contradition, without being able to move forward and without being dragged backwards to some place where the hard-earned freedoms we have won are betrayed. I did consider inviting you all to stand for the duration of my address to make my point more viscerally, but decided against it! Rather, I want to explore with you, to play with, this metaphor of 'standing' to see if it might provide us with some insight into the kind of spirituality that we require in this place in which we find ourselves.

'Standing', of course, is a common enough term, part of everyday parlance. *The Shorter Oxford English Dictionary* has four dense pages covering the history of usages of the term. Let me highlight a few that may have particular resonance for us. We speak of taking a stand, standing one's ground, standing a chance, standing watch. Figuratively, to stand can mean to remain steadfast, firm or secure; to endure, last, to remain valid, to hold good. By extension, in the sixteenth century, 'standing' could refer to a state of checked or arrested movement, a state of being unable to proceed in thought, speech or action, a state of perplexity or nonplus (and this is exactly how it can feel to be LGBTQI+ in the church) – from which we get the term 'standstill'. In its transitive usages, standing can mean to confront, face, oppose; to resist, bear the brunt of; to endure, undergo, be submitted to a trial or test; to face or encounter without flinching or retreating.

It is instructive to consider the social and ritual occasions on which we stand. We stand in the presence of greatness: for royalty (if we are monarchists), for those in high office, for the living and the dead. We stand at the entrance of the bride and the coffin; for the reading of the Gospel and for the Eucharistic Prayer. We stand in the presence of the holy, the numinous, the liminal; for those moments of passage, of crossing over, when we move from one fundamental state or condition to another. As one might expect for a word with such a wide range of usages, it crops up often enough in popular sayings, songs and hymnody. From 'Stand and deliver!' to 'Stand by your man' and 'Stand up, stand up for Jesus!' there are plenty of examples that come readily to mind.

When we turn to the Bible, we find that the terms 'stand' and 'standing' are also frequent. Standing in the presence of God denotes the nearness and holiness of God; the angels and archangels are those who stand in God's presence (Luke 1.19), as do the prophets and friends of God. Moses takes off his shoes on Mount Horeb because he stands on holy ground (Exodus 3.5); Elijah repeatedly refers to the God 'before whom I stand' (1 Kings 17.1; 18.15; 2 Kings 3.14; 5.160). By contrast, those who are aware of their sin ask, 'How then can we stand?' (2 Kings 10.4). 'If you, O LORD, should mark iniquities, LORD who could stand?' (Psalm 130.3). (See also Psalm 1.5; 24.3; 76.7; Malachi 3.2; Revelation 6.17.) A particular favourite of mine is the story in Exodus 17, when Moses grows weary from standing on the hilltop at Rephedim and holding his arms up – which God has instructed him to do to keep the Israelite army winning the battle against the Amelekites – and has to sit down on a stone and get Aaron and Hur to hold up his flagging arms. The Bible is realistic about the wearisome work of standing!

Standing in the Bible is also a stance of witness and testimony, as well as of solidarity. Peter in Acts 1 stands to address the crowd (Acts 1.15), and this is more than a pragmatic action. As the Egyptians pursue the Israelites on their escape from slavery, and the people fear for their lives, Moses tells them, 'Do not be afraid, stand firm, and see the deliverance that the LORD will accomplish for you today' (Exodus 14.13). Their task is only to stand still and look; God does the rest. This same service of standing and looking is offered by the women at the cross, who stand at a distance, watching and enduring Christ's death when the men have deserted (Mark 15.14; Matthew 27.55; Luke 23.49).

Ultimately, it is God and God's Word – the self-expression of God – that alone stands: 'The grass withers, the flower fades, but the word of our God will stand for ever' (Isaiah 40.8). Job looks forward to the revelation of God in the latter days: 'I know that my Redeemer lives, and that ... he will stand upon the earth' (Job 19.25); and Stephen, the first martyr, sees the heavens opened and the Son of Man standing at the right hand of God (Acts 7.56). Because God stands and God's truth will for ever stand (see Psalm 33.11: 'The counsel of the LORD stands for ever'), 'standing' is also used as a metaphor of judgement. 'See, the Judge is standing at the doors,' proclaims James 5.9; and Ezekiel is called to 'stand up on your feet' in order to hear what God will proclaim to him (Ezekiel 2.1). (It is a great irony that, in his trial, Jesus – the judge of the whole earth – stands before Pilate to be judged (Matthew 27.11).) In Jeremiah 6.16, standing at the crossroads is used as a metaphor for discernment: 'Thus says the LORD, "Stand at the crossroads, and look, and ask for the ancient paths, where the good way lies; and walk in it".'

Equally, because God stands and God's truth stands, those who stake their life upon God may also stand, and this sense of enduring faithfulness (primarily that of God and derivatively of the believer) is found frequently in Paul. In Romans 5.2, Paul speaks of 'this grace in which we stand', and it is precisely because he is confident of this grace in which the believer's life is rooted that he can make the frequent appeal to Christians to 'stand firm in your faith' (Galatians 5.1; 1 Corinthians 16.13; Philippians 1.27) or, similarly, 'stand firm in the Lord' (1 Thessalonians 3.8; Philippians 4.1). Paul's exhortatory use of the metaphor echoes Jesus' command to the paralytic to 'stand up and walk' (Mark 2.9), as well as the same command given by Peter and John to the lame man in Acts 3. The command in both instances is performative of the act, and the result is healing and release.

The most extensive usage of the metaphor in Paul is, of course, the famous passage in Ephesians 6, when the apostle calls the believer to 'put on the whole armour of God, so that you may be able to stand against the wiles of the devil', so that, 'having done everything' the believer may 'stand firm' (verses 10, 13). It is this passage, of course, which gave rise to hymns such as 'Soldiers of Christ, arise' and 'Stand up, stand up for Jesus'. It should be noted, however, that in Ephesians, the military imagery is used in an entirely defensive way, that is, to describe the protection of the Christian against the attacks of the evil one, and is not used to suggest or condone an aggressive or offensive stance. To return to Exodus 14, there is no need for the believer to fight, for 'The LORD will fight for you, and you have only to keep still' (Exodus 14.14).

All these biblical associations were taken up in the early church's practice of praying in the standing posture, continuing the custom of standing in the synagogue and Jesus' own practice, if gospel hints are anything to go by (Luke 9.28–32; John 17.2a). Standing was the favoured posture for prayer, as we see in the earliest catacomb frescoes which show figures standing with arms held aloft, in the gesture familiar to many of us in liturgical or charismatic prayer. Mary and the saints are frequently shown in this orans posture, in icons and other representations. The upright posture for prayer – which is still the normal position in the Eastern Churches – speaks powerfully of a stance of respect, attentive alertness, readiness for action, as well as endurance. For feminists such as Marjorie Procter-Smith,[3] standing to pray with eyes open and with head unbowed has become symbolic of a stance of watchful alertness and a refusal to adopt a passive or compliant posture in a patriarchal church where it is not safe to close one's eyes or bow one's head. If I may quote myself:

We must pray with eyes wide open, refusing to see nothing of what is hidden, secret – blatant lies.

We must pray with heads held high, refusing to bow in obsequiousness to prelate, priest or pope.[4]

Alongside such resistant, counter-cultural meanings, standing can also token gratitude, joy and praise when the heartfelt thanksgiving of the believer wells up and compels one to one's feet. Perhaps it was such an overflowing of joy, as well as the sense of being in the presence of greatness, that inspired King George ll to get to his feet when he first heard Handel's 'Hallelujah' chorus. No one really knows why he stood, but I do know that something quite indescribable and palpable is added to the impact of that astounding music by rising to one's feet with every other member of the audience.

I hope to carry all of these associations and resonances, and others that you will be bringing, with us, as I turn now to sketch out what I see to be the key elements of a spirituality of standing. I will attempt to portray a spirituality that is generous and compassionate, prophetic and playful, contemplative and engaged, costly yet transformative – rooted in the reality of God and the gospel, as well as the world in which we are set.

A spirituality of standing

First and foremost a spirituality of standing is a *spirituality of presence*. Standing offers no more and promises no less than simply staying put, being with the other.[5] Let us be present to and for and with each other, in the presence of that 'present, ever-present Presence' who has, in the words of the poet Kathleen Raine, 'never … not been/ Here and now in every now and here'.[6] We do not have to justify ourselves, explain ourselves or defend ourselves – to ourselves, to one another or to those who deny or assail our presence. We simply have to stand; as Henri Nouwen puts it, 'standing in the world with head erect, solidly rooted in the knowledge of who we are, facing the reality that surrounds us and responding to it from our hearts'.[7] Let God be our defence, if we need one. The fact that we are here today, sharing presence in the Presence, says far more than any words can. We are queer and we are here. We stand here for ourselves and for the ones who are not here but wish to be or perhaps don't dare to be. We are here *as* church; as Christ's presence and body in the world in all its queer erotic beauty and desirability. And when I talk about 'queer' I don't mean primarily a category of sexual identity so much as a way of being in the world that is marked out, in Hopkins' lovely phrase, by being 'counter, original, spare, strange'.[8] However we choose to name or define ourselves (or not) – whether as gay, lesbian, bi, trans, queer, fluid, straight or some combination of any or none of these – we are here in all our unfinished, singular and beautiful human particularity, each one of us mirroring and manifesting something of the strangeness, beauty and, yes, queerness, of God, as surely as every other creature in the cosmos does; perhaps, in some way, *more* than other creatures, simply because we are part of that great company of the *anawim*, God's excluded little ones, those Jon Sobrino names among 'the poor' – not in any financial or material way (look at us, for goodness sake!) but in the sense that we are among those excluded from access to the centres of power and significance, at least in the ecclesial sphere[9] – who therefore, simply by their exclusion (and not through any particular moral or religious virtue of our own, thank God) point to the Queer God who is always and everywhere squeezed out from the centre, rejected by the establishment and crucified by the powers that be – and whose very being is ceaselessly oriented towards all who are similarly excluded. I find myself wanting to say, aren't we *all* at least a little queer? 'There's nowt as queer as folks,' as the saying goes. It's just that some of us are able and willing to manifest our queerness, in all its quirky originality, more openly and obviously than others – not, as some seem to think, in order to confirm the rest of humankind, the straight folk, in their heteronormativity, but precisely as a signal and an invitation to all to enter into the playful possibilities of their as yet unexplored queerness. Now there's a thought for the primates to play with!

Simply to *be*, then, and to stand as we are, for who and what we are, is a witness, an invitation and, at the same time, a protest against the norm and the status quo – whatever the norm is; a protest against any and every attempt to limit or restrict or control the gracious free gift of God. Presence is a testimony, points beyond itself to something or someone signified. I'm reminded of those extraordinary standing figures of Anthony Gormley's that have begun to people our landscape and city scapes and can also be found in some churches. They are naked and mute, some obviously gendered, others more featureless; mysterious and utterly arresting, compelling attention. They are a presence that speaks, even if we are not sure exactly what they are saying. In some such way, a spirituality of standing is also a *spirituality of witness and, by that token, a spirituality of protest*. We are called to stand in the open; to stand tall; to stand up to be counted; to stand so that we may be seen. In so far as we may. Gene Robinson quotes Harvey Milk, the first openly gay supervisor of San Francisco, who said, 'The most political thing any of us can do is come out.' And Robinson adds, 'it is also the most religious thing we can do'[10] – because our identity as queer sisters and brothers called and loved into being by God speaks, in and of itself, of divine grace and mercy and of God's election of the most unlikely and the least: most especially in contexts where that reality is denied. As is often said, and as many of us know, in the end it is not argument or evidence that convicts and converts (important as it is to engage with the debate) but the sheer intractability of human presence and story: knowing someone who is good, honest, upright, whose love of God and others cannot be doubted – and who just so happens to be gay, lesbian, bi or trans.

I said we need to stand tall 'in so far as we may'. Coming out can only be an individual imperative, not something we impose on others (I do not believe in outing others), and there are many sane reasons why many of us do not do it, or if we do, only partially and selectively. Gene Robinson again:

in dioceses and provinces around the globe headed by very conservative leadership, there are no safe places for anyone to talk openly about these issues without fear of negative consequences, and gay or lesbian people would have to be crazy and virtually suicidal to come forward to tell their story.[11]

The fact that no small number of us *are* willing to be visible and to claim our names and our identity and share our stories is testimony to the empowering Spirit of God in our midst and a challenge to those who do not yet feel they can join us. Respecting those who, for good reasons, remain in the closet, I want at the same time to challenge each of us to take whatever steps we can towards increasing visibility because it is this in the end that will compel change. In particular, in the present climate, it behoves those of us who are lay and whose livelihood does not depend on the church, to take a lead in standing up and speaking out when we know that it is so much more dangerous for our ordained sisters and brothers to do so. I want, too, to salute all those who are willing and have been willing over many years to stand up and be counted, often at great cost and no small risk – today, in particular, we are saluting Richard Kirker for his tireless willingness to stand, but we can think of many others too, here and worldwide – bishops, clergy, theologians, writers; the well known and the less known – those who show us what it means to take a stand, and who empower and encourage us to do so by their boldness.

Such saints also remind us that we never stand alone, and that a spirituality of standing is therefore a *spirituality of solidarity*. We stand by and alongside and for one another, especially for those who cannot stand, but whose presence is nevertheless palpable and powerful – a silent, invisible company of the spirits of the just who compel those of us who may stand to do so. Gene Robinson tells of meeting with a gay and lesbian fellowship group in Hong Kong and of the enormous significance to them of his willingness simply to meet with them and stand with them. 'They wanted to thank me, they wanted to touch me, they wanted to tell me their stories.'[12] The memory of that fleeting visit of the gay Bishop of New Hampshire will surely inspire and embolden them for years to come. When we feel terribly exposed and alone, we do well to remember those others around the globe who are standing with us. And, by the same token, when we are wearied of having to stand up once more and give account of ourselves, fed up of our sexuality being constantly in the spotlight – when heterosexual marriage and celibacy are rarely problematized within ecclesiastical discussions as the oppressive and abusive patriarchal conditions they often are – we need to remember that our brothers and sisters elsewhere look to us for courage and depend upon us for their very lives.

So, then, a spirituality of standing has to be a *spirituality of endurance*, a spirituality of the long haul, a spirituality that refuses to give up, however joyless the present seems or bleak the prospect of change. We must stand and keep standing, like those crazy saints that stood on pillars for decades in the desert or up to their thighs in freezing Celtic seas while barnacles grew on their toes and they went right on praying and praising the Almighty. It is unfashionable in many circles – including those shaped by queer discourse – to speak of asceticism, but there is a necessary asceticism to Christian spirituality. The fact that it has often been distorted is no reason to abandon it but a compelling reason to reshape what we mean by it. The kind of asceticism I am talking about here is the asceticism of holy Saturday, the asceticism of watching and waiting in the place of apparent hopelessness and death, what David Wood in his book *Dark Prayer* calls the 'prayer of silence in the dark chasm'.[13] This is not primarily an asceticism of the body (although it might be), certainly not a denial of our sexuality, but it is a deep and profound asceticism of the spirit, and it is a suffering in the body ecclesial, the collective body, which leaves its marks on all of us who share the long night – marks, we might dare to hope, that are akin to those transfigured wounds the risen Christ shows to his disciples, marks that therefore speak of hope. But before we speak of resurrection too quickly, let's not delude ourselves. Not all have endured, or remained standing. Some have been felled, like mighty oaks brought down by lightning. Others have been irreparably stunted or wounded in ways that don't speak of risenness – and we can all think of members of the company of the fallen. Those who do remain standing don't do so painlessly, as cattle or horses do; most of us limp or lean against each other, rest in each other's arms for a while or take turns at sitting down and sleeping for long stretches. We don't have to all keep standing all the time, thank goodness, so long as there are always some of us doing it.

More than standing? The joy of dancing

Is a spirituality of standing sufficient? Doesn't it sound just a little passive, defeatist, joyless even? I don't think so. Paradoxically, when undertaken with intentionality and commitment, standing isn't mere loitering, standing around vaguely waiting for something to happen. It is labour, it is work; it is a way of inhabiting the present when the present appears not to admit of movement; but it bears its own strange fruit in its own – or better in God's – time. Standing and carrying on standing literally grounds us and roots us; as we stand, so we find the power in our standing. As Audre Lorde has written, 'When I dare to be powerful, to use my strength in the service of my vision, then it becomes less important whether or not I am unafraid.'[14]

And standing bonds us to the others with whom and for whom we stand; we learn a solidarity in the struggle that cannot be given any other way. And such standing can also, I believe, effect change – in others, in the world, as well as in ourselves.

What good does it do to stand and keep standing? Well, for one thing, it encourages others who have been sitting on the fence to come off and stand with us – as many have done over recent events in the Anglican Communion. And, as I have already suggested, the stance of ordinary fallible but faithful LGBTQI+ Christians holding on and holding out in our everyday places of work, worship and witness, does have an extraordinary power to convert – a power that we ourselves can't always see but that, like the silent leaven in the lump, transforms the whole. On the larger political scale, we can call to mind irreversible changes that have come about through the sheer persistent pressure of ordinary members of the populace who simply refused to give up and go home: the downfall of apartheid in South Africa, the Good Friday Agreement in Northern Ireland and so on.

Even so, all this is not quite enough and I can't finish here. Our bodies are made for more than standing. Perhaps most particularly at a time when we can feel boxed in, constricted, unable to move, stoical standing will not suffice. We need also to dance! Dance is possible in the smallest space: anyone's living room, a hermit or prison cell, the meanest sanctuary. We can do it alone, for the sheer joy of it, or better, with others; with strangers, as well as with friends and lovers, even with opponents. You don't have to agree anything with anyone to dance with them; all you have to do is be willing to be in the same space together, to risk shared bodily presence and let those bodies move together. Donald Eadie, in his wonderful book *Grain in Winter*,[15] reminds us that we need parties for the creation and sustenance of both community and hope; and that the best parties don't happen in palaces or the corridors of power but on the streets, under motorways and around the makeshift altars that human beings are always making whenever food and drink is shared with strangers. And, just occasionally, in churches.[16] And aren't parties one of the places where we do routinely stand around, eating, drinking and chatting, with absolutely no intention of getting anywhere? And we dance: shaking it all about, jiggling our bits, looking as strange or as gorgeous as we may. We dance to express joy, or to make it. We dance in celebration of life and in defiance of death. We energize and revitalize the work of standing by our dancing. And we learn, as we dance, what the trees know, how to bend without breaking, how to sway and move with the storms when they come, and, while taking the battering, to remain standing.

We don't have to wait for the party to begin to start dancing. Yes, we stand in the place of tension between the unfulfilled 'now' of deep yearning and the tantalizing 'not yet' of the kindom[17] banquet, when all hungers will be sated and all God's queer children set free. And in our standing we feel the tension, one foot in both camps, and it fatigues us to our bones. Like Moses at Rephedim, we have to sit down on whatever stones are to hand and ask brothers and sisters around us to lift up our arms. Or maybe not. Instead of sitting down, in dejected exhaustion, why not leap up and join the dance? And why not invite others, even and including our opponents, to dance with us? Can you imagine all the bishops and primates at the Lambeth Conference at a huge all-night disco, and what might not emerge out of them dancing together? We don't have to wait for the party to begin to start dancing. Just do it. In our dancing we pre-empt the joyous freedom of the children of God, we enter into the joy of our God, we give our yes to the party invitation that Christ ushers ceaselessly – to all who are childlike and eager enough to want to party. When others might expect us to give up and go home, we are those who are deciding not only to keep standing but to start dancing.

I can't think of a better way to end this reflection than by reading a poem by my partner Rosie Miles which captures just the spirit of exuberant, subversive and passionate faithfulness that we need to keep us standing and dancing where we stand.

So here we are
Dancing on the edge,
The dangerous and delightful edge.

So here we'll be
The irritant in the eye
Of the church:
The cracked lens through which it needs to see.

So here we'll not be silent, or invisible,
But we'll say our names
And show our colours
And others will know
Who we are.

So here we'll laugh and love and dance
And sing and play and drink and
Whose edge is it anyway?

This edge, we say,
Is ours; and we will
Fill that edge
To overflowing:
Loving it with passion,
Embracing it with desire,
And flirting unashamedly with the centre.

This dangerous and delightful edge
Is the edge where we are dancing,
So, here we are.[18]

Notes

1 For a recent excellent analysis of the lives of partnered lesbian and gay Christians, see Clare Herbert, *Rethinking the Theology of Same-Sex Marriage: Squaring the Circle* (London: Jessica Kingsley, 2020).

2 Nelson Mandela, *Long Walk to Freedom* (London: Abacus, 1995).

3 Marjorie Proctor-Smith, *Praying With Our Eyes Open: Engendering Feminist Liturgical Prayer* (Nashville, TN: Abingdon Press, 1995).

4 Nicola Slee, *Praying Like a Woman* (London: SPCK, 2004), p. 1.

5 And for this reason, while I am aware that the metaphor of 'standing' might be ambivalent for persons for whom physical standing is problematic or impossible, I consider it applicable to all, however differently able bodied we may be. Some of those who most exemplify the characteristics of a spirituality of standing are, in fact, those who do not and cannot literally and physically stand. It's possible – indeed necessary – to stand tall spiritually from a variety of physical postures.

6 Kathleen Raine, 'The presence', in *The Presence: Poems 1984–87* (Ipswich: Golgonooza Press, 1987), p. 30.

7 Henri Nouwen, *Can You Drink the Cup?* (Notre Dame, IN: Ave Maria Press, rev. edn, 2006), p. 88.

8 Gerard Manley Hopkins, 'Pied beauty', in W. H. Gardner (ed.), *Gerard Manley Hopkins: Poems and Prose* (Harmondsworth: Penguin, 1963), p. 31.

9 Jon Sobrino SJ, 'Getting real about the option for the poor', in Julian Filochowski and Peter Stanford (eds.), *Opening Up: Speaking Out in the Church* (London: Darton, Longman & Todd, 2005), p. 26.

10 Gene Robinson, *In the Eye of the Storm* (Norwich: Canterbury Press, 2008), p. 97.

11 Robinson, *In the Eye of the Storm*, p. 143.

12 Robinson, *In the Eye of the Storm*, p. 137.

13 David Wood, *Dark Prayer: When All Words Fail* (Harlech: Cairns Publications, 2004), p. 11.

14 Audre Lorde, *The Cancer Journals*, in *The Audre Lorde Compendium: Essays, Speeches and Journals* (London: Pandora, 1996), p. 9.

15 Donald Eadie, *Grain in Winter* (Peterborough: Epworth, 1999), chapter 22.

16 For example, in the wonderful Church of St Gregory of Nyssa, San Francisco, where much of the liturgy is danced and where the walls are decorated with images of dancing saints and a dancing Christ. See www.saintgregorys.org.

17 I speak of 'kindom' in preference to 'kingdom', as a number of feminists and others do, to avoid the monarchical associations of the latter and suggest the bonds of affection and connectedness that characterize the former.

18 Rosie Miles, 'So here we are', in Geoffrey Duncan (ed.), *Courage to Love: An Anthology of Inclusive Worship Material* (London: Darton, Longman & Todd, 2002), pp. 78–9.

PART 4

A Feminist Practical Theological Poetics

Words for the journey

Some I'll write with a wooden pen
in my recycled cotton journal
where they'll sink into softness.

Some I'll read in whatever collection
of poems I must have with me
(Levertov, Jennings, Herbert, Hopkins).

Some I'll croon and sing and pray
in my office book of psalms
that mark the milestones of night and day.

Some are locked inside me, like preserved fruit
that will sweeten the way: rhymes from childhood,
nonsense chatter that lovers and children chant.

Some are waiting to be gathered along the road
from strangers who will offer greetings,
shout out news or warning, sharp benediction.

Many more will be missed
in a language or a tongue I can't decipher
in a turn of the road or sharp incline I won't take.

Yet other walkers will hear them,
receive them, throw them back
into the air for onward travel.

as well as to the mother; this process of labour is experienced as one of profound loss, akin to death; giving birth is still one of the most dangerous of human endeavours and is, for that very reason, a powerful analogy for religious conversion.

Non-metaphorically, immersion can point to the holiness of an appropriately 'worldly' spirituality. Our default model of holiness or spirituality still tends to be one of withdrawal, involving long periods of quiet, focused reflection, dark churches, and dignified liturgies – as Janet Martin Soskice describes it in her essay 'Love and attention':

> In its higher reaches it involves time spent in contemplative prayer, retreats, and sometimes the painful wrestlings with God portrayed by John Donne or George Herbert. Above all, it involves solitude and collectedness. It does not involve looking after small children.

As this last comment makes clear, this default model of holiness, predicated on the lonely, detached, rational and controlling Enlightenment male self, disenfranchises many people, especially women. Soskice herself, along with others such as Margaret Hebblethwaite, offers an alternative model of engaged, embodied spirituality that is practised in the management of ordinary life and the realm of necessity. Through attention to the minute particularities of caring, feeding and cleaning, for instance, Soskice argues that parents learn and practise essential spiritual disciplines of self-mastery, patient humility, and disinterested love. In the process being bodily as well as spiritually changed. Rather than try to escape the overwhelming demands of parenting, the mother or father of a newborn infant immerses willingly in the task, both losing and finding themselves in attending to that overwhelming reality.

Feeling the time/holding the tension

Immersion within the forces of overwhelming implies this second stance or posture, as we experience and bear within ourselves the extraordinary buffeting, tension and constriction of being, in the place where the forces of overwhelming meet and mingle. Rather than collapsing the tension of trying to resolve the confusion in favour of one overwhelming or simple solution, a spiritually mature response to multiple overwhelmings require one to hold the space at the intersection of the forces of overwhelming, to reside in the place of greatest tension in the conviction that, out of this place of intersection, a new reality may be envisaged and birthed. Continuing the birth imagery, this is the work of labour which requires enormous concentration and suffering in the interests of new life; it requires a willingness to reside, at least for a time, within the birth canal where the forces of life and death converge.

9

Poetry as Divination:
What Poetry Means for Faith

The text of this chapter originally formed a lecture for the Severn Forum[1] in May 2012, under the title 'Poetry as a Means of Theological Reflection' and has been honed over a number of presentations including to the Leicester and Suffolk Theological Societies. Parts of the article draw on my Audenshaw Paper, 'The public use of poetry', AP215, 2005, The Hinksey Network.

Introduction

All Christians (and the same could be said about other faiths, but I restrict myself to my own tradition) are shaped by poetry, whether they realize it or not, and poetry both informs and expresses our profoundest convictions and experiences of the holy. The Bible is full of poetry. Most obviously, the poetry of the psalms has formed Christian prayer from the very beginning, but biblical poetry has also formed religious consciousness and theology more widely: much of the prophetic and wisdom literature is poetry; the creation narratives in Genesis are profound poetry (rather than scientific accounts); Jesus' parables and teaching are more akin to poetic discourse than much of what we would today describe as religious or theological discourse. Hymnody, too, is poetry – some of it rather bad doggerel, but some of it very fine. Many Anglicans have learnt the poems of George Herbert through singing them, for instance, and Methodists are shaped by the poetry of Charles and John Wesley. Those of us who have received some kind of classical liberal arts education have doubtless been introduced to the riches of the canon of western poetry, much of which has deep Christian roots: from Herbert and Donne and the metaphysicals to Milton and Blake and Hopkins, from Rossetti and Tennyson to Dickinson and Eliot.

All this is obvious, but provides something of a backcloth to what I wish to attempt in this lecture, namely a consideration of the nature and characteristics of poetic speech itself, what kind of language poetry is and what significance poetry and the poet might hold within our wider social life, particularly in articulating religious and spiritual truth. I want to suggest that poetry has a crucial role to play in renewing language and speech in our time, in witnessing to the freedom of human creativity which cannot be contained by any ideology or institution, in holding before us the glory as well as the suffering and fragility of the cosmos and in recalling human beings to truths about our condition that we might otherwise conveniently ignore. More than this, I want to suggest that poetry, like all the arts, witnesses to the transcendent, to the beyond in our midst, to the 'more than' that beckons human beings beyond the demands of the immediate, the functional needs of the moment – and that this is so whatever the professed beliefs of the individual poet or the content of the poetry. It is easy to assent to the view that poetry may be a form of theological exploration in the work of poets who have a clear religious conviction and who write 'religious verse', or perhaps in the work of those who, while they may not confess religious belief, nevertheless address themselves to religious, philosophical or spiritual matters in their writing. Yet I want to say that the capacity of poetry to be a means of theological exploration and insight is not dependent on the religious belief of the poet or the religious content of the poem. Overtly religious poetry may or may not be good poetry, and may or may not be good theology.

Rather, I want to say that poetry, *in and of itself, and to the degree in which it is good poetry,* is a way of knowing, of seeing and becoming that takes us close to the heart of religious faith and has much in common with the concerns and functions of good theology. Katherine Venn, a poet interviewed in the *Church Times*, speaks of the relationship between poetry and faith in the following way: 'Poetry is truth-telling, a mode of thought and self expression. Faith is ultimately concerned with truth; so perhaps they are cousins with something to say to each other.'[2] Poetry shares many of the core characteristics of the language of prayer, the sensibilities of the mystic and the vision of the prophet. Poetry has its origins in music, in dance, in the organic rhythms of the breath, but also in ancient ritual and liturgy, in the healing work of the shaman and the priest. Conversely, it is difficult to imagine the practice of any religious faith that does not call on the poetic for its articulation of a sense of the divine, for its means of address to the divine, for its expression of its vision of the world and of reality.

Up until modern times, it was common to regard the poet as a seer, one inspired – inbreathed – by the Spirit and the spirits; one who, like the priest, was both a part of the common humanity to whom and for whom he (and it usually was a 'he') spoke, but also, to a degree, one set apart from the community, residing in the liminal boundary between the sacred and the profane, a conduit of the transcendent. This higher vision of poetry reached its apotheosis in the Romantic tradition in Shelley's notion of the poet as the 'legislator of the world'; a tradition subsequently tempered within the Victorian era and finally dismantled by modernism's project of desacralizing the universe and making humanity the measure of all things. In our current, postmodern context of pluralism and fragmentation of belief, in which we have lost any sense of a shared, coherent meta-narrative and in which the arts have largely abandoned any sense of spiritual vocation, nevertheless it is not unusual to come across echoes of this earlier tradition in the writing of many contemporary poets and in the motivations of many contemporary readers of poetry, both of whom look to poetry for that 'something more' – not simply an expression of a vision of reality that is more than functional, mechanistic and materialist, but also an *experience* of heightened attention and awareness that might once have been found in prayer or meditation but many now find in the arts.

Perhaps for many in our time, then, poetry is a primary form of spirituality; this is suggested by Clare Brown's definition of poetry as 'spirituality without going to church',[3] and by Wallace Stevens' claim that poetry is 'a means of redemption', with the poet as 'the priest of the invisible'.[4] It is certainly notable that, at liminal moments in individuals' lives, at times of crisis – whether of ecstasy or agony – at births, deaths and the solemnizing of relationships, many people who would never otherwise read poetry turn to the poet to put into words what otherwise cannot be expressed.[5]

What I seek to do in what follows is to consider some of what I see to be key characteristics of poetry, and explore how poetry can function in a variety of ways as a form of exploration, divination, revelation and insight that is not far from the way in which religious faith functions. There are, of course, very many different forms and traditions of poetry, ranging from the tightly disciplined set forms of classic poetry (the sonnet, villanelle, ballad, and so on) to the less obviously patterned free verse of much modern poetry, from epic narrative poetry that has been a traditional means of enshrining and transmitting stories to the brief lyric poem. While my hope is to reflect across the breadth and range of poetic forms and texts, it is probably true to say that there is something of a bias in what follows to modern, lyric traditions of poetry rather than to some of its older, epic forms.

A kind of speaking ...

'There is a kind of speaking that places us into relation with the ground of the depth of being, and without this attentiveness we are capable neither of beauty nor truth.' So says Dorothee Soelle,[6] poet, theologian, political activist and mystic. Such is the vocation of all speaking, we might want to say, and certainly it is what the preacher and the pray-er aspire to: language that not only speaks *about* some thing or state of affairs, but mysteriously effects that of which it speaks, causing the hearer not only to think new thoughts but to feel passions and aspirations and to sense a reality of which they might previously have been unaware. Poetry, at its best, is such a species of language: speech that pierces through the superficial, the ephemeral and the transitory and arrests the hearer, awakening desire and awareness, compelling us to attend to the concrete particular, yet, at the same time, leading us beyond the particular to some larger vision of things.

In one sense, of course, poetry – like any of the arts – resists any instrumental or utilitarian appropriation. I would want to say that poetry is gloriously and utterly superfluous, like all the arts, and perhaps, too, like religion. Auden famously said, 'Poetry makes nothing happen',[7] and he was right in the sense that wars are not waged over poetry, poetry does not put governments in or out of power, and poetry has little, if any, economic power. Soelle has spoken of prayer as 'this superfluous activity, this unproductive waste of time' which 'happens *sunder warumbe*' (without any why or wherefore); and I would want to say the same of poetry. 'It is as free of ulterior motives as it is indispensable. [Poetry] is its own end and not a means to obtain a particular goal.'[8] This is to insist on the freedom of the artist, whose creative impulse cannot be controlled or limited by any political or religious agenda nor set to serve institutional power. And this is why some 'Christian poetry' is bad poetry, because it is too much concerned with an ulterior motive – to preach or convert or drive home a particular ethical or religious standpoint – and too little concerned with the craft of poetry, and with the subtlety, multivalency and integrity of poetic speech itself. It is not that poetry can't do theology – I very much believe it can, and it has become one of the primary forms in and through which I do my own theology – but it doesn't do it like prose, otherwise what would be the point of writing a poem? If I can tell you what I want to say in straightforward prose, there is no need for the poem; the poem merely acts as a shell in which the kernel of dogmatic truth is hidden – once we get to the husk, we can discard the shell. In good art, conversely, the form and the content are absolutely indispensable, they are intimately integrated and it is not possible to have one without the other. The poem's meaning is inseparable from the poem itself – which is one reason why it is very hard to say what a poem 'means' and why we can all read a poem differently, so that any one interpretation of a poem can never exhaust the poem's possibilities (if it is, indeed, a good poem).

Because, of course, poetry is so much more than 'meaning' – if by that we infer something narrowly cerebral or propositional. Poetry, like any other art form – music or art or theatre – is an experience, an encounter, an invitation into awareness that is not primarily addressed to the rational mind, although because language is its primary medium it certainly includes such an address. Yet poetry's concern with language is deeper than the surface meaning of the words; poetry is first and foremost an aural experience, not simply words on a page, and a good poem will arouse our senses, emotions and imagination as much as our minds. Poems can, of course, raise profound ethical, spiritual and existential questions about the nature of reality, about what it means to be human, about awe, mystery, beauty and pain in the world; poetry can equally engage religious narratives and topics, can be 'about' faith in an overt sense; but poems usually come at such themes in a manner very different from the way a theologian or a preacher might – indirectly, through concretion, symbol and narrative, often not naming the largescale abstracts (Truth, God, Love, War, and so on) that is their ultimate concern, leaving the reader to discern the significance of what may be presented piecemeal, a fragment of experience close-up, like the zoom lens of a camera.

Another way of putting this is to suggest that the *process* of reading or writing the poem is as significant for theology as its content. Although reading and writing poems are two distinct activities, I believe they share a range of characteristic attitudes and stances – not only towards the creative act per se but more fundamentally towards life and reality themselves – and it is to these characteristic features of the poetic craft that I now turn, not only because they deserve close attention in their own right but also in the conviction that they can illuminate aspects of the life of faith and the work of theology. By a careful study of the *processes of reading and writing poetry* we may come across clues or signs of the transcendent and a way into the realm of the sacred. In what follows, I will suggest six significant features of both reading and writing poetry that might be illuminating for the life of faith and the work of theology.

Poetry as *lectio divina*, contemplative practice

Because poems are typically dense, compressed speech, language pared down to the minimum, in which each word is *working* in a particularly charged and concentrated way, it requires a very particular kind of reading or listening: a measured, intensely concentrated attention, in which all the faculties are alert and working – brain, senses, intuition, heart. One cannot hurry a poem on the page, it demands to be read slowly, and generally invites rereading many times, rather like early Christians read the scriptures and contemplatives still do today in the practice of *lectio divina*. Poems do not yield their meaning quickly or easily; or at least, if they do make an immediate impact, there is much more that can only be accessed or approached through slow, careful reading. We might say the same about other forms of highly disciplined, concentrated writing: academic writing of various kinds, including theology and philosophy, which demand sustained and tutored concentration. The difference may be one of degree rather than kind, and what makes the slow reading of poetry distinctive from other kinds of concentrated reading relates to other features of the poetic form explored further below.

Such concentrated, contemplative reading is a skill many people do not possess in a digital age where speed and easy access to information are prized over slow, unhurried leisure to read. Under the pressures of timetabling, the compulsion to 'cover the curriculum', the demands to read widely rather than deeply, educational establishments that might induct students into such contemplative reading may, in fact, compound the problem. Yet such an approach towards texts as well as towards human beings and the world more generally is essential if we are to have any chance of becoming persons of faith. Poetry may be one place – not the only one – where we may be taught to slow down, to pay attention, to search out the freight and nuance of every word on the line, to look at the shape of the poem on the page, the gaps and spaces between words, the pattern the poem makes on the page, and the rhythms and patterns it makes on the ear as it is read.

Poetry as embodied knowing

I have already suggested that poetry demands a kind of reading and attention that brings into play the brain and the heart, the ear and the eye, the body and the intelligence. The best poems do require full intellectual engagement: they make the reader work hard to pull together surface and deeper meanings, to investigate the system of metaphors or images in the poem, to work out the identity of the speaker (by no means always obvious) and the perspective(s) from which the speaker is viewing the situation, to tease out the layers of meaning under the surface. At the same time, poems require more than analytic ability; they demand the engagement of the body and the senses, as the poem utilizes visual and visceral imagery, triggers feeling and memory, and appeals to the ear in its use of rhythm, metre and rhyme. Unlike more academic forms of discourse, poetry is typically concrete, narrative, visual and episodic, working with fragments of a situation rather than attempting to give a systematic overview of the whole, and crafting meaningful patterns out of those fragments.

The impact of a poem is often visceral, as well as intellectual, calling to mind Emily Dickinson's famous dictum:

> If I read a book and it makes my whole body so cold no fire can ever warm me, I know *that* is poetry. If I feel physically as if the top of my head were taken off, I know *that* is poetry. Those are the only ways I know it.[9]

Precisely because poetry is rooted *in* the body, with an organic connection to the breath, the passions, the emotions as well as the subconscious, it has this power to awaken feeling and sensation in the hearer. Perhaps in this sense it can have a similar impact to music: the aural qualities of poetry, mixed with its dense, compacted intensity, create a visceral reaction – the hairs can stand up on the back of the neck, the body can give an involuntary shudder.

Gillian Clarke speaks of the way in which poetry draws on 'the well-spring of language', 'grounded in the earliest experiences in memory too deep to name, stored in the senses rather than in the filing-system of the conscious mind'.[10] She goes on: 'For me, poetry is a rhythmic way of thinking. It is thought informed by the heart, informed by the body, by the rhythms of breathing, walking, moving ... It is breath, pace, gait, gesture.' This brings us very close to the rhythms and movements of liturgy, and speaks of the origins of poetry in religious ritual.

As the writer draws deeply upon such pre-conscious, pre-verbal sources, so the impact of the poem on the reader is on the *whole person* – intellect as well as feelings, soul and will as well as desire and senses. Adrienne Rich emphasizes the way in which poetry can 'break open locked chambers of possibility, restore numbed zones to feeling, recharge desire'.[11] Its intensity, along with its originality and freshness, can awaken deadened desire in the hearer, can stir not only the imagination but also the overstimulated or jaded capacity for feeling in the hearer.

Poetry as empathic awareness

The emotional stirring created by good poetry may be to feelings and desires within the self that have gone unattended or unnoticed, or the poem may awaken us to a strong empathic connection to the other. Here is another gift that poetry, along with fiction and theatre, offers: an access to the thoughts, feelings, experiences and situations of others far removed from us in time and space, in gender, age or social class, in extremity of pain or joy. The best poems, like fiction and much visual art and cinema, teach an empathic attention to the particularity of human characters and situations, calling on the reader's compassion and a commitment to understand, as fully as she or he is able, the life-experience and perspectives of another with whom they may have little or nothing in common. In this sense, poetry – like all good art – takes us out of ourselves and into the reality of another place, person, situation and so on, but in doing so enlarges the world of the self. Thus David Constantine defines poetry as 'a widening of consciousness, an extension of humanity'.[12] Through the poem, we weep with those who weep and laugh with those who laugh (Romans 12.15); but more than that, we may be enabled to feel and begin to understand more complex human emotions and situations – the compulsion to hurt or maim another; the need to possess or control; the terror of vulnerability; the pity of mental anguish, and so much more.

Nor need poetry only offer access to empathy within the human world; poets have also ventured into the animal kingdom and the natural world of trees, plants, rivers, sea, sky, stars and planets, not merely describing creation from the outside but seeking to inhabit it from the inside. Think of Hopkins' 'Binsey Poplars', or Ted Hughes' evocation of the otherness of 'Pike', or of Plath's fascination with bees and mushrooms, of Alice Oswald's bringing to life of the many sounds and voices of the river Dart, or ... The list could be extended indefinitely. There is no limit to the range of the poet's curiosity and imagination; indeed, the search to find authentic expression for that which lies well beyond the human realm, while resisting colonization or appropriation of what is properly 'other', is perhaps one of the more challenging tests of the poet's craft. When successful, the poem that speaks the life of the forest or river, the bird or bear, the desert or canyon, may take the reader on an imaginative journey that births an attitude of respect, insight and awe at the sheer prodigality and diversity of the created order. Of course, prose can do this too – from *Watership Down* to *War Horse* – but that does not take away from the particular skill of the poet.

Poetry as divination, revelation, epiphany

Seamus Heaney speaks of poetry as 'divination', 'revelation of the self to the self' and 'restoration of the culture to itself':[13] in other words, as an instrument of discovery, a means of exploration. I think this is true for both the writer and the reader of poetry. The act of writing is itself a discovery, as much for the writer as for the reader. It's not that I know what I want to say before I begin writing the poem; the poem will tell me something about my own life – often something I was only dimly aware of. I sometimes say, 'I don't know what I think until I start to write about it', but the poem tells me more than my thoughts or ideas. Precisely because the poem comes from the deeper places of the subconscious, it often knows more than the conscious mind knows. Thus Adrienne Rich says, 'poems are like dreams, in them you put what you don't know you know ... poems are more like premonitions than conclusive'.[14] I may have the sense with some of my poems that they are way ahead of my life, that they know something I don't know yet, and the challenge is to live into the truth of the poem. Again, Rich comments, 'the meaning of a poem becomes clear to me as I see what happens in my life'.[15]

As a reader, I come to poetry for all kinds of reasons – for the sensual musicality of the language, for its beauty and balance and order, for its quiet, contemplative qualities (but poems can rouse and rage too, of course), but also to discover the truth about my own life and the life of the world – to be taken deeper into reality and to engage in a process of exploration and discovery. I'm not the same person at the end of the poem as I was at the beginning, even if I can't articulate what the poem has affected in me. I have learnt something, I have been moved, or comforted or cleansed. I may have been shaken and disturbed, but in a way that leads me to a different place or awareness than before the poem started. And whatever discovery I have made cannot be had apart from the poem itself. As soon as I try to state what the poem tells me in prose terms, something is lost; because the poem works as a whole, and it is as much the sound of the words, the visual power of the images and metaphors, the subtle associations of memory and the senses which lead to the experience of recognition or revelation in which the reader senses being spoken to by the poem.

Poetry as healing art, as reconnecting what has been divided

Poetry brings together and fuses many aspects of our experience that we often regard as separate, even in polar opposition to each other. It brings together and integrates body and mind, emotions and intellect, concretion and universal meaning. It works with sound, rhythm and shape, as well as the meaning and association of words. We might say it combines the two realms of discourse of which Julia Kristeva speaks: the symbolic and the semiotic, where the symbolic represents the network of signifiers that constitutes language and culture (identified with the masculine) and the semiotic represents the physical basis of language – 'its sounds, cadences, tones, and rhythms, originating in the body',[16] and identified with the maternal feminine. In other words, poetry combines the rational discourse of the mind with the nonsense babble of pre-language infancy, speaking to both realms and integrating them.

One of the key ways in which poetry functions as 'liberative language' is in its capacity to connect what has been disconnected or severed in us. This is something that feminist poets in particular have emphasized. Thus Rich pioneered a female poetics in which she insisted on bringing together politics and personal relationships, sex and social reform, thinking and feeling. In a 1998 interview she asserts this capacity of poetry to

> connect the fragments within us, connect us to others like and unlike ourselves, replenishing our desire. It's potentially catalytic speech because it's more than speech: it is associative, metaphoric, dialectical, visual, musical; in poetry words can say more than they mean and mean more than they say.[17]

Elsewhere she speaks of wanting to write poetry that is 'intellectual and moral and political and sexual and sensual – all of that fermenting together'.[18]

Because of this capacity to integrate what is often divided, poetry may perform a therapeutic function – not only for the individual but for wider society too. This is not separate from its prophetic, political function but another aspect of it. While it holds out the promise of integration and reconciliation of opposites, at the same time it exposes and critiques the way in which society functions to perpetuate these divisions. Like all good art, it holds up a mirror to the society of which it is a part and from which it yet also stands somewhat apart, magnifying, compressing, framing and simplifying what it sees in such a way as to function as a prophetic and mimetic word.

Poetry as witness to the irreducible, transformative Word

Poets perhaps more than other crafters of the word are the custodians of language, those who purge language of its dross, renew and revivify speech; and we have never needed them as we do now. In a sound-bite culture where words are proliferated endlessly and demanded on cue, where most written text is transitory and quickly consigned to the dustbin, the poet stands for the word that has to be waited for. Like the contemplative, the poet utters a word out of silence, out of long wrestling with speech – and is thus able to speak a counter-cultural word that is freighted with the power of the wait. Against those who seek to manipulate language for political victory or religious ideology, the poet stands for the power and beauty of words and, ultimately, for the freedom of the Word itself: the *dabhar* of which Jews and Christians speak that is the divine source of all creativity and knowledge, that cannot be possessed or controlled, that manifests as both reason (Logos) and wisdom (Sophia) and is endlessly uttering itself in the world in every fresh manifestation of truth and beauty and longing for justice.

Whether or not they subscribe to a religious world view, poets speak for this Word whenever they witness to the irreducible variety, particularity, glory and beauty of the world and whenever they evoke the glory and pity of human life, enabling the reader or hearer to break out of the limitations of their own little world and envisage lives and concerns not theirs, yet part of our common humanity. This sense of serving a wider vision is well expressed for me by Jeni Couzyn speaking about the deepest motivation of her writing: 'Asked by a journalist whom I write *for*, I found myself answering, "I write for God" – meaning I write for the deepest eye and ear within myself that I am able to reach.'[19] And Kathleen Raine speaks of the absolute necessity of the strange, elusive mystery of poetry in our lives (a need that many do not recognize):

People need poetry in their lives, not just a few unbalanced neurotics and misfits, but the poet, that is to say the soul, latent in everyone. We really cannot live by bread alone but by every word of God ... and is that not another name for poetry? ... The poetry of life is not a luxury, it is a necessity.[20]

Again, this sense of the vocation of the poet to witness to the spiritual is not separate from the prophetic or political dimension of the poet's witness. Rich speaks of the vocation of the poet to 'bear witness to a reality from which the public – and maybe part of the poet – wants to turn away'.[21] The poet, like the political agent, has the gift of 'radical imagination' – 'the radical imagination of the not-yet, the what-if'.[22] Despite its apparent fragility and insignificance, Rich insists that poetry 'makes a difference', cutting across the loneliness of those who have felt 'like monsters', challenging 'the idea that there is no alternative', giving voice to a different way of being or doing things in the world. 'Through its very being, poetry expresses messages beyond the words it is contained in; it speaks of our desire; it reminds us of what we lack, of our need, and of our hungers. It keeps us dissatisfied. In that sense, it can be very, very subversive.'[23] We might name this unsettling, disruptive, hunger-rousing work of poetry as part of the transformative work of the Spirit, though Rich would not.

Notes

1 See www.thesevernforum.org.uk for information about the Forum.

2 *Church Times*, 23 September 2011, p. 40.

3 Original source unknown. Quoted in the Aldeburgh Poetry Festival Programme, 2002, p. 18.

4 From 'Adagia', in W. N. Herbert and M. Hollis (eds.), *Strong Words: Modern Poets on Modern Poetry* (Tarset: Bloodaxe, 2000), pp. 58, 62.

5 Evidence for this is partly anecdotal, but supported by the popularity of anthologies of verse dedicated to birth, love and death and websites providing suggestions of poems for naming ceremonies, weddings and funerals. See, for example, Hugh Morrison, *Non-Religious Readings for Naming Ceremonies* (London: Montpelier Publishing, 2015); Hugh Morrison, *Non-Religious Wedding Readings* (London: Montpelier Publishing, 2017); Neil Astley, *Do Not Go Gentle: Poems for Funerals* (Newcastle: Bloodaxe, 2003); Janet Morley, *Our Last Awakening: Poems for Living in the Face of Death* (London: SPCK, 2016); Janet Morley, *Love Set You Going: Poems of the Heart* (London: SPCK, 2019).

6 'Breaking the ice of the soul: Theology and literature in search of a new language', in Sarah K. Pinnock (ed.), *The Theology of Dorothee Soelle* (Harrisburg, PA: Trinity Press International, 2003), p. 32.

7 From 'In memory of W. B. Yeats', in W. H. Auden, *Collected Poems*, ed. Edward Mendelson (London: Faber & Faber, 1976), p. 197.

8 Dorothee Soelle, *The Silent Cry* (Minneapolis, MN: Fortress, 2001), p. 294.

9 Emily Dickinson, letter to Thomas Wentworth, 1870, in Mabel Loomis Todd (ed.), *The Letters of Emily Dickinson* (Mineola, NY: Dover Publications, 2012).

10 Gillian Clarke, *At the Source: A Writer's Year* (Manchester: Carcanet, 2008), p. 9.

11 Adrienne Rich, *What is Found There: Notebooks on Poetry and Politics* (London: Virago, 1995), p. xiv.

12 Original source unknown. Quoted in Neil Astley (ed.), *Staying Alive: Real Poems for Unreal Times* (Tarset: Bloodaxe, 2002), p. 18.

13 Seamus Heaney, 'Feeling into words', in *Finders Keepers: Selected Prose 1971–2001* (London: Faber and Faber, 2002), p. 14.

14 Quoted in Peter Sansom, *Writing Poems* (Tarset: Bloodaxe, 1993), p. 61.

15 Adrienne Rich, in Sansom, *Writing Poems*, p. 61.

16 Grace M. Jantzen, *Becoming Divine: Towards a Feminist Philosophy of Religion* (Manchester: University of Manchester Press, 1998), p. 195.

17 Ruth E. C. Prince, 'The Possibilities of an Engaged Art: An Interview with Adrienne Rich' (1998), available at www.english.uiuc.edu/maps/pets/m_r/rich/onlineints.htm (accessed 11.4.13).

18 Michael Klein, 'A Rich Life: Adrienne Rich on Poetry, Politics and Personal Revelation', *Boston Phoenix,* June 1999. Previously available on www.poets.org, but no longer.

19 Jeni Couzyn (ed.), *The Bloodaxe Book of Contemporary Women Poets: Eleven British Writers* (Newcastle: Bloodaxe, 1985), p. 215.

20 Kathleen Raine, 'Earth's Children', *Resurgence* 135 (1989), pp. 4–5.

21 Rich, *What is Found There*, p. 115.

22 Prince, 'The Possibilities of an Engaged Art'.

23 Adrienne Rich, interview with Matthew Rothschild, *The Progressive* 58 (January 1994), pp. 31–5.

10

(W)riting Like a Woman: In Search of a Feminist Theological Poetics

This chapter was originally published in Making Nothing Happen: Five Poets Reflect on Faith and Spirituality, *co-authored with Gavin D'Costa, Eleanor Nesbitt, Mark Pryce and Ruth Shelton (Farnham: Ashgate, 2014, pp. 9–47). Gavin, Eleanor, Mark, Ruth and I have been meeting as 'the Diviners', a group of poet theologians, from around 2000 onwards (and, for a short period at the beginning, Rowan Williams was a member of the group). We meet three or four times a year, for the best part of a day, taking time over a leisurely meal (they are often works of art in themselves!) to gather and share news, before settling down to read poems and respond to them. This group has been a constant source of life, joy, encouragement and, at times, respite from the ridiculous pressures we all seem to live under. Working on a shared book was one of a few collaborative projects the group has taken on; we also co-led a BBC Radio 4 Morning Service in 2006 from St James Priory Church in Bristol and jointly gave the Anne Spencer Memorial Lecture[1] at Bristol University in February 2014. In* Making Nothing Happen, *we each included a selection of poems alongside our essays. For the sake of brevity, I have omitted these here, along with comments in the essay on those poems.*

Introduction

In what follows, I want to tell something of how poetry and faith have been significant in my life and how I perceive their interrelationship. Underlying this story is a sense that both poetry and theology have funded and nourished my sense of self from earliest days – taught me who I am, where I belong in the world and how to speak into and of the world. At the same time, poetry and theology have been arenas in which I've struggled to come to authentic speech as a woman – a pervasive theme in much second-wave feminist writing from the 1960s onwards, where there has been considerable debate about what it means to write, think and speak (even throw and climb!) 'as' or 'like a woman'.[2] The debate has centred around women's struggles to find an authentic female tradition or traditions of writing, to take up a subject position (rather than be the object of the male gaze or male writing) and to develop distinctively feminine forms of literature without buying into limited, essentialist notions of gender. My own struggle has been to find traditions of theology and poetry into which my own particular voice can speak; and to find a way of integrating poetic and theological discourse, without prioritizing one over the other or re-inscribing oppressive dualisms – emotion versus intellect, concretion versus abstraction, feminine versus masculine – on to the poetry–theology relation. In this piece, I seek to write in a way that is confessional and reflexive, as well as thematic, as a way of honouring this struggle and attempting to hold the tension between different modes of thinking and speaking. My aim is to stay close to my experience of both reading and writing poetry, as well as to draw on my commitment to prayer and public liturgy, my work of teaching theology and spirituality (in which poetry has a place), and my research into women's faith lives (which employs ethnography in ways that link with poetry), for it is out of these contexts that my own writing has been shaped and to which it seeks to speak. I shall also make some reference to the wider feminist literature that has pursued the discussion about what 'writing like a woman' can mean.

Poetry and prayer: language of the depths

Poetry and faith have always been there, from as far back as I can remember, and have always been intertwined, though it is perhaps only with hindsight that I can recognize how significant have been their interconnections – and these have not always been capable of articulation, precisely because the roots of each go deep and have been as much lived as reflected upon, wellsprings of vitality and creativity that have not required inspection. Part of the attraction, as well as the challenge, of writing this piece and engaging in the collective enterprise of this book, is to seek to find a way of unearthing and articulating the relationship between poetry and faith which might go at least some way towards doing justice to their depths, without killing off what remains elusive, mysterious and properly beyond rationalization.

I wasn't brought up in a particularly literary household, but my upbringing was one that gave me an instinctual, uncomplicated love of language, poetry, rhythm and music. Both my parents had been compelled to leave school in their early teens, but both sides of my family held as precious the written and spoken word, and handed on to me different forms of literary and religious tradition which shaped my sense of self, community and world. My Scottish mother came from a generation that learnt poetry by heart and recited reams of the Border poets to me and my siblings, as well as classics of the English canon, in her broad brogue. I didn't understand much of it, but I loved the *sound* of it and the way it made the hairs stand up on the back of my neck; I imbibed the sense that words are visceral things, and can *do* things – charm, sooth, rouse, amaze, infuriate, lodge in the body and subconscious in such a way as to continue their mysterious reverberations. From as far back as I can remember, I was taken to the Methodist chapel a mile along the road from where we lived – largely peopled by my Devonian father's relatives – where I heard the King James Version read Sunday by Sunday and sang rousing Wesley hymns. I learnt something about the reverence and holiness of words, the respect sacred texts were accorded, but also the love of scripture and hymnody.

These early formative experiences root the sense I have always had that poetry and prayer are very close to each other, are both forms of speaking that, as Dorothee Soelle puts it, 'place us into relation with the ground of the depth of being'.[3] There is a quality of attentiveness, of language honed to the essential in both poetry and prayer, that I recognized in the rather motley mix of Robbie Burns, Moody and Sankey hymnody and the cadences of the King James Bible that made up my child's repertoire of tongues. In each of these different forms of oral poetry, I experienced something of the out-of-the-ordinariness of poetic diction, the denseness and compactness of words working at full tilt, the intricacy of sound patterns and rhythms that didn't need to be spelt out to me because they were doing their own magical stuff. They also taught me something of the discipline and restraint of poetic speech, of language working with the spaces, pauses and silences between and beneath the words.

Both poetry and prayer are more than the words themselves, they call us to something else, *someone* else perhaps, above and beyond the words – and they do this as much by what is *not said* as by what is said, by their rhythms and sounds and patterns as well as their obvious content. The gaps and pauses in poems, as well as in liturgy, are breathing spaces, fertile places where the words take on extra freight. For me, the sound of poetry is extremely important and I often *hear* the first line of a new poem, as if spoken to me from another source (although it is, of course, my own self speaking); the sound of the line leads me into the whole poem, often without any conscious sense of what it is I am writing until after I have written it. There is a sense, which perhaps all poets feel, that one's own work comes from a deeper source than the conscious self and knows more than the conscious self knows. As Adrienne Rich has written, 'poems are like dreams, in them you put what you don't know you know'.[4] The poetic word, like God's creative *dhabar* that utters the world into being in Genesis, is a fiat, a performative word that does what it speaks. Thus a poem works as much through its subliminal impact on the ear, the memory and the unconscious as on its appeal to the rational mind. I have learnt to appreciate that the 'meaning' of a poem is far more than any moral, religious or political 'message' that might be summarized on the basis of the poem. Any poem that can be translated into prose terms without loss, is hardly a poem worthy of the name. The poem is a totality of sound, rhythm, association, image and voice, of which the surface 'meaning' is only one perhaps relatively insignificant dimension – which is why 'nonsense' poems have such appeal on the one hand and, on the other, it is more or less impossible to say exactly why and how a poem makes an impact on one person but not on another. 'A poem should not mean/ but be';[5] more viscerally, David Constantine suggests that: 'A poem, like the clitoris, is there/ For pleasure.'[6] The sensuous discourse of poetry by and large eschews abstraction and philosophical distance (although plenty of poems are intellectually demanding) in favour of concretion. 'For all the history of grief/An empty doorway and a maple leaf.'[7] Constantine's sexual metaphor also suggests that poetry belongs to the realm of the feminine and to the female body – themes to which I will return.

We could speak of this sensual particularity of poetry in theological terms as coming close to what Christians understand by incarnation and sacrament, themselves an outworking of the doctrine of creation,[8] which speaks of the physical world as an expression of the being and longing-to-be-in-relation of God. The universe is created not as some kind of extension of God but as something that is truly its own self, multiple and various and complex as it is, free to be separate and apart from God, and yet imbued with the qualities and characteristics of its maker. Any artist knows something of this relation between themselves as creator and the work of art as an independent, separate thing-in-itself which must be let go to live its own life in the world, and yet which has emerged from the being of the creator and is an authentic expression of the person. In incarnation, as in creation, God gives Godself to the created order without reservation, in total vulnerability and trust, in openness and in commitment, in self-giving and in love – and this giving is expressed in God being born in human flesh, becoming a discrete, particular, embodied part of the creation, subject to all its limitations and laws. The God who is the source and origin of all that is becomes a newborn whelp, utterly dependent on other creatures for very existence. This bespeaks a divine self-offering that gives to the uttermost, that risks not only rejection but annihilation. If there is some kind of aesthetic parallel to incarnation in the work and life of the poet, it is perhaps to be seen in the costly struggle the poet must wage with the slippery and intractable stuff that is language in order to compress the most profound experiences and apprehensions of the self into a frail, limited body that is the poem. Every poem, we might say, gestures towards incarnation and has a sacramental quality about it, in so far as it succeeds in becoming a vehicle for revelation, a place where grace and truth are compressed and encountered.[9]

This is the kind of second-order theological reflection on poetic creation that has only come later, after decades of writing and reading poetry, as I have learnt to stand back from the process in order to reflect on it. Nevertheless, it is clear to me that my own poetry is deeply embedded within, and nurtured by, the specific forms and texts of the Christian scriptures and liturgy, particularly Anglican forms of worship but also other, more experimental and 'alternative' forms of liturgical expression. Much of my poetry addresses consciously 'religious' subjects, stories and texts, has often been written for liturgical use and, even when neither of these is true, draws deeply on scriptural forms – particularly the language and rhythms of the psalms (repetition, parallelism, chorus and so on) and makes use of liturgical forms such as the confession, canticle and litany.

Much of my poetry, perhaps all of it, is written, whether consciously or not, against the backdrop of divine presence or absence and is addressed, whether consciously or not, to a divine 'Thou'. My poems, as well as more overtly liturgical texts, are constantly in search of more authentic ways of addressing, naming or evoking the Thou who becomes not less mysterious and elusive with time but more. I find myself returning to certain elemental images – water, the sea, the abyss, darkness, the erotic, the wilderness, death – in poems that gesture towards the divine, but also drawing on more playful terms and names for God: God as stroppy middle-aged mother, as hiker, spinster, quester, jester, as the female Christ figure, the Christa who, herself, appears in many diverse forms. I am also learning to be more adventurous in the voices, tones and forms I use in my poetry, moving out from a predominant use of the contemplative, respectful stance of the worshipper from which much of my earlier poetry was written, to occupy a greater range of stances – the sceptical, the quizzical, the angry, the humorous, the stoical. Nor, of course, should the poet's voice be assumed to represent the 'I' of the person who writes, at least not in any direct, confessional sense. Although much of my own writing is, in fact, strongly confessional, I have also experimented with the dramatic monologue as a form for inhabiting other voices, particularly as a way of bringing to voice the anonymous, invisible or ignored women of scripture, tradition and the contemporary world (a strategy common among feminist poets and liturgists; see below).

Interestingly, much contemporary British poetry is written in a tone of detached, ironic distance – more than is the case in contemporary American verse, say – and the use of the passionate voice in poetry, including a religious voice of adoration and worship, is rare. Yet if, as Penelope Shuttle suggests, part of the purpose of the poet is 'to go on loving the world', even 'when it deals you severe blows',[10] then the voice of praise and blessing needs to be present in contemporary poetry, however mediated and translated. This is a language that is basic to religion, and part of what religious poets have to offer the wider contemporary scene might be a capacity to bless the world and all that is in it. Yet for a language of blessing to be authentic in the contemporary world, it needs to speak to those for whom religious vocabulary and speech are not only foreign but also empty and redundant, devoid of symbolic force. It is notable that many contemporary poets, most of them without overt religious faith, frequently employ religious or liturgical forms to address weighty matters, investing them with new, secular meaning at the same time as calling on and utilizing their ancient, totemic power for their own meanings and ends. Carol Ann Duffy's much-anthologized sonnet, 'Prayer',[11] composed of entirely secular expressions of what might be considered forms of prayer, is an obvious example of this tendency of secular poets to pick up and use traditional, religious forms. Adam Zagajewski's 'Try to praise the mutilated world', published in *The New Yorker*[12] in the aftermath of the Twin Towers' collapse on 9/11, is another.

Just as in the wider cultural setting there are myriad ways of religious faith and poetry speaking to, or drawing from, each other, so in my own development as a poet and a theologian, the ways I have experienced and understood the relationship between poetry and faith have shifted and changed. The intertwining of poetry and religion continued throughout childhood and into adolescence, where it became more tutored and self-conscious. My schooling introduced me to a sampling of the riches of the western canon of literature, with all its glories and limitations. English was always my first love in school, although I was intensely pious too and I'd have been hard pressed to choose between the Bible and the great religious poets (John Donne, George Herbert and most especially Gerard Manley Hopkins were my heroes). I was also learning more about a critical study of religious texts through Theology A level, though it took me years to permit critical theological reflection to shape and inform my practice of faith. When I came to have to decide what to read at university, I finally opted for Theology because I knew that I'd never stop reading literature and poetry, whereas if I had chosen Literature, I doubt I would have carried on reading much theology. Indeed, when at university, I often used to bunk off theology lectures to sneak into the English department to hear poets and literary critics. So there was always this pull between religion and literature, sometimes experienced as a tension or something I needed to choose between (as if it was not possible to have them both!) – but they were always both there, speaking to each other, informing each other, feeding each other or fighting with each other.

Throughout childhood and adolescence, too, I was writing poetry. Most of it was undoubtedly terrible; although we did do written composition at school, no one seemed to think there was any need to instruct us in the craft of writing. It was either something one could do, or not. Both writing and faith now seem to me essentially disciplines to be practised rather than a therapeutic outpouring of thoughts and feelings (on the page, to God), and much of this can be learnt – or at least, improved by practice. Both prayer and poetry are a repeated practice concerned with as profound an attentiveness as I can muster (as Simone Weil has characterized the essence of prayer in her classic study[13]): attentiveness to my own life, both inner and outer, as well as attentiveness to other people, objects and events in all their mysterious otherness, and, in and through each of these, attentiveness to the source of all life and creativity, the Word uncreated and incarnate.

Feminist critique and struggle: learning to write and pray 'like a woman'

At some stage in my developing love affair with poetry and theology, there began a gradual conscientization process as I became increasingly aware of the deeply patriarchal nature both of the religious tradition I was part of and the literary/cultural heritage I was steeped in. I began to realize in my early twenties how the texts and traditions I'd inherited and that had formed me were largely those of a privileged western male elite. While many of my teachers had been women, all the poets I'd learnt about and read were male, with the exception of Christina Rossetti and Sylvia Plath. With one or two notable exceptions, all my theology teachers were men, and certainly all the texts and ideas I was introduced to were from male writers and thinkers. I could not have named a single female theologian – it had not dawned on me even to ask the question of whether any existed. The only exception to this gaping female absence was being introduced to the writings of Julian of Norwich while I was working in my gap year at Lee Abbey in North Devon and, through her, to the existence of other medieval women mystics. But neither Julian nor any of the other female saints featured in my theology degree. At that time, in the late 1970s, feminist theology was only just beginning to emerge, not in academia at first but in small, grassroots networks of which I began to be a part. Groups like Women in Theology (a national network for women wanting to explore theology in new ways), as well as local and regional groups, met to do theology in a wide variety of ways, employing methods borrowed from academia (seminars, lectures and so on) but also using the arts, imaginative forms of reflection, body work, therapeutic methods, role-play and so on, as a way of seeking to engage politically and holistically with emerging feminist theologies.[14] In company with other women who were part of this early feminist theological and liturgical movement, I found myself writing in a variety of modes as an expression of feminist theological exploration. My first published article was a rereading of the parables of Jesus from the perspective of women's experience,[15] and this seems significant because the parables themselves might be seen as a prime scriptural form which combines the poetic and the conceptual, provocative metaphors (whether brief, riddle-like koans or more developed, narrative forms) that engage imagination, brain, heart and will. At the same time, I was writing poems and prayer texts, often for collective use in feminist theology and worship groups. Much of the content of my first collection,[16] though published much later, comes from this period.

Throughout my twenties and thirties, then, I kept both poetry and faith alive – or should I say they kept me alive? I was deeply engaged in both, but sometimes inhabited them as if they were separate compartments, coming from different parts of me: the rational versus the affective, the professional versus the personal, the academic versus the spiritual. Theology was associated with the former, poetry with the latter (though personal faith was more akin to poetry, being associated with feelings, an intense personal relationship with God, and so on). There was, for a long time, a huge split between these different parts of myself, and the tension created by this produced enormous paralysis – a big theme of my twenties and thirties. I was working – or trying to work – in two modes, two forms of writing: the academic and scholarly, on the one hand, and poetic and liturgical on the other; both were essential and yet I experienced them as pulling in different directions, and it was almost impossible to keep both alive at the same time. When I engaged in scholarly writing, the poems seemed to die a death and go far away, underground, and much of my own imaginative life and creative power died with them. When the poems returned – often with ferocious, almost violent, assertiveness, bringing havoc and a painful return of feeling in their wake – they were greedy in their demands and would only accept centre stage, not content to share the limelight with my academic writing.

This experience of struggle between different parts of the self and different forms of writing is not, I have come to recognize, merely a private or personal dilemma – one of the reasons for recounting it here in some detail. The struggle to overcome false polarities and to forge an authentic 'voice' that does not simply reinscribe the dualisms is a recurring theme in the lives of many other women students, scholars and writers – something I explored in my doctoral research into women's faith lives, where metaphors and narratives of alienation, paralysis and dividedness were pervasive.[17] It has been a major theme in both literary and theological feminist discourse, addressed in rather different ways by Anglo-American feminists and French feminists such as Hélène Cixous, Julia Kristeva and Luce Irigaray. Embedded within an intellectual tradition of French philosophy and psychoanalytic theory, French feminists have sought to respond to Jacques Lacan's thesis that postulates the symbolic order of language as essentially masculine, dominated by the phallic Law of the Father. In Lacan's scheme, language, rationality itself and all that flows from them – law, religion, science and civilization – are structured by the masculine symbolic. The feminine has no subjectivity or voice within this order, but is relegated to the realm of the unconscious. In Lacanian terms, to speak at all is to enter the masculine realm, and women themselves have no language of their own. As Grace Jantzen puts it, 'in order to speak, women must use men's language, play by men's rules, find themselves in a foreign country with an alien tongue'.[18] Exploring this theme in a highly concrete fashion, Elaine Showalter argued that, in the American university system of the early 1970s, women students were taught to 'think like a man'; studying texts and traditions supposedly representative of the best of the literary canon, women students were 'estranged from their own experience and unable to perceive its shape and authenticity'. Expected 'to identify as readers with a masculine experience and perspective ... presented as the human one', women students learnt to doubt and even hate their own selves, becoming 'timid, cautious and insecure' when enjoined to 'think for themselves'.[19]

What, then, does it mean to write or think 'as a woman', and how may women claim a space – a room, a tradition and a voice – of their own? This is the central question of 1980s feminism, and even though in more recent debate gender has been radically destabilized by theorists such as Judith Butler,[20] as well as by increasing awareness of the complexity and fluidity of gender identities and relations, the question is still a fruitful and creative one for the female writer – at least for this one.

Feminists themselves propose various solutions to the dilemma of 'writing as/like a woman'. Cixous, Irigaray and Kristeva all, to some extent, accept Lacan's thesis of language and culture as the realm of the masculine yet, at the same time, seek to disrupt and subvert it through a range of creative, writerly and linguistic strategies. Cixous proclaims woman as the source of life, power and energy and announces the advent of a new, female form of language – écriture féminine – which subverts the patriarchal binary. In 'The Laugh of the Medusa', she urges women to 'put herself into the text', to 'write her self', to 'write as a woman, toward women', claiming the female body as the source of their writing.[21] Irigaray offers a variety of tactics that she believes can undercut phallocentric logic: mimeticism, or the mimicry of male discourse; female mysticism understood as a space in western history where women have spoken and acted publicly, and 'le parler femme' or 'womanspeak', a spontaneous form of feminine speech that emerges when women speak together. Kristeva proposes a new distinction between the 'semiotic' and the 'symbolic', to replace Lacan's distinction between the Imaginary and the Symbolic Order, and reconceives their relation. The symbolic represents the network of signifiers that constitutes language and culture (identified with the masculine), while the semiotic represents the physical basis of language – 'its sounds, cadences, tones, and rhythms, originating in the body'[22] and identified with the maternal feminine. For Kristeva, the monolithic structure of the symbolic

> can be disrupted by the irrepressible semiotic with its multiple meanings and sounds ... The sober intellectual narrative where words and meanings are rigorously pinned down is subverted by the rhythms, intonations, repetitions, and sound-plays of the semiotic, which is a *jouissance*, a 'transgression' of the symbolic order.[23]

The struggle for the woman writer, the woman thinker, is how to inhabit patriarchal discourse without doing fundamental violence to her sense of self, without reinforcing her very absence and silence or positioning herself as stereotypically 'feminine' – passive, receptive, occupying the affective domain, maternal and caring (roles that, of course, religion has legitimized and theologized over centuries). In order to speak or think at all, the woman writer has to find a new language, make new maps, revise and reverse the patriarchal myths – and Kristeva in particular considers poetry, with its roots in ritual, to have a peculiar potency to subvert and recreate the symbolic order. Adrienne Rich, one of the foremost feminist poets and thinkers whose work can be seen as a forging of just such a new form of discourse, speaks of the profound alienation experienced by the woman poet: 'The rules break like a thermometer ... the maps they gave us were out of date/ by years.'[24] The female poet, like the political agent, is required to exercise 'radical imagination' – 'the radical imagination of the not-yet, the what-if'[25] – in order to give birth to new forms of perception, new ways of speaking. Even while, in more recent debate, critics have problematized the notion of 'writing like a woman' (or, indeed, a man), just as gender itself has been radically destabilized by theorists such as Judith Butler, the exploration of how gender is constructed in texts is still a fruitful and creative one.

Feminist poets, like feminist theologians, have found themselves engaged in many kinds of critical and revisionary tactics in order to remake the language. Both poets and theologians have employed invective, lament, irony and humour to undo the assumptions of patriarchal texts and traditions, and feminist liturgies of denunciation and protest use such strategies. Both poets and theologians have revisited patriarchal (including scriptural) texts and stories, rewriting them from different perspectives of female protagonists: Carol Ann Duffy's The World's Wife[26] is a recent example in poetry; Sara Maitland has employed the medium of the short story to do the same thing in fiction;[27] and feminist biblical hermeneutics, from Elizabeth Cady Stanton's ground-breaking Women's Bible onwards,[28] provide myriad examples of this tactic in theological mode. Rich, in a much-quoted essay, described this kind of 're-vision' by women as 'an act of survival'.[29] My own attempts to rewrite biblical or liturgical texts from a female perspective stand firmly within this tradition of feminist revisionist mythology. Yet, although there are many parallels between the work and intentions of feminist poets, fiction writers and theologians, there is little literature addressing the relationship between feminism, literature and theology[30] – another reason, perhaps, why many of us have struggled to integrate these forms within our own work and lives.

Poetry as a means of prayer and theological reflection: a place of integration

Integration of the forms and voices, then, has become an urgent and domin-ant concern of my middle years. Gradually, over the past decade or so, more or less successfully, I've begun to integrate theology, poetry, spirituality and feminism into my own life as some kind of a whole. My writing, I hope, mirrors something of this integration but is also the place where I practise it. The work of integration has been, at one level, a slow, developmental process of trial and error; but it has also required some particular choices, including some refusals of inauthentic ways of being/writing/speaking, as well as some options for greater risk-taking, visibility and putting-myself-out-there – not only in my writing, but also in my teaching, public speaking and life choices. I had to lay down a long, painfully abortive attempt to write the definitive PhD thesis, give up trying to please daddy (gain approval in the male academy) in order to release a more authentic writing voice which expressed itself both in poetry and in a more engaged feminist practical theology. Having aborted one endlessly protracted, drily theoretical PhD, I began another, this time employing qualitative research methods as a way of listening to women speak about their spiritual lives and analysing their metaphors, narratives and ways of speaking as a way of discerning pattern and shape within them. This piece of research became a forum for the work of integration as I drew on scholarly literature from theology, psychology, literary studies and feminism, and developed a method of data analysis that read interview transcripts in similar ways to the ways I read poems, paying close attention to vocabulary, rhythm, metre and imagery, as well as to the gaps and silences within the text. Although at this stage I was not aware of it, there is a growing interest in such a use of poetry in data analysis in the qualitative paradigm.[31] Poetry was coming out of the intensely personal realm of my 'private life' and 'going public' as I employed poesis as part of my research methodology.

Not long after completing the doctorate, I published my first collection of poems, prayers and liturgical texts under the title *Praying Like a Woman*. At the time, this felt like an enormous exposure of the self, with nowhere to hide and the risk of disapproval from the male hierarchy (both ecclesial and academic). Yet this risking of the poetic voice freed me to rediscover a more authentic theological mode of writing. Theology gradually moved out of the realm of (someone else's) abstract, clever ideas into the language of poetry, prayer and liturgy. With many feminists, I am convinced that 'the master's tools will never dismantle the master's house', as Audre Lorde famously put it.[32] If theology and poetry are to be capable of bearing women's lives and meanings, their forms will have to change. It is not enough to simply 'add women and stir' to existing patriarchal traditions, whether we are talking about literature or theology. The traditions themselves have to be dismantled, recreated and reformed, with women finding new ways of speaking, thinking and writing – from the body, from our own diverse realities, from our own sense of the sacred. These are themes that are at the heart of feminist theology and literature, of course, and with which much of my own writing has been intensely engaged. My poem 'Writing the body'[33] seeks to explore and interrelate these themes. Drawing on Cixous' 'Laugh of the Medusa', I seek to suggest how writing as a woman, from a woman's body, is connected both with 'righting' the body – the long, painful process of undoing and correcting patriarchal control of female bodiliness, sexuality and self-expression – and 'riting' the body: ritualizing women's experiences through lament, celebration, feminist sacrament and ritual actions. The title of this essay is also intended to gesture towards these interconnections.

Bringing poetry more and more into my teaching, public speaking and retreat work has also been an important part of the journey towards integration, and I have become self-conscious in my intention to utilize the tradition(s) of women's spiritual poetry in my teaching. These traditions are much less known, in both theological and poetry circles, than the canon of men's religious poetry. A number of commentators have traced the English tradition of men's religious poetry, in which the Anglican poet priest has a particular part,[34] and I would want to place alongside this a much more diffuse and hidden tradition of women's religious/Christian poetry, which has been, of necessity, until very recently, a lay and therefore less 'official' tradition. The work of women poets such as Stevie Smith,[35] Kathleen Raine,[36] Elizabeth Jennings,[37] Denise Levertov,[38] and many others[39], has been enormously important in my own development as a woman poet who chooses to write about faith and spirituality, legitimizing and demonstrating some of the range of ways in which women can write about faith *as women*, in and through the particular lenses of their own embodied lives. I have also found that bringing women's poetry into the classroom, the pulpit and the retreat centre is a potentially liberating and empowering force in women's lives. Hearing, engaging with and responding to women's poetry can be a key means for women students and seekers to have the courage to claim their own voices and speak their own truth. Over many years, I have been running retreats and courses for women (as well as some for mixed-gender groups) that explore spirituality in contemporary women's poetry. Again and again, I have discovered how the words, as well as the lives, of women poets can speak profoundly to contemporary spiritual seekers, offering not only a language to express the inarticulate struggles and hopes of women in search of the sacred but also a company of sisters who have walked the way of faith before and have forged authentic expression for their own faith lives. It is not, of course, that men's poetry cannot also speak to, and nourish, women; I would not be without the poetry of Donne, Herbert, Hopkins, not to mention R. S. Thomas, Wendell Berry, Charles Causley, and many others. Yet, as a woman of faith seeking my own language of faith, men's language alone cannot substitute for the women's tradition I need to know and inhabit. Nor is gender, of course, the only relevant factor. I am conscious that most of the poets I have mentioned as significant in my own development are white and British, reflecting the bias of my own education and reading. Nevertheless, black poets such as Maya Angelou,[40] Alice Walker[41] and Jean 'Binta' Breeze[42] are also part of the great tradition of women poets I have more recently discovered and would wish to celebrate and affirm.

So, without really planning to do so, I realize that I've come, over more recent years, to use poetry quite deliberately and intentionally as a means of doing theology from my own specific context and location as a feminist Christian in search of women's literary as well as religious traditions and seeking to forge a contemporary feminist theological poetics. Poetry offers a form of theological reflection and exploration that allows me to work with a multiplicity of sources, experiences and questions, in a disciplined yet playful, even subversive, kind of way, with a freedom and quality of intense engagement that is less easy (for me, at least) to sustain in prose. Poetry has become a medium in which to explore some key theological questions, and to do so drawing on some of the same sources that theologians use (scripture, tradition – in the form of doctrines, creedal statements, visual images, lives of the saints and so on – and academic theology itself) but engaging them in a more free-flowing, unsystematic, episodic kind of way.

Sometimes a passage of scripture might be the starting point for a poem; sometimes an idea, suggestive phrase or image from a theological text might prompt the poem. Along with many contemporary poets, a visual image or artefact can often invite poetic response: for example, I wrote a sequence of poems responding to various images of Mary in Southwell Minster, performed as part of the 2002 Southwell Poetry Festival.[43] Poetry has been the place where I've wrestled with what it means to 'pray like a woman', not by reflecting on this question in any kind of systematic, second-order way (though I have also done that), but precisely by writing prayers that are grounded in the reality of my own life and that attempt to speak truthfully about my life (its childlessness, for example, or my struggle with low-level sickness and fatigue). Poetry has helped me to shape a language of prayer that is offered from a stance that is honest – 'with eyes open', to use Marjorie Procter-Smith's evocative phrase,[44] adopting a posture of standing as often as kneeling, using names and terms towards the divine that seek to honour how I understand and perceive that relation. Thus, along with other feminist liturgists, I find myself using hierarchical terms such as 'Lord' and 'Father' sparingly and critically, if at all, preferring terms that invite mutuality and co-creatorship – Friend, Sister, Christa, and so on – though even new names can also become habitual, unthinking, and constantly need to be subverted and renewed, or held in tension with other images and names for the divine.

After my first collection – a gathering together of pieces written over a 20-year period, crystallizing around the theme of *Praying Like a Woman* – I've become more ambitious in my engagement with poetry as a means of theological exploration. I've deliberately set out to write a book of poems, a long sequence, exploring a particular theological topic or theme – Mary, in the first case,[45] and the idea or image of the female Christ, or Christa, in the second.[46] In either case, I could have set out to explore Mary or the Christa in prose terms – and indeed, both books do contain significant prose passages – but using the poetic medium has encouraged in me a freedom, an imaginative creativity, the possibility of engaging with a wide range of diverse perspectives and voices, that would not have been possible in an extended prose treatment. A collection of poems allows there to be space as well as connection between the individual poems – in the same kind of way as, within a single poem, there is connection and space between the stanzas, the lines, the images. This is true, of course, of good prose, though in a different way. Poetry, I think, does it more elusively, more enigmatically, without spelling out so clearly the conceptual or metaphoric patterns. Poems leave the reader to do more of the work than most prose; although there can be a kind of elitism in poetry that I don't admire, a refusal to leave any traces for the reader to follow so that reading a poem becomes a detective work of hunting down all the allusions and references. I have, in my own poetry collections, provided ample notes to indicate at least some of the sources of my poems and to provide links to significant resources which readers might not otherwise access.

Not all poems are written as part of a larger project, and not all my poems are consciously 'about' gender in any obvious way. Poems often arise in response to everyday events as well as to liminal, critical incidents. In recent years, I've found myself writing more poems about my family – the death of a brother, relations with my parents, memories of my childhood in North Devon. These poems are working with my own particular family history, a way of integrating both the wounds and the gifts of my genetic and familial inheritance. They are not separate from the larger engagement with and critique of patriarchy, so much as a mapping of the intimate setting in which I learned those larger patterns.

Whether small-scale or large, intimate or public, poetry is for me a form of discourse that holds together and may even on occasion resolve the tensions and opposites of my life. Poetry is a way of speaking and thinking that is rooted in the (female) body, utilizing the kind of emotional intelligence that emerges from feeling. Utterly visceral, good poetry also engages the brain and requires the reader to think hard, to bring all the faculties of sense, knowledge and critical acuity to bear on the page. Poetry is a form of discourse in which *desire* plays a key role, in which feeling and passion are often strongly present, though may also be refracted through distillation and reflection – there is no one emotional tone or stance of a poem, any more than there is one topic or form. Poetry, at its best, is a way of speaking and thinking that stays close to narrative and concretion, as of course much scripture and liturgy does, and yet offers the reader symbolic, universal and representative truth through the particularity of the concrete/narrative (we're back to poetry as sacrament). Poetry is a way of speaking and thinking that offers both tight discipline yet huge opportunities for freedom, experimentation and play – it is at one and the same time a very small arena and a vast, free space, a kind of playground of the imagination. Poetry offers a way of speaking and thinking that is authentic yet need not be straightforwardly confessional; it can allow the poet to take on a variety of voices and perspectives, being both 'oneself' and yet moving behind or within other voices and identities, inhabiting multiple perspectives as a way of reflecting truth from different vantage points. Poetry is a way of speaking and thinking that is a close companion to prayer; like prayer, it pushes at the edges of language, it inhabits absence and silence as willingly as the word.

For all these, as well as other, reasons, poetry is a way of speaking and thinking that may be peculiarly fraught with potential for women who seek a form of discourse that integrates the symbolic and the semiotic without having to give up on either. In poetry, language both means/speaks and also stutters, *un*speaks, makes a kind of speaking that is as much non-sense as sense; this is particularly obvious in the work of poets who subvert the usual conventions of meaning-making, who push at the edges of the way words normally work, who play with the sound and arrangement of words and lines on the page. Gertrude Stein's[47] highly inventive use of repetition, stream-of-consciousness and bizarre word associations come to mind as an example of poetry functioning at the interface of the symbolic and the semiotic, whose poetic speech likes to inhabit the irrational or the non-rational, speaking with voices that do not make logical sense but proffer other kinds of meanings. Such poetry shares more than a little in common with glossolalia as well as faith's extravagant languages of praise, blessing, lament and confession, all of which may be considered redundant, extraneous, 'making nothing happen' in the world. Yet, for all that, I am encouraged by Grace Jantzen's suggestion, building on Kristeva's analysis, 'that it is from new liturgies and creative metaphor and poetry, in the expansion of a feminist imaginary, not with a preoccupation with truth-claims and justification of beliefs, that the masculinism of western Christendom can be transformed'.[48]

Perhaps, after all, it is not necessary to have to make a stark choice between the intellectual endeavours of theologians who address themselves to the truth-claims and logical coherence of religious beliefs, on the one hand, and the offerings of poets and liturgists, on the other, who seek to remake the Word that can serve the deepest needs of people's prayer, reflection and action. Both need each other; feed off each other, scrutinize, correct and critique each other, although, if Kristeva is correct in her analysis, it is poetic discourse arising from the semiotic that births the rational thought of the symbolic, rather than the other way round. So perhaps it is necessary to conclude that poetry makes a great deal happen, and births the symbolic systems by which faith lives.

Notes

1 This is an annual lecture hosted by the university's multi-faith chaplaincy in memory of a lecturer at the university, Anne Spencer.

2 Themes of silence and voice have been pursued in feminist literary criticism, feminist psychology and feminist theology, for example: Tillie Olsen, *Silences* (New York: Deacorte, 1978); Adrienne Rich, *On Lies, Secrets and Silence: Selected Prose 1966–1978* (London: Virago, 1980); Carol Gilligan, *In a Different Voice: Psychological Theory and Women's Development* (Cambridge, MA: Harvard University Press, 1982); Rosemary Radford Ruether, *Sexism and God-Talk* (London: SCM Press, 1983); Mary Field Belenky et al., *Women's Ways of Knowing: The Development of Self, Voice and Mind* (New York: Basic Books, 1986). For discussion of throwing, reading and writing 'as' or 'like' a woman/man, see Peggy Kamuf, 'Writing like a woman', in Sally McConnell-Ginet, Ruth Borker and Nelly Furman (eds.), *Women and Language in Literature and Society* (New York: Praeger, 1980), pp. 248–99; Iris Marion Young, 'Throwing like a girl: A Phenomenology of Feminine Body Comportment, Mobility and Spatiality', *Human Studies* 3 (1980), pp. 137–56; Jonathan Culler, 'Reading as a woman', in *On Deconstruction: Theory and Criticism after Structuralism* (London: Taylor & Francis, 1982), pp. 43–63; Terry Lovell, 'Writing like a woman: A question of politics', in Frances Barker, Peter Hulme, Margaret Iveson and Diana Laxley (eds.), *The Politics of Theory* (Colchester: University of Essex,1983); Robert Scholes, 'Reading like a man', in Alice Jardine and Paul Smith (eds.), *Men in Feminism* (New York: Methuen, 1987), pp. 214–18; and Dianne Chisolm, 'Climbing like a girl: An Exemplary Adventure in Feminist Phenomenology', *Hypatia* 23 (2008), pp. 9–40.

3 Dorothee Soelle, *The Silent Cry* (Minneapolis, MN: Fortress, 2001), p. 294.

4 Rich, *On Lies, Secrets and Silence*, p. 40.

5 Archibald MacLeish, 'Ars Poetica', in *Collected Poems 1917–1982* (Boston, MA: Houghton Mifflin, 1985), p. 106.

6 David Constantine, 'Pleasure', in *Collected Poems* (Newcastle: Bloodaxe, 2004), p. 326.

7 MacLeish, 'Ars Poetica'.

8 See Gavin D'Costa, 'The miracle of poetry: divine and human creativity', in Gavin D'Costa, Eleanor Nesbitt, Mark Pryce, Ruth Shelton and Nicola Slee, *Making Nothing Happen: Five Poets Explore Faith and Spirituality* (Farnham: Ashgate, 2014), pp. 171–209, for an elaboration on the theology of creation.

9 This is perhaps less true in certain kinds of epic, narrative poetry than in lyric poetry; though, even in long poems, this element of compression is present.

10 Penelope Shuttle, *Redgrove's Wife* (Tarset: Bloodaxe, 2006), back cover.

11 Carol Ann Duffy, 'Prayer', in *Selected Poems* (Harmondsworth: Penguin, 1994), p. 127.

12 Adam Zagajewski, 'Try to Praise the Mutilated World', *New Yorker*, 24 September 2001, www.newyorker.com/magazine/2001/09/24/try-to-praise-the-mutilated-world (accessed 24.3.20).

13 Simone Weil, 'Reflections on the right use of school studies with a view to the love of God', *Waiting on God* (Glasgow: Collins Fount, 1977).

14 For an account of the development of feminist theology networks in the UK, see Jenny Daggers, *The British Christian Women's Movement: A Rehabilitation of Eve* (Aldershot: Ashgate, 2002).

15 Nicola Slee, 'Parables and Women's Sexperience', *The Modern Churchman* 26.2 (1984), pp. 20–31. Republished in *Religious Education* 80.2 (1985), pp. 232–45, translated as 'Gelijkenissen en de ervaring van vrouwen', *Voorwerk* 1 (1987), pp. 2–15, and reproduced in A. Loades (ed.), *Feminist Theology: A Reader* (London: SPCK, 1990), pp. 41–7.

16 Nicola Slee, *Praying Like a Woman* (London: SPCK, 2004).

17 Nicola Slee, *Women's Faith Development: Patterns and Processes* (Aldershot: Ashgate, 2004).

18 Grace M. Jantzen, *Becoming Divine: Towards a Feminist Philosophy of Religion* (Manchester: University of Manchester Press, 1998), p. 42.

19 Elaine Showalter, 'Woman and the Literary Curriculum', *College English* 32 (1971), pp. 855–7.

20 Judith Butler, *Gender Trouble: Feminism and the Subversion of Identity* (New York and London: Routledge, 1990).

21 Hélène Cixous, 'The Laugh of the Medusa', *Signs: Journal of Women in Culture and Society* 1 (1976), pp. 875–93.

22 Jantzen, *Becoming Divine*, p. 195.

23 Jantzen, *Becoming Divine*, p. 196.

24 Adrienne Rich, 'Twenty One Love Poems', XIII, in *The Dream of a Common Language: Poems 1974–1977* (New York and London: W. W. Norton, 1993), p. 31.

25 Ruth E. C. Prince, 'The Possibilities of an Engaged Art: An Interview with Adrienne Rich' (1998), available at www.english.uiuc.edu/maps/pets/m_r/rich/onlineints.htm, p. 1.

26 Carol Ann Duffy, *The World's Wife* (London: Picador, 1999).

27 For example, Sara Maitland, *A Book of Spells* (London: Michael Joseph, 1987) and *Angel and Me: Short Stories* (London: Mowbray, 1995).

28 Elizabeth Cady Stanton, *The Women's Bible* (New York: European Publishing Company, 1985 reprint of the 1898 original).

29 Adrienne Rich, 'When we dead awaken: Writing as re-vision', in Rich, *On Lies, Secrets and Silence*, pp. 33–49.

30 There are, of course, some significant exceptions; for example, Susan Alicia Ostriker, *Stealing the Language: The Emergence of Women's Poetry in America* (London: Women's Press, 1987) and, in the UK, the work of Heather Walton, in, for example, *Imagining Theology: Women, Writing and God* (London: T&T Clark, 2007) and *Literature, Theology and Feminism* (Manchester: Manchester University Press, 2007).

31 See, for example, Rich Furnam, Cynthia Lietz and Carol L. Langer, 'The Research Poem in International Social Work: Innovations in Qualitative Methodology', *International Journal of Qualitative Methods* 5.3 (2006), pp. 1–8.

32 Audre Lorde, 'The master's tools will never dismantle the master's house', *Sister Outsider*, in *The Audre Lorde Compendium: Essays, Speeches and Journals* (London: Pandora, 1996), p. 158.

33 Slee, *Praying Like a Woman*, p. 97.

34 For example, L. William Countryman, *The Poetic Imagination: An Anglican Spiritual Tradition* (London: Darton, Longman & Todd, 1999) and Malcolm Guite, *Faith, Hope and Poetry: Theology and the Poetic Imagination* (Farnham: Ashgate, 2012).

35 Stevie Smith, *Collected Poems* (London: Penguin, 1975).

36 Kathleen Raine, *Collected Poems* (Ipswich: Golgonooza, 2000).

37 Elizabeth Jennings, *New Collected Poems* (Manchester: Carcanet, 2002).

38 Denise Levertov, *New Selected Poems* (Newcastle: Bloodaxe, 2003).

39 For examples of collections of women's spiritual/religious poetry, see Marilyn Sewell (ed.), *Cries of the Spirit: A Celebration of Women's Spirituality* (Boston, MA: Beacon Press, 1991) and *Claiming the Spirit Within* (Boston, MA: Beach Press, 1996); Veronica Zundel (ed.), *Faith in Her Words: Six Centuries of Women's Poetry* (Oxford: Lion, 1991); Julia Neuberger (ed.), *The Things that Matter: An Anthology of Women's Spiritual Poetry* (London: Kyle Cathie Ltd, 1992); Jane Hirshfield (ed.), *Women in Praise of the Sacred: 43 Centuries of Spiritual Poetry by Women* (New York: HarperCollins, 1994).

40 Maya Angelou, *The Complete Collected Poems* (London: Virago, 1995).

41 Alice Walker, *Collected Poems: Her Blue Body Everything We Know: Earthling Poems 1965–1900* (London: Orion, 2005).

42 Jean 'Binta' Breeze, *Third World Girl: Selected Poems* (Newcastle: Bloodaxe, 2011).

43 All in Nicola Slee, *The Book of Mary* (London: SPCK, 2007).

44 Marjorie Procter-Smith, *Praying With Our Eyes Open: Engendering Feminist Liturgical Prayer* (Nashville, TN: Abingdon Press, 1995).

45 Slee, *The Book of Mary*.

46 Nicola Slee, *Seeking the Risen Christa* (London: SPCK, 2011).

47 Gertrude Stein, *Gertrude Stein: Selected Writings* (London: Vintage, 1990).

48 Jantzen, *Becoming Divine*, p. 196.

II

Theological Reflection *in extremis*: Remembering Srebrenica

This article arose out of a workshop given at the British and Irish Associ-
ation of Practical Theology (BIAPT) 2018 annual conference on 'The
Practical Theologian as Reflective Practitioner', and was a means of bear-
ing witness to colleagues at BIAPT of my recent experience of participating
in a women's delegation to Bosnia, as the article recounts. I include it
here for a number of reasons, not least to reflect on the core activity of
theological reflection, about which there is much debate among practical
theologians, but also to demonstrate that poetry can be a means of witness
and response to traumatic suffering on a large scale, and not only a way of
capturing personal experience and insight. The article was originally pub-
lished in Practical Theology *12.1 (2019), pp. 30–43. I am deeply grateful*
to the charity Remembering Srebrenica for the invitation to participate in
the delegation to Bosnia in March 2018, to each of the women from the
UK who participated in the visit with me, as well as to Amy Drake, the
Director of Remembering Srebrenica, who accompanied the delegation,
to our local guide Rešad Trbonja and to each of the women and men of
Bosnia I encountered.

Introduction

In this article, I offer a worked example of autoethnographic theological
reflection (TR), picking up BIAPT 2018's conference theme of 'the practical
theologian as reflective practitioner'. This case study of TR emerges out of
a European context of recent civil conflict marked by violence, atrocity,
trauma, war, rape and ethnic cleansing (not to mention contested narratives
about what really took place and the causes of the events) – what I am
calling, in shorthand, theological reflection *in extremis*. The example comes
from my recent visit to Bosnia, as a guest of the British charity Remembering
Srebrenica.[1] This visit, brief as it was, by no means qualifies me to write or
speak about the complex history of the break-up of the former Yugoslavia, or the Bosnian war, as any kind of expert, theological or otherwise.[2]
Rather, I offer these reflections on my experience, along with my endeavours to reflect on them theologically, in the spirit of autoethnography.

Graham, Walton and Ward write of 'the reflexive self using writing to bring to light the experience of life in order to deepen self-awareness and generate understanding of God',[3] and this is an apt description of what I seek to do, both in the article as a whole and in the poems that form a part of my autoethnographic reflection. Ellis, Adams and Bochner define autoethnography as 'an approach to research and writing that seeks to describe and systematically analyze (*graphy*) personal experience (*auto*) in order to understand cultural experience (*ethno*)'.[4] In what follows, I am engaged in writing as an act of personal, political and theological exploration of my own subjective experience, in a context of *extremis*, as a way of seeking to understand broader cultural experience. Ellis, Adams and Bochner go on to reflect that such an approach 'challenges canonical ways of doing research and representing others and treats research as a political, socially-just and socially-conscious act'.[5] I hope that readers of this journal do not need persuading of the importance of research that intentionally sees itself as 'a political, socially-just and socially-conscious act', although some readers may be less familiar with a highly personal, autoethnographic approach to such research. As a feminist practical theologian, I refuse any sharp binary between the personal and the political, believing that the personal is always rooted in larger dynamics of power and, conversely, that the political assumes and depends on dynamics of personal relationship, even if these are (still) not often acknowledged or analysed. This article also owes a debt to autoethnographic research that is intentionally making use of poetry as a method of research.[6]

What I seek to do in this article, then, is to narrate something of the visceral experience of visiting such a context as Bosnia, and to describe my own attempts to respond theologically to the place and the people I met: a response that has only become evident to me in retrospect, but that in hindsight I am now able to analyse and break down into several component parts. I will highlight the part that the arts can play – in this case, poetry in particular, though I shall also refer to the visual art of Margaret Argyll – in expressing, responding to, staying with and processing events and experiences that did not seem to allow immediate cognitive response.

While few TR texts offer resources for reflecting on large-scale situations or incidents of war, ethnic cleansing, systematic rape and so on – something that practical theologians working in the field might ponder – their models and methods of TR, as outlined in key texts, could readily be applied to my experience and subsequent reflections. In broad terms, I had an experience that seemed to me to be pressing towards theological response and articulation; I describe and seek to enter more deeply into that experience; I have sought to learn from the experience by drawing on theological resources from my own Christian tradition and placing them alongside the experience in order for each to speak to, and interrogate, each; and finally, I am seeking to enact the learning through my own changed praxis (the process of TR as described by Robert L. Kinast[7]). O'Connell Killen and de Beer's[8] model of TR – with its close attention to the feelings stimulated by an experience from which images may arise that then, in turn, may give birth to insight and thence to action – is particularly helpful in highlighting the creative, potentially artistic nature of TR, and what follows seeks to develop their account of TR.

The context

The day of 11 July is Srebrenica Memorial Day, recalling the genocide of thousands of men and boys in July 1995 at the so-called UN safe haven outside the small village of Srebrenica, as well as the systematic rape of thousands of women and girls in designated camps throughout Bosnia. Twenty-three years after those events, in March 2018, I was privileged to take part in a women's delegation to Bosnia, organized by the British charity *Remembering Srebrenica*. I joined a multi-ethnic, multi-faith (Christian, Jewish, Muslim, secular/no overt faith) team of senior British women, including a war correspondent from *The Times*, a *Guardian* journalist, senior CEOs of charities working with survivors of domestic abuse, the Principal of Leo Beack College and a city councillor working with local faith communities. Over a period of a few days, we visited major sites associated with the atrocities, met survivors and heard something of their stories, and engaged with leading activists who are working for peace and justice in a country that remains deeply scarred by the events of the war. As this was a women's delegation, the trip focused in particular on women activists working with female survivors of the rape camps and the loss of multiple members of their families and communities, although we also met male survivors.

While by no means untouched by postmodernity, Bosnia remains a deeply patriarchal society, not least shaped by its religious traditions, ethical mores and strong emphasis on family and kinship. As in all wars, the Bosnian war was profoundly gendered: the experiences of men and boys was quite different from that of women and girls. Although some women did participate in the armed struggle, most did not. Women and girls in large numbers underwent sexual violence and rape, collectively organized (as did some men and boys); they were the main targets of the systematic programme of ethnic cleansing and rape as a weapon of war.[9] While more women than men survived the war, many of them have remained deeply scarred by their twofold experiences of loss (of sons, husbands, fathers and male relatives) and sexual violation. The trauma of sexual violence has been compounded by the strong taboos against speaking of such experience, even within the intimacy of marriage and family life. Many women are only now, more than twenty years after the events, being enabled through therapeutic support, to speak of the trauma they underwent during the war.

My brief visit to the beautiful country of Bosnia continues to haunt me. I struggle to absorb and make some kind of theological and spiritual sense of it. I had never been to Bosnia before, though I do remember vividly watching the nightly news on TV in the mid-1990s as the war unfolded and as the truth about the murder of thousands of Bosnian Muslims gradually emerged. In the ensuing years, up to December 2017 when the International Criminal Tribunal for the Former Yugoslavia was finally dissolved, the trials and indictments of war criminals at the Hague have been broadcast throughout the globe via mass media, many of whom have now served their terms and been released back into society.[10] Many Serbian leaders and ordinary Serbs have never acknowledged the genocide and still regard Slobodan Milošević, Radovan Karadžić and General Ratko Mladić as war heroes (although it is important to recognize that there are others who resisted the aggressive Serb nationalism of their leaders and stood in solidarity with their Muslim neighbours; and it is also important to acknowledge the deaths and suffering of civilian as well as military Serbs).

The experience of travelling to Bosnia and engaging in an intensive programme of visits and meetings to hear and learn more about survivors' experience of the war and the ways in which they are seeking to recover and reclaim their history, was an intense and in many ways overwhelming one. There were few opportunities for reflection and response at the time, although there were some: travelling by coach from Sarejevo out to Srebrenica allowed time to talk to my fellow delegates; mealtimes allowed further conversation; and the meetings with various survivors and activists always included opportunities for questions and dialogue. As writers on TR emphasize, the process of absorbing experience, attempting to make some kind of sense of it, and finding ways of responding to it, is normally a shared, communal experience and requires to be practised in community. I am immensely grateful to the women who shared the trip with me, including key workers from the charity, and our local (male) guide, Rešad, who accompanied us throughout the visit.

Although we all responded very differently to the various events and to learning more about the Bosnian war, we did what women very often and habitually do when thrown together by chance and circumstance: we talked, we wept, we laughed, we got angry and upset, we talked some more, we were reduced to silence by much of what we heard. We remained with each other throughout this demanding visit – without which it is inconceivable that I, at least, would have managed the journey at all. I include in this description of shared communal support the local Bosnian women activists we met, very briefly, at therapeutic and support centres. Although frequently divided by language and working through interpreters, the British delegation experienced extraordinary hospitality, compassion and support from our Bosnian hosts.

I emphasize the collective, communal nature of reflection at the outset because much that I go on to describe may appear as my own solitary, individual activity; and at one level, that is right. Part of my own response to my experience was to write a sequence of poems narrating various encounters with individuals and places; these poems are, of course, my own highly personal expressions. Yet they come out of the shared experience of the visit, as do all the other aspects of TR I analyse below.

The processes of theological reflection, identified in hindsight

The invitational nature of TR

TR is never automatic or coerced. It arises out of a response to an invitation, to undergo some experience and to enter into it. This might be an invitation to personal, interpersonal or broader socio-political encounter. The invitation often has an imperative quality to it – although it can always be refused. It may well be to go to some place – either literal, physical or emotional, psychological – where we would not have chosen to go, where faith challenges or requires us to go. In my own case, I was invited to go to a place that was strange to me, well beyond the shores of my known world, and to encounter others whose stories of rape, ethnic cleansing and unimaginable loss could not be distanced or switched off. The first challenge was allowing myself to respond positively to the invitation, and to risk all that would attend the going.

The consent to being overwhelmed and to powerlessness

I have written elsewhere of a spirituality of multiple overwhelmings.[11] While not unconnected, the primary sense in which I am using the term here is to refer to the demand that faith may make of the believer to allow oneself to be overwhelmed by suffering on a scale previously unimagined or unvisited, and to consent to the very real undoing that such suffering effects on the psyche and on the meaning-making imperative of theology. Part of my own dread of going to Bosnia, even while I felt I must, was that I would be devastated by the overwhelming reality of genocide and mass rape, that I would not be able to bear or cope with the degree of pain and suffering I would meet in others, that my response to their stories and pain would be utterly inadequate. Essentially, this was a fear of my own powerlessness and capacity for pain; a fear that I could only meet by consenting to the very real possibility of being overwhelmed. Interestingly, Heather Walton suggests that scariness may be a fundamental characteristic of good practice in TR, and that the degree to which something is alarming or worrying may be the degree to which it permits of significant theological reflection.[12]

The powerlessness I had to consent to was not merely affective; it was also cognitive. The literature of TR seems to be frequently driven by a goal to find meaning or make theological meaning out of experience, but what cognitive response is it possible to make in situations of mass atrocity that we might name as evil? Events such as the Holocaust or the Bosnian genocide render any endeavour to 'make meaning' highly suspect, if not abhorrent; they challenge the very notion of divine presence and agency, at least in any obvious or immediate sense. The consent to powerlessness and overwhelming demands the ability to 'live with the questions'[13] that admit of no answers and to feel the force of such questions. Why did Serbs who had lived peaceably with Bosnian neighbours for centuries claim their land and seek to purge the nation of their ethnic presence, in the process raping and killing them? Why did the rest of Europe look on and do next to nothing? Where was God on the day when more than eight thousand men and boys were taken into woods near Srebrenica and shot, then buried roughly in mass graves? These questions may be the wrong kind of questions, yet they are ones many feel compelled to ask, and the powerlessness of there being no credible theological answers may be part of the overwhelming TR requires of those who seek meaning in the crucible of history's undoing.

The undefended posture of Christian hospitality

Christian hospitality (other faiths may have a similar imperative, but I speak out of my own faith tradition) requires a radical openness to the other, to the neighbour and the stranger who, tradition tells us, is frequently Christ incognito, God coming in the flesh and garb of the outsider. TR requires the willingness to encounter, in as undefended a pose as we can manage (and this will vary according to a range of factors), the other who may be poor, smelly, unhinged, dying, excessively demanding or simply annoying. This is the encounter with alterity (another of Walton's characteristics of TR, as is the degree to which it touches the pain of the world[14]), the willingness to open one's heart, mind and, potentially, purse to the grief, wound and loss of the other. To engage with the suffering other is almost always to consent to being overwhelmed, if only by the enormity and intractability of their suffering. The vain hope that we might be able to 'cure' or 'solve' someone else's pain is one of the first casualties of self-armour that the would-be minister has to relinquish. At the same time, if we genuinely give our full attention to the neighbour, we may well find they ask much of us by way of patient presence and listening. Admitting Christ incognito into the home and the heart is a dangerous activity.

The pedagogy of material things

Heather Walton calls attention to the materiality of TR,[15] and her work enriches practical theology with insights drawn from scholars of the new materialism who critique anthropocentrism, rethink subjectivity and emphasize the self-organizing potential of the non-human within human affairs. I experienced this in a visceral way on my Bosnian trip. Although I had taken as much time as possible before the trip to read up about the context and situation, and to watch TV coverage and documentaries (readily available on YouTube), nothing could prepare me for the materiality of the place and the impact of *things* upon the feeling, thinking human agent.

Little things, concrete and material things – rather than large or abstract concepts – undid me and, at the same time, ate their way into my consciousness and instructed me, demanding my attention and respect:

- The pock-marked buildings of Sarajevo, smeared with oil and what looked like blood, standing next to shiny new skyscrapers without a hint of recent history inscribed on them.
- The sweet, sickly smell of the morgue in Tuzla where forensic anthropologists are still identifying human remains.
- The Bosnian hillsides strewn with primroses, a native plant of my home county of Devon, connecting me powerfully to this new landscape.
- Tiny cups of hot, sweet coffee and glasses of mint tea, offered to us wherever we went, along with platefuls of dates, nuts and cake.
- The sadness in the eyes of survivors who have lost brothers, fathers, sons, sometimes waiting years to recover a few body parts, sometimes finding no trace of loved ones to bury.
- The strong embraces of women survivors and campaigners, reaching out to visiting strangers in connection and compassion.

As both poet and theologian, I am doubly convinced of the material, incarnational nature of Christian faith. The God of Jesus Christ is a God who is embodied in human flesh, who suffers human devastation and loss, who works within the world unceasingly, in and through the Spirit, for the healing of ruptured relations and for the liberation of truth. This is a God who has wept and screamed in agony at the brutal torture of fragile human bodies; a God who has dwelt in the silence of untold stories of rape and given the power to break that silence; a God who has cradled a dead child in her arms; a God who has gone seeking for signs of the beloved and found only unnamed bones in a mass grave. This is a God whose many faces for me will now for ever include those of the remarkable Bosnian women, men and children I met on my all too brief visit, as well as the women and our one local male guide, Rešad, with whom I was honoured to travel.

Poetry as a form of attention, solidarity and witness

In inviting us to Bosnia, the charity 'Remembering Srebrenica' requested of each delegate that we make a pledge to 'remember Srebrenica' on our return and, more than that, translate the experience of our visit and the learning from it into some kind of commitment to act against conflict, violence and the 'othering' of ethnic or religious groups in our own professional, cultural and social contexts. Part of my pledge was to write about my experience as a way of sharing some of my learning; I knew that this was likely to involve writing poems. Although there was little time for writing on the trip, on our final morning there was a bit of free time in Sarejevo. A small group of us went to a local cafe; I suddenly realized this presented an opportunity to write. Excusing myself from the group, I found a quiet table and wrote, very quickly, the draft of three or four poems.

It felt important to begin the poems while I was still in the country; while I was close to the individuals I had met, still surrounded by the material actuality of the landscape, the cityscape of Sarajevo and the towering, thickly wooded hillsides surrounding the city. I was aware that, once I left, I would immediately begin to re-engage with my home life. There was a danger of distancing myself from all I had experienced. I wanted to get my experience down, raw, immediate and urgent, while I was there.

Of course, these were very rough-and-ready first drafts, and required a lot of editing and reworking on my return home. Nor were they the only poems I wrote. More came as I worked on the first set, reflected on and talked about my experience of the trip to friends and colleagues at home. I had no overt theological intention in writing the poems, other than – and this, of course, is a theological intention – to bear witness, to honour the people I had met and to enshrine in writing something of their lives, their courage as well as their suffering. I wanted to pay homage to their resilience and resistance. I certainly did not want the poems to preach, or to be overtly didactic. I also knew that poems, like stories, could communicate, through their density and immediacy, to others who had not shared my experience, in a way that scholarly or academic prose might not.

Here, then, is a sample of the poems (not all of them), with a brief introduction to each, setting the scene and explaining any necessary background.

On our first evening at our local hotel in Sarajevo, we met and heard from one of the country's most prominent activists, Bakira Hasečić, speaking through an interpreter.

Bakira Hasečić

She refuses to keep silent, will speak of her shame
although it is not she who has anything to be ashamed of.
She tells of the day when she watched her daughter raped
and was taken away and raped herself, three times.
To this day, her husband has never asked her about it.
She speaks of it repeatedly to strangers.

Her two main occupations, she tells us, are smoking
and hunting down war criminals. For twenty-five years
she has been amassing evidence from women's broken
narratives to convict the men living with impunity
in flats and streets all around. She never goes out without a camera.
She knocks on neighbours' doors, urging them to testify.
She will not take no for an answer.

She sits at the hotel table, clutching her gold designer bag
looking beyond us at some point in the distance which might be
a past long demolished or a future still over the horizon.
Her voice is dry and brittle with an urgency that drives her.
Her eyes keep shifting about the room.

On our final day, travelling from Sarajevo to Srebrenica, we stopped at
Tuzla, to visit the International Commission for Missing Persons, where
forensic scientists are still assembling and identifying human remains.

Visiting Tuzla

Nothing has prepared me
for the sweet stench of death.
It almost knocks me off my feet.
Around me, the body bags are labelled,
sorted, placed on their shelves.
Brown paper bags containing clothing
and personal items, so much luggage
on overhead racks. At our feet,
two metal stretchers with the skeletal
outlines of persons who lived and breathed
and laughed in this beautiful land.

Dragana Vučetić, Senior Forensic Anthropologist,
describes her work in minute detail.
She speaks in perfect English, politely,
persistently, looking straight into our eyes.
One person's remains may have been scattered
to fifteen separate locations, she tells us.
Primary mass graves were roughly broken up,
bodies shovelled by huge diggers
and taken to secondary graves
in an effort to obscure evidence.
Every day she returns to the scene
and continues with her matching of fragments,
counting all the bones, storing every tear in her bottle.

Meanwhile, I am gripping Deborah's hand for dear life,
to keep me upright in this factory of death.

At Srebrenica itself, where the UN base has been left largely untouched,
some of the cavernous aircraft hangers have been converted into museum
spaces, with images and stories from the war displayed around the walls.
Here, we were privileged to meet Hasan Hasanović, one of the few men who
survived the so-called 'Death march' from Srebrenica to the free territory
of Tuzla, and is now Museum Curator at the Srebrenica Memorial Centre.
I found his account of the massacre of thousands of his compatriots, with
accompanying footage, so distressing that I had to leave the memorial
centre and walk away, out into the fresh air. I found myself walking in
the large memorial garden which has been erected opposite the UN base,
where the remains of more than eight thousand men and boys killed in the
Srebrenica genocide are buried. Although the site of so much bloodshed, it
is now a deeply peaceful site marked out by row upon row of simple, white
marker stones. The Mothers of Srebrenica, like similar groups of mothers
around the world, turn up every day at the site to honour the dead and to
meet visitors, selling souvenirs. The final poem tells of my meeting with one
of the mothers.

The mothers of Srebrenica

In the kiosk selling souvenirs, opposite the cemetery,
I meet one of the mothers. She speaks no English
and I, of course, have no Bosnian. Her face –
the face of grandmothers of every race, generation
and religion – gazes into my sixty-year-old face,
her eyes into my sad eyes. She beholds me

with an infinite gentleness containing not one jot
of blame or recrimination. We hold each other's
hands, hug each other lightly. She speaks
to me of the prices of postcards and sewn items,
and it is the most exquisite poetry pouring over
my head and bathing me in forgiveness. I need
no translator to tell me her story, or she mine.
Each to each, in a place far out beyond language,
we become mothers to the motherless, in the kiosk
opposite the parking bay at the UN safe haven
where eight and a half thousand finally rest in peace.

The possibility of revelation, gift and insight within the overwhelming

Margaret Argyll, a textile artist who created the Bosnian Christa during the
mid-1990s as her own theological and artistic response to the mass rape of
Bosnian women in the war, speaks of how the artistic process of making
the Christa led to new theological insight and faith which would not have
been possible apart from the artistic process.[16] She speaks of her initial
resistance to creating 'a Christa which would speak about the obscenity of
rape clearly and graphically', even regarding such a notion as 'obscene'. As
she began work on stitching the image, she reflects, 'I don't think I knew
what I was doing; my hands did the thinking at that stage. I suppose my
hands were teaching me something about the nature of God – though I
didn't realize this until much later.'[17] Argyll's experience is typical of a process that artists and poets down the ages attest: that the image gives birth
to the insight, as the title of a recent collection of William Hart McNichols'
icons puts it.[18]

In a similar way, the writing of poems while I was in Bosnia, and subsequently on my return, led to a recognition of theological insight that would
not have come about without the writing. Poetry (and art more generally),
I want to insist, is a form of revelation, what Seamus Heaney describes as
'divination',[19] rather than merely a means of expressing something already
perceived or understood. The poet only discovers in the making of the
poem what it is he or she sees, senses, knows. In this sense, the poem can
be as much a gift and a surprise to the poet as it is to anyone else. Perhaps
one reason for this phenomenon, widely recognized by poets and artists, is
the way in which artistic activity comes at least as much from the unconscious as the conscious mind, and thus poems and other forms of art can
have a revelatory quality to them similar to that of dreams or images given
in meditation or prayer. This may also suggest one of the deep reasons we
are driven to prayer and find sustenance and meaning in prayer: not that
prayer provides any ready or easy 'answers' to extreme suffering or social

injustice, but that in prayer – as in poetry and art – we may be given a glimpse of the compassionate nature and purposes of God, an image or experience that keeps us from despair and supports our own endeavours to act compassionately and hopefully in the world.

Having written the sequence of poems, and through later rereadings and sharing of the poems with others in a variety of liturgical and ritual contexts,[20] I began to recognize an implicit theology at work within them: a kind of mirroring back to me of a theology latent within each of those momentary and material encounters. I didn't, and couldn't, realize it at the time, but the poems enabled me to perceive ways in which each of those encounters, turned into speech and text, were tiny glimpses of the presence and activity of God in that apparently godless place. The individuals named and honoured in the poems have become for me icons and embodiments of the redemptive, salvific presence of God – whether or not they believed in God or had any sense of such a faith perspective. If an icon is a visual representation of the sacred that mediates the divine,[21] my poems might, perhaps, be seen as verbal icons that, unwittingly, mediate something of the presence of the sacred in the persons I encountered. The work of art – in whatever medium – is a sacralizing act that lifts up the human or material encounter and offers it as more-than-itself, a kind of sacrament, a dense and condensed vehicle of transcendence, a captured moment in time which reflects something of enduring significance.

Thus, in my poem, the bloody-minded tenacity of Bakira Hasečić, refusing to keep silent, hunting down war criminals in order to bring them to justice, becomes an emblem of something more than her own personal resistance and insistence on justice. Without for a moment being less than her own work and commitment, she is also for me an embodiment of the restless, justice-seeking imperative of the God who will not rest until righteousness is restored throughout the world – whether or not Hasečić would, herself, profess religious faith or recognize God at work in her political actions. Similarly, the minute precision and attention to macabre detail of the senior forensic anthropologist at the morgue at Tuzla becomes, in the poem, and by virtue of being made poem, an expression of divine attention to the detail of every human life and creature, even in death and dismemberment. And the face of the elderly mother selling souvenirs in the kiosk opposite the cemetery at Srebrenica is, if only fleetingly, immortalized by being turned into text. Her face is lifted up to readers and hearers of the poem as the infinitely compassionate face of our grandmother God, who looks on our own grief and loss with infinite compassion no less than on the faces of all those in Bosnia and throughout the world who have lost sons, brothers, husbands and lovers to violence.

The refusal of each of these individuals to leave their devastated homeland, their refusal to give up on the painstaking work of retrieval and recovery, their belligerent pursuit of justice, became for me not only emblems of the ongoing work of God in redeeming and healing, but living embodiments, incarnations, of that ongoing work. It is this that I attempt to honour and compress in language in my poems. They are the people who survive, who remain, who will not leave, who cannot forget; and God in them remains, remembers, retrieves, refuses to give up, redeems the time.

Even the members of my own women's delegation, so briefly *there*, yet endeavouring to stand with and beside the suffering women and men of Bosnia, became also living guarantees of divine presence and resistance. The stout body of Rabbi Deborah Kahn-Harris, enfolding and holding me for dear life as I wept uncontrollably at the UN base at Srebrenica and gripping my hand to help me stand upright in the morgue at Tuzla, will always be to me the dependable body of God my tender friend. And it is Deborah's voice I hear, singing the kaddish for the departed in the snow-covered Jewish cemetery on the hills of Sarajevo, as the voice of God which will not cease its singing until every body unaccounted for, in war, rape or natural disaster, is named and honoured and known.

Sarajevo in snow[22]

Slip-sliding down the steep steps
to the Jewish cemetery, snow silences
the sound of traffic. The peace is profound
in this place of the four thousand dead.
Deborah recites the mourners' kaddish
in Aramaic as the rest of us huddle round.
Hard to imagine the Serb soldiers crouching
here among the headstones, aiming guns
and mortars at Muslim neighbours
a few streets away. Four years the Bosniacs
lived in this city, without water, electricity,
no warmth against the winter snow.
Rešad does not speak of it, brushes
our enquiries aside. 'I'll tell you about
that later', he says; but later never comes.
You can see the dead place in his eyes,
behind the smile, where he seldom goes.
It's scattered with too much pain
and too many shattered bones.

Turning insight into action: a renewal of praxis

Theological reflection does not end with insight, however profound; it demands to be turned into action, so that the process of praxis (reflective action or active reflection) is renewed. Experience offers the opportunity for engagement with a context, a people and the complex political and theological issues arising from that context; the engagement leads to multiple encounters and to a series of stories and images; the image or story gives birth to insight; and insight demands response and action, which itself leads to new questions, reflection and engagement. As many have noted, the process of theological reflection is a spiral rather than a circle that is ever completed.

What have been the actions attendant upon my own experience of visiting Bosnia and the ensuing reflection? They have taken a variety of forms, and continue to evolve. I only knew when I accepted the invitation of the visit that I was likely to write as part of my pledge, and this I have been doing – and this article, of course, represents one such out-working of my pledge to 'remember Srebrenica'. Behind the writing lies reading that I would not have expected to demand my attention before my trip – and our choices about what we read are, of course, moral and religious as well as intellectual choices. There have also been educational, liturgical and ritual events in which I have shared something of my own experience of the visit and invited others to respond to it: a workshop at BIAPT 2018 conference (out of which this article has grown), a memorial event in Birmingham Town Hall, a sharing of experience at a local deanery chapter, a service of remembrance at Queen's as part of our marking of the season of remembrance. On each occasion, the response of others – in deep, attentive listening; in good, probing questions; in silence, tears, touch and hugs; in ritual action and prayer – has deepened my own engagement with the Bosnian context and renewed the moral, political and theological questions arising out of that context. As I have taken action to share something of my own, limited and inadequate knowledge and experience, so what little insight I had gleaned from the experience of the visit has been stretched, challenged, deepened and renewed. The spiral of learning is ongoing and I have no idea where it will lead or end.

Notes

1 See www.srebrenica.org.uk/.

2 For eye-witness accounts of the war, and historical, political, ethical and religious analyses of the conflict, see, for example, Noel Malcolm, *Bosnia: A Short History* (London: Macmillan, 1994); Ed Vulliamy, *Seasons in Hell: Understanding*

Bosnia's War (London: Simon & Schuster, 1994); Erich Weingärtner and Elizabeth Salter (eds.), *The Tragedy of Bosnia: Confronting the New World Order* (Geneva: World Council of Churches, 1994); Ivo Andrić, *The Bridge on the Driva* (London: Harvill Press, new edn, 1995); Laura Silber, Allan Little and Aleksander Ciric, *The Death of Yugoslavia* (London: Penguin, 2nd edn, 1996); Bülent Diken and Carston Bagge Lausten, 'Becoming Abject – Rape as a Weapon of War', AMID Working Paper 34 (Aalborg OE: Academiet for Migrationsstudier I Danmark, 2004); Selma Leydesdorff, *Surviving the Bosnian Genocide: The Women of Srebrenica Speak* (Bloomington, IN: Indiana University Press, 2011); Michael Ipgrave (ed.), *Building a Better Bridge: Muslims, Christians, and the Common Good* (Washington, DC: Georgetown University Press, 2008); Julian Borger, *The Butcher's Trail* (New York: Other Press, 2016); Hasan Hasonović, *Surviving Srebrenica* (Tarland: Lumphana Press, 2016). See further resources at www.srebrenica.org.uk/.

3 Elaine Graham, Heather Walton and Frances Ward, *Theological Reflection: Methods* (London: SCM Press, 2005), p. 32.

4 Carolyn Ellis, Tony E. Adams and Arthur P. Bochner, 'Autoethnography: An Overview', *Forum: Qualitative Social Research* 12.1, p. 1: www.qualitative-research.net/index.php/fqs/article/view/1589/3095 (accessed 24.4.20).

5 Ellis, Adams and Bochner, 'Autoethnography', p. 1.

6 See, for example, Melisa Cahnmann-Taylor, 'Poetry in qualitative research', in Lisa M. Given (ed.), *The Sage Encyclopedia of Qualitative Research Methods* (London: Sage, 2008), pp. 637–40; M. Prendergast, C. Leggo and P. Sameshima (eds.), *Poetic Inquiry: Vibrant Voices in the Social Sciences* (Rotterdam, Boston and Taipei: Sense Publishers, 2009); Carol Gribch, *Qualitative Data Analysis* (London: Sage, 3rd edn, 2013): chapter 11; and for further reading, qualpage.com/poetry-in-qualitative-research/ (accessed 24.4.20).

7 Robert L. Kinast, *Let Ministry Teach: A Guide to Theological Reflection* (Collegeville, MN: Liturgical Press, 1996), pp. x–xi.

8 Patricia O'Connell Killen and John de Beer, *The Art of Theological Reflection* (New York: Crossroad, 2004).

9 For an insightful analysis of rape as a weapon of war, see Diken and Lausten, 'Becoming Abject'.

10 For an account of the pursuit and capture of the Balkan war criminals indicted by the International Criminal Tribunal for the former Yugoslavia (ICTFY), see Borger, *The Butcher's Trail*.

11 'A Spirituality of Multiple Overwhelmings', *Practical Theology* 10.1 (2017), pp. 20–32; and chapter 6 in this book.

12 Heather Walton, in Judith Thompson with Stephen Pattison and Ross Thompson, *Theological Reflection: SCM Studyguide* (London: SCM Press, 2008), p. 30.

13 Rainer Maria Rilke, *Letters to a Young Poet* (New York: Vintage, 1987), p. 34.

14 Walton, in Thompson, *Theological Reflection*, p. 30.

15 Heather Walton, *Writing Methods in Theological Reflection* (London: SCM Press, 2014), pp. 31–42; and 'The Consolation of Everyday Things', *Lir Journal* 4 (2015), pp. 138–52.

16 Julie Clague, 'Interview with Margaret Argyle', *Feminist Theology* 4 (1995), pp. 57–68.

17 Clague, 'Interview', p. 59.

18 John D. Dadosky and William Hart McNichols, *Image to Insight: The Art*

of William Hart McNichols (Albuquerque, NM: University of New Mexico Press, 2018).

19 Seamus Heaney, *Finders Keepers: Selected Prose 1971–2001* (London: Faber and Faber, 2002), p. 14.

20 For example, I read a couple of the poems at a memorial event organized by Remembering Srebrenica at Birmingham Council House in July 2018, and again at a service jointly devised with the Revd Jess Foster at Queen's in November 2018, as part of our institutional commitment to remember and honour the war dead.

21 Dadosky and McNichols, *Image to Insight*, pp. 1–2.

22 This poem won third prize in the Manchester Poetry Competition 2018, and is available, with other winning and commended poems from the competition, at www.manchestercathedral.org/poetry/purchase-a-poetry-booklet/ (accessed 24.4. 20).

PART 5

Feminist Theological Practices: Teaching, Reading, Writing and Research

The pleasure of reading

This is not work, my father said
who never read a difficult book in his life.

A real man labours all day
comes home with dirt in his hair

to sit at a table laden with food
prepared by the woman of the house.

After he eats he moves to his chair by the fire,
closes his eyes, having earned the right

while the mother and daughter
clear plates and food away.

Later, in her own room,
the daughter reads hungrily,

stretches the contours of her mind
growing ideas that will take decades to fruit

in a territory and climate
far from the farmer's reach.

There is nothing to show for her work
beyond a certain fatigue.

Her hands remain smooth.
Her skin is pale, untouched by sun.

12

Presiding in the Classroom:
A Holy Work

Teaching has been a constant in my life, either in the role of student or that of teacher, and I have always regarded teaching as core to my own vocation. I owe a huge debt to a number of teachers who have been inspirational role models. This essay, originally published in 2010 in Presiding Like a Woman *(London: SPCK, pp. 156–65), co-edited with my friend and colleague Stephen Burns (who is, himself, a very fine teacher), reflects on the work of teaching through the prism of the ministry of presiding.*

Introduction

In what follows, I would like to reflect on my experience as a teacher to see in what ways this experience might offer insights into what it means to 'preside like a woman'. I will explore the notion of presiding to focus on the different ways in which teachers offer a mediating, enabling, priestly ministry within the classroom. I have chosen to broaden the perspective beyond specifically liturgical settings for at least two reasons: first, to affirm and demonstrate the claim that has been made in several places in this book, that women preside in a wide range of contexts, not only the ecclesial and liturgical; and second, to suggest that experiences of presiding outside the liturgical assembly might inform liturgical presidency, at the same time as allowing liturgical presidency to illuminate and inform leadership in other spheres. In doing so, I invite recognition of teaching as 'holy work', in every way as sacramental as liturgical presidency, and 'teachers as ministers of personal and social transformation', as Gloria Durka puts it[1]. Much of the history of women's teaching, like that of women's priesthood, has been hidden, and women's authority as 'teachers of the faith' denied or downplayed. Yet,

> For every woman
>> denied the voice to speak out her own religious truth,
>> refused the opportunity to teach her wisdom
>> and ridiculed for her theological insights and ideas

> we can and should celebrate
>> every woman
> who claimed her authority in vision, prophecy and dream,
> who spoke out her truth in hymnody, verse and story.[2]

Starting with Mary, the teacher and priest par excellence,[3] Christian tradition is replete with a venerable tradition of women teachers, 'doctors of the church' (even if not acknowledged as such) – from the unnamed Syrophoenician and Samaritan women in the Gospels who helped to form Jesus' mind to renowned theologians such as Hildegard of Bingen and Teresa of Avila; from mothers who nurtured and instructed the faith of their more famous offspring (not only Mary, but Monica and Macrina come to mind) to pioneering scholars (such as Elizabeth Cady Stanton in the USA and Maude Royden in Britain) who paved the way for contemporary feminist scholarship.

Teaching is core to my own sense of vocation. It is in this context more than any other that I have the experience of 'sitting in front of the assembly', occupying the seat of authority, exercising superintendence, conducting and directing the company of learners, to call on some of the dictionary definitions of 'preside'.[4] Feminists have suggested a wide variety of metaphors that might articulate a feminist vision of teaching – the teacher as midwife, voice coach, contemplative artist and reticent outlaw, for example;[5] here I offer one more, the teacher as presider. While it is not usual to speak of the activity of teaching in terms of 'presiding', I suggest that this can be a helpful term for focusing on the ways in which the teacher manages, directs and shapes the processes that operate within the learning environment.

I am not thinking primarily here of lecturing, because, although the didactic delivery of material has a role to play in adult learning (particularly in the inspiration of learners), and although it has its analogy in liturgical presidency (the delivery of the sermon being analogous to the delivery of a lecture), it seems to me the least interesting form of teaching, from a pedagogical point of view, and the least potentially illuminating of the work and ministry of the presider. Rather, I am thinking about teaching situations in which learning is more participative and fluid, a shared enterprise between facilitator and learners, although no less formed than a good lecture. I am thinking of a wide range of learning situations from my own experience: informal Bible study groups; postgraduate research seminars; residential courses and retreats in which the focus is on personal learning and where much of the learning takes place in groups; experiential workshops in which participants practise creative writing or work to put together an act of worship; and so on. In all these settings, I am working with adults, sometimes in formal academic settings but often not; sometimes in women-only contexts; almost always with very mixed groups of learners who represent a wide variety of educational, social, cultural, ethnic and ecclesiastical backgrounds.

Presiding as a commitment to liberative praxis

What is the work of the teacher in such settings? In what does 'presiding' consist? Above any specific function, the teacher's skill and her very being must be oriented towards education as the practice of freedom, and her teaching must be informed at every turn by a commitment to the liberation and empowerment of the students. It is this commitment that grounds and holds the teacher's work, channels her power and offers protection against the abuse of that power for her own self-aggrandizement. Feminist pedagogy is rooted in this commitment to education as emancipatory, transformative praxis, what Rebecca Chopp names 'saving work',[6] and what Brita Gill-Austern describes, simply, as 'pastoral care' – where the 'practice of teaching deepens authentic, just and life-giving connection in all spheres of life'.[7] Such teaching is, perhaps, modelled most clearly in Christian tradition by Mary: it is her secret work during the hidden years of his childhood that tutors Jesus in prayer, in a sense of God and in the demands of justice that we see coming to full flower in his public teaching and practice.[8] Similarly, I would suggest that liturgical presidency, to be authentically feminist, must grow out of and be rooted in a fundamental commitment to church as a community of emancipation and liturgy as the place where that freedom is enacted in embodied word, ritual, interaction and sacrament.

Rather than be focused on her own *teaching*, the feminist teacher is centred in and on the *learning* of those she seeks to enable, as Mary's teaching of Jesus demonstrates most powerfully. Simple as it sounds, this distinction is crucial. It is not that her own expertise is insignificant, but that it is always to be put at the disposal of the group's learning, and her own authority employed to release and bring to expression the gifts, knowledge and power of the group and of each individual within it, rather than to call attention to herself. This is not to say that the facilitator's role is not crucial; it is, and without it the life and energies of the group are likely to become dissipated, disruptive and dysfunctional. Indeed, the group cannot function as what they are called to be – in this case, a learning community – without the teacher. There is a paradox in the work of presidency which means that, very often, the more effective it is in enabling the life of the group, the more inconspicuous and unselfconscious it will be. The effective group facilitator, like the effective priest, enables the group to claim its own learning and power, to know *itself* to be empowered and effective and to find her own satisfaction in that reality. This is to speak of the essential kenotic quality of all teaching, though it is important to use such language carefully so as not to reinforce the powerlessness of women, and to affirm that the exercise of self-emptying that lies at the heart of all Christian ministry is dependent on a strong and secure selfhood.[9] The teacher who seeks to enable learning as liberative praxis must exercise strong leadership, challenging power where it is misused, including the abdication of power or voice, teaching students to transgress, in bell hooks' suggestive phrase[10] (or what Gill-Austern describes as 'becoming partners in resistance'[11]), where compliance would mean a diminishment of their agency. It is the feminist teacher who can say to her students,

> Dare to
> declare
> who you
> are[12]

and model in her own claiming of voice the authority of a subject position authentically claimed.

The teacher works always for an enlargement of students' vision, imagination, potential and subject power, as does the person presiding in the liturgical sphere. Strong leadership is required for such teaching, but it is a leadership focused on the enabling of the learners rather than on the interests, needs or agenda of the teacher. Undergirding such teaching, such presidency, is a spirituality of profound attention – to the needs, gifts and wounds of the community in which the teacher serves; to her *own* needs, gifts and wounds, and the ways in which they must be cared for (requiring deliberate and intentional self-reflection), and attention to the missio dei, the gospel call to justice and freedom in which her own vocation and that of the whole laos are rooted.[13]

Presiding as the creation of safe and creative space

A first calling of the teacher is, simply, to gather the learning community and to create a space in which learning can take place – a space that is safe,[14] boundaried and clearly focused on the active pursuit of truth and freedom. The president does not *create* the community, but she is frequently the one to call the community together and to issue the invitation to the risky, adventurous process of learning. The president has the responsibility to make sure the space is safe and conducive to the activity the community is gathered to share. In learning situations this usually means paying attention to the physical space in which learning takes place and arranging that space in a way that will maximize learning,[15] allowing participants to introduce themselves and state their own hopes and fears for the event, setting clear boundaries around timing, roles, conduct, confidentiality and so on – effectively negotiating a 'contract' for the life of the group. All of this is necessary for individuals to have a sense of knowing who and where they are within the group, to feel safe in the knowledge that the facilitator will take care of these things, and to be enabled to take the necessary risks they will be called upon to take – for all genuine learning involves the risk of entering into the unknown, not only the unknown and unexplored territory of new knowledge but, more significantly, the unknown power and potential of the learners themselves, both as individuals and as a group. While the invitation to enter more deeply into one's own power and into the larger truth of God's reality is an ultimately liberating gesture, it is frequently also deeply disturbing – which is why learners often resist learning, or seek to inoculate themselves against deep change in all kinds of ways. Part of the work of the teacher is to keep the invitation to genuine transformation open to the students at each stage of learning, however often that invitation may be resisted, and to keep the space of the learning environment an open and clearly boundaried one in which students know that they will be supported and encouraged in their quest for truth. Both openness and boundedness are important in this creation of community; safety is necessary for genuine, transformative learning to take place,[16] but there is always a danger of a learning community becoming too closed in upon itself, so the teacher has a right 'concern always to be expanding the circle of who belongs to that community', and 'bringing into substantive dialogue those who have been perceived to be on the margins'.[17]

Although such contracting of the boundaries of the group's life does not take place overtly when the ecclesial community gathers, this is part of what is going on, unconsciously probably, at the beginning of every act of worship, and it is part of what the president needs to attend to in gathering and greeting the assembly. Rather than being a mere formality, the opening greetings and prayers of the liturgy are essential for the community to sense and know who we are in Christ, why we are gathering and to trust that the president will 'hold' the space and time we have given so that each person may be welcome, may have a place at the table, may give and receive as they are able, and may participate in the conduct of worship. Much of this is conveyed subtly and unconsciously through the ordering of the physical space, the care and attention paid to the material objects and symbols in the space, and above all through the embodied being of the one presiding: through tone of voice, body language, eye contact and the sense they convey within themselves of being at home in their role as president and of welcome and inclusion. There must be a willingness to occupy the seat of authority, not in any controlling or authoritarian sense, but in the sense that the presider needs to sit comfortably and securely in their own selfhood, taking clear responsibility for the group, so that everyone can relax and let go into the work each one has come to do and claim their rightful authority within the group – rather than competing for power, as often happens in groups where there is no clear leadership. The presidency can be shared, can be passed from one person to another, in both liturgical and educational settings, and very often is in feminist liturgies as well as in feminist pedagogy; yet whether shared or exercised by one person, attention to the power dynamics within the group and careful management of those dynamics is essential if the community is to function well.

Presiding as an embodied holding, a work of form-giving

The presider holds a creative tension between the needs of the individuals, the dynamics of the group, and the purpose of the group's life. As a teacher, my work is to focus the group on the particular learning they have contracted to do and to maintain that focus, not allowing individuals or the group to deflect from task, continuing to hold the invitation and the challenges before the group. I do that in any number of ways: by presenting material to them in a variety of ways (sharing my expertise and knowledge, such as it is), by directing them to other sources of learning (books, articles, websites and so on), by encouraging and challenging them to engage actively with the material (asking questions, setting exercises, directing small group work) – but also, beyond specific 'teacherly' activities, in and through my own being as a learner myself: through my passion and enthusiasm for my subject, thus incarnating subject matter in ways that make the subject 'live' and that are potentially revelatory for the learners; through my demonstrable commitment to ongoing learning in the field (both through a commitment to research and publication but also to other forms of embodied learning, such as social justice or political engagement); and, perhaps above all, through the intangible quality of my person as a learner and teacher. The teacher is almost certainly the one person least conscious of what this quality might be and how it communicates, because they inhabit it as a norm, but it is this intangible 'presence' that we hold before the group when we teach (as the priest offers their priestly presence to the liturgical assembly) and that calls out from the students an answering quality of being, as they discover themselves anew as learners, as those whose hunger for learning is reawakened, as those with the power to know and to shape their learning in life-giving ways.

This work of holding, enabling and shaping the learning process involves the coordination of many elements: the management of time and space, the encouragement of each person to participate fully as they are able, the gathering of the dispersed gifts of the community and offering of them so that each person is enriched by the gifts of all, and so on. When this is working well there is a sense of organic development and dynamic flow, which is both within and beyond the control of any one person, even though the presider may be the one 'holding' the flow. The learning has a shape and structure to it, one that is both spontaneous and scripted. Unlike a lecture with a set text, most of such teaching is a more spontaneous interaction between the teacher and the learners in the group. Far from being less prepared, the facilitator in such a setting needs to be *more* prepared, needs to know their material better, so that they can use it and adapt it according to the needs and interests of the learners. It is a skill to be able both to 'hold' the group to task and yet also be open to the dynamic energy and flow of the group itself, to allow someone to take the group off at a tangent, perhaps, or to play with what might at first seem a whacky idea offered by someone from 'offside', in order to discover some new insight or come to some new place that is only reached by following the unexpected diversion. In order for this to happen, the presider has to trust and believe that the learning belongs to the group as a whole, rather than being her own sole possession. The teacher is one who can testify:

> I do not possess the truth
> but with others to witness to what they know
> I will be able to discern what is right.[18]

Sometimes this trust requires active intervention on the presider's part – inviting the quiet person to speak, encouraging the talker to desist from talking, say; sometimes it requires a more receptive letting go and letting be of whatever is emerging in the group. Whether active or passive, this is truly a work of form-giving, as Maria Harris names it, an essentially aesthetic practice of finding an appropriate form for the learning that is emerging from the interaction between the learning subjects, the subject matter in which all are engaged, and the teacher. To speak of this theologically, this is 'the incarnation of subject matter that leads to the revelation of subject matter'.[19] This process requires profound attention on the part of both learners and teacher, each to the other, each to the subject matter in which they are engaged, and each to the interaction that is taking place within and among them. Good learning, like good liturgy, emerges from the life of the group that is more than the sum of its parts, that is the mysterious culmination of the shared hunger, knowledge, questing and offering of each member of the group interacting with the material and the other learners. This is why no two group seminars are ever the same, even when the material is exactly the same and even if the learners are the same individuals – just as no act of worship is ever the same, even when the script is identical.

Presiding as costly, transformative work

The work of presiding, either at the liturgy or in the classroom, is a costly work which often doesn't look like 'work' from the outside, because much of it is hidden and internalized. It is a bearing in the body of the presider of the life of the group, gathered and focused in time and space around a particular set of actions. It is a labour of praying the hungers of the community, sifting their stories, assuaging their desires, offering one's own knowledge, longings and presence as food to nourish the people.[20] Much of this work is unconscious as the gathered community projects on to the president their hopes, fears, angers at the church (or the academy), frustrations, deepest longings, joys and griefs, and looks to him or her for healing, feeding, cleansing, renewing. Without needing to know the content of these hopes, joys and griefs, the president absorbs within her own body the weight of all these mixed and potent realities, and takes them into herself, lives them for the duration of the group's gathering, and mediates them, offers them back in the form of words, gestures, actions, looks, sighs even, which have the potential to meet the hungers of the community. At the same time, the president herself receives from the group; it is not a one-way process. Looking around, she sees the struggles and wounds of those gathered with her; she notices and absorbs the triumphs of learning, of the living and praying of individuals whose stories she may or may not know, the glory of relationships forged and celebrated, the gifts each one brings, whether hesitantly or confidently – and she is both blessed and burdened by that flow of life that comes towards her, meets within her and flows out again through her.

In the Eucharist, there is a mysterious exchange that takes place between the gathered assembly and Christ, as the offering of all this brokenness and potential is made on the table and the gifts of bread and wine offered back to the assembly, the same and yet not the same. Just this same kind of transformation and exchange can and often does happen in the classroom, as learners offer to each other the fruits of their costly learning and receive back from each other what they have offered and shared, mysteriously transformed in the interchange, mediated in and through the body of the teacher as presider. This is why Maria Harris speaks of teaching as a work of 'religious imagination' that requires both aesthetic and theological categories, as well as pedagogical ones, to explicate its potential for transformation. When teaching is conducted as 'an activity of religious imagination', when subject matter is incarnated authentically to lead to 'the revelation of subject matter', then learners discover that they themselves 'are the primary subjects of all teaching', and they 'discover themselves as possessing the grace of power, especially the power of re-creation, not only of themselves, but of the world in which they live'.[21] Such teaching and such learning are truly sacramental, sites of divine revelation and thus of profound empowerment, places where we make and know Eucharist:

O come and eat, O taste and see:
How good a feast.
How rich a guest.
How lavish a host.
How ravished a hunger.

I am met. I am meat. I am ate.
I am full. I am fed.
I am juice, I am joy, I am all golden peach.[22]

The gender question

Is there anything specifically gendered in this work of presiding I have been describing? I want to say both yes and no. No, in so far as both women and men can, and do, exemplify this kind of priestly teaching, just as they exemplify eucharistic leadership in other contexts and vocations. Yes, in so far as women are frequently those who have learnt, through socialization into roles of caring, nurturing and sustaining of relationships, how to exercise this kind of ministry of bearing and empowering of others in and through the bodies we inhabit – often in ways that are not recognized as priestly or authoritative, yet are. This is one part of the gift that women can bring to the exercise of priesthood, as well as to the vocation of teaching. Many feminists have spoken of the role of the priest or teacher as midwife,[23] and, while this is not the exclusive preserve of women, when women do such work – supporting, empowering, holding and directing the birth of the new, releasing and transforming incipient life – they bring to that work a particular character and skill that is rooted in their own gendered histories, embodiment and identities, and they mirror and reflect the *imago dei* in specifically gendered ways.[24] As others have suggested in this collection, women image forth the Christa, the female Christ figure, who does not have any one face or form, but is a new manifestation of the being and the passion of Christ in the world. When I preside in the classroom in such a way as to enable the liberative praxis of the community towards a greater justice, freedom and wholeness, I am, in that holy work, *in persona Christa*, holding before the gathered community the challenging, gracious, enabling presence of Christ/a as one who calls us to freedom – but so are they to me, and each to the other, as we each in our various ways respond to the invitation to the liberation and empowerment of one another, and as we incarnate for each other the call of Christ/a into ever new forms of freedom.

Notes

1 Gloria Durka, *The Teacher's Calling: A Spirituality for Those Who Teach* (New York and Mahwah, NJ: Paulist Press, 2002), p. 1.

2 Nicola Slee, 'A litany of grief and gladness (2)', in *Praying Like a Woman* (London: SPCK, 2004), p. 85.

3 See my discussion of Mary as teacher and priest in Nicola Slee, *The Book of Mary* (London: SPCK, 2007), chapters 6 and 7.

4 Rebecca S. Chopp, *Saving Work: Feminist Practices of Theological Education* (Louisville, KY: Westminster John Knox Press, 1995).

5 Brita L. Gill-Austern, 'Pedagogy under the influence of feminism and woman-ism', in Bonnie Miller-McLemore and Brita L. Gill-Austern (eds.), *Feminist and Womanist Pastoral Theology* (Nashville, TN: Abingdon Press, 1999), pp. 151–9.

6 Chopp, *Saving Work*.

7 Gill-Austern, 'Pedagogy under the influence of feminism and womanism', p. 150.

8 See my poem, 'Mary teaching the child Jesus', in Slee, *The Book of Mary*, p. 66.

9 Feminists have strongly criticized notions of sacrifice as they have been employed in Christian tradition to legitimize the powerlessness of women and other groups, although recent debate indicates some rapprochement and a more nuanced reclaiming of notions such as kenosis and sacrifice. See, for example, Kerry Ramsay, 'Losing one's life for others: Self-sacrifice revisited', in Susan Frank Parsons (ed.), *Challenging Women's Orthodoxies in the Context of Faith* (Aldershot: Ashgate, 2000), pp. 121–33.

10 bell hooks, *Teaching to Transgress: Education as the Practice of Freedom* (New York: Routledge, 1994).

11 Gill-Austern, 'Pedagogy under the influence of feminism and womanism', p. 165.

12 Nicola Slee, 'Conversations with Muse', in *Praying Like a Woman*, p. 60.

13 I have tried to spell out and exemplify something of what such attention might mean in the context of listening to women's narratives of faith in my study *Women's Faith Development: Patterns and Processes*. The principles that under-girded the development of my research methodology in that study are similar to those I am articulating in this essay, and indeed I see close analogies between the practice of feminist qualitative research and the practice of feminist pedagogy.

14 For a feminist analysis of the notion of 'space', see Elaine Graham, 'From space to woman-space', in *Words Made Flesh: Writings in Pastoral and Practical Theology* (London: SCM Press, 2009), pp. 27–44.

15 Jeanne Stevenson-Moessner speaks of 'rearranging the furniture', both liter-ally and metaphorically, as a way of translating feminist values from seminary to parish, in 'Feminist values from seminary to parish', in Miller-McLemore and Gill-Austern, *Feminist and Womanist Pastoral Theology*, pp. 211–21.

16 Safety will be particularly important for those who have been abused or wounded – thus Carol Lakey Hess speaks of the necessity of '"safe-houses" for raising girls in families and communities of faith', in *Caretakers of Our Common House: Women's Development in Communities of Faith* (Nashville, TN: Abingdon Press, 1997), chapter 4.

17 Gill-Austern, 'Pedagogy under the influence of feminism and womanism', pp. 164, 165.

18 Nicola Slee, 'With others: A statement of interdependence', in *Praying Like a Woman*, p. 66.

19 Maria Harris, *Teaching and Religious Imagination: An Essay in the Theology of Teaching* (San Francisco, CA: Harper & Row, 1987), p. 167.

20 See my poem, 'Mary bakes bread', in Slee, *The Book of Mary*, p. 82.

21 Harris, *Teaching and Religious Imagination*, p. xv.

22 Nicola Slee, 'Word', in *Praying Like a Woman*, p. 117.

23 For example, Mary Field Belenky et al., *Women's Ways of Knowing: The Development of Self, Voice and Mind* (New York: Basic Books, 1986), pp. 217ff. Gill-Austern, 'Pedagogy under the influence of feminism and womanism'.

24 See Emma Percy, 'Reverend Mother: How Insights from Mothering can Inform the Practice of Leadership in the Church' (parts 1 and 11), *Modern Believing* 44.2 and 3 (2003), pp. 33–44 and 24–36, for an exploration of similar themes, drawing on the experience of motherhood for an illumination of leadership. These ideas are developed in Emma Percy, *Mothering as a Metaphor for Ministry* (London: Routledge, 2014).

13

Research as Transformative
Spiritual Practice

This chapter, and the subsequent one, form the substance of lectures given at the Practical Theology Professional Doctorate Summer School at the University of Cardiff, in July 2015. Over the past number of years, the professional doctorate in practical theology has taken off in a big way in a number of British universities. The shared summer school brings together around one hundred doctoral students (probably more by now) from different universities, with core staff. There is usually an invited guest who offers keynote lectures and I was very glad to have the opportunity, on this occasion, to reflect on core aspects of research – reading and writing, in particular – which often do not receive a great deal of attention, beyond a study skills approach. As I was addressing doctoral students, my focus in this and the following chapter is on undertaking doctoral studies, specifically within practical theology – although much of the discussion is applicable to other contexts and other levels of research. Although previously unpublished, some of this material also forms the substance of online resources produced by a small working party from Queen's as part of a Common Awards Seedcorn project, 'God and Study Skills'. I am grateful to my colleagues Ash Cocksworth, Dave Allen, Jen Smith, Al Barrett and Ruth Harley for stimulating and fruitful conversations on research and study as theologically significant activities.

Introduction

In this, and the following chapter, I reflect theologically on the processes of doing research, paying detailed attention to some of the activities and practices that constitute research. These are things, like reading and writing, that we habitually do as researchers and to which we may or may not pay considered attention, practices that form our craft and, I want to suggest, form us as persons. Research forms us, not only as scholars and researchers but also simply *as* persons; and this includes, for many of us, being persons of faith, however we understand, define or practise that.

As Terry Veling has suggested, in a fine reflection on reading and writing as spiritual practices: 'The activities that teachers and students engage in –

reading, writing, reflection, conversation, teaching, learning – are activities that can be spiritually formative, filled with love and desire, rather than driven by fear and competitiveness.'[1] He is thinking broadly of learning and teaching in the university context, not specifically of higher-level research, but much of what he writes is applicable to the processes of research as well as learning generally. In what follows, I want to pay attention both to the practices of research and how they may be expressions of our own religious and spiritual commitments, and to how they may shape our religious and spiritual values. In doing so, I am aligning myself with recent developments in contemplative education and contemplative inquiry that seek to ask, 'What might happen if we try to frame the central questions of our discipline as spiritual questions and to deal with them in light of our spiritual understanding?'[2]

In this chapter, I want to reflect broadly on the nature of research and how it may embody a set of moral and spiritual virtues and thus help to form us as spiritual persons. In principle, this applies to any and all research, whatever the subject matter, but should be particularly true of research in theology and even more true of research in practical theology! I shall consider our motivation and desire in the pursuit of research, the kind of activity that research is and the discipline and determination it requires of us, as well as the challenges and testing of moral resolve that research frequently involves.

Desire in the process of research

Why do we undertake research? There are all kinds of reasons – professional, personal, academic – some of which we will be aware of when we sign up for a research degree or begin a piece of research, but many of which only become apparent as the process of research evolves, and some of which we may never really know.

I started a PhD in my early twenties (and only completed a second PhD much later in my early forties) for a whole set of very bad reasons (because I'd got a good first degree and my teachers said, 'Have you thought of doing a PhD?', because I hadn't really got a clue what to do with the rest of my life, to name only two). As I look back, I sense that I was sleepwalking through my life with very little ownership of my decisions. Attempting a PhD in such a state nearly destroyed me. I spent three of the most miserable years of my life locked in libraries and in my room, having very little clue what I was supposed to be doing, reading endlessly and trying to write but finding that I couldn't. I had the wrong supervisors, I was at the wrong university for the kind of topic I was trying to pursue, and I did not possess the emotional maturity to see me through the struggles and challenges. Any sense of myself as a thinker, a writer, a person with something to say, naive and untested as it was, simply evaporated, shrivelled up and died. I lost my voice, I lost any capacity to write, I lost all my academic confidence. I felt an inordinate sense of shame that, for the first time in my life, I could not perform successfully in the academic arena, and the shame grew greater the longer it went on. I carried this abortive PhD around with me for years, neither finishing it nor abandoning it, stuck in a place of fearful paralysis (although, oddly, I began publishing articles during this time and could do this; the deadlock was specifically in relation to the PhD). Eventually, I managed to resolve the paralysis through an intensive process of therapy, which gave me the courage to put the PhD down. Only when I did so, did an entirely new desire and vision for the research I really wanted to do emerge. By then, I was older, I had knocked about a bit, I was teaching and loving it, I had published some articles in academic journals. More significantly, I knew what I wanted to do and why I wanted to do it (I wanted to research women's faith lives, and I wanted to do this as an expression of my commitment as a feminist practical theologian and as an outworking of my own feminist faith). My motives and reasons were good ones, and were strong enough to hold me through the ups and downs of the research journey.

I've spent some time on this autobiographical exploration of motivation for doing research because I've become aware, through my own experience and that of others, that doing research for the wrong reasons, or at the wrong time, can be immensely destructive and distressing (who determines what are 'wrong' reasons or the 'wrong' time is, of course, significant – these seem to me judgements only the researcher can make, although others may help to shape that judgement). Undertaking doctoral research is a huge decision and I always say to prospective students, 'Don't do it unless you are desperate to do it, unless your life depends upon it.' You can't do a PhD through sheer determination or simply because it will look good on your CV or enhance your career – at least, *I* couldn't do a PhD for those reasons and I don't know many other people who have done (there may be a few, perhaps in disciplines where doing research is less self-involving, as it usually is in theology and the humanities).

Desire is significant, both in the process of research and in the life of faith. Something, or perhaps someone, draws us into this journey. We are led by desire for knowledge, truth, wisdom, and ultimately to the ultimate source of all truth and life, whom many of us name God, although we may or may not articulate it as clearly as this. The lure and love of the topic of our research draws us, its intrinsic significance and worth apart from any extrinsic value that may come out of it, such as promotion and the title of 'Dr'. If we don't love our research in some sense, why are we doing it, for heaven's sake? It takes years of one's life, huge amounts of energy and time, not to mention money, and there is no reason for this massive investment unless we are passionately committed to our subject.

Simone Weil emphasizes joy in intellectual work:

> The intelligence can only be led by desire. For there to be desire, there must be pleasure and joy in the work. The intelligence only grows and bears fruit in joy. The joy of learning is as indispensable in study as breathing is in running.[3]

It's not simply the *topic* or content of our research that is the lure. The process of study and research is also and perhaps even more of a draw. We wouldn't be doing research if we didn't love study itself or, at least, *want* to love it. For some of us, the interiority of research is the main draw: the solitude, quiet, the interiority of reading and writing, and a justification for withdrawing from the external world for a few hours a day or a day a week into our 'inner room'. May Sarton, at the beginning of her *Journal of a Solitude*, speaks of 'taking up [her] "real life" again at last' as she resumes her solitary writing life after a period of travel and giving talks. 'That is what is strange – that friends, even passionate love, are not my real life unless there is time alone in which to explore and to discover what is happening or has happened.'[4] If we live hectic, busy lives with a great deal of external, outward-facing activity, research – like prayer or meditation – can offer a turning aside from the relentless demands of jobs, families and faith communities, a closing of the outer door. We can allow ourselves to immerse in books, ideas, the otherness of something we don't understand and want to know better but, at the same time, may also be a study of our own lives. While there may be some fields in which the subject of research bears no direct relation to our own lives, this is not so in practical theology, and most of us are researching something that is close to our own lives, in one way or another.

In her classic 1942 essay 'Reflections on the right use of school studies with a view to the love of God', written for school children,[5] Simone Weil argues that study of any kind has the capacity to teach us the faculty of attention, which is an essential component of prayer, of love of God and love of the neighbour. Even when the focus of our study has nothing overtly to do with God or faith, the very practice of concentrated attention on something for its own sake, in order better to comprehend it, is an exercise in loving contemplation that prepares us better for love of God and neighbour.

For others, the conversational, interactive, outward-facing dimensions of research are what most draws and excites. The opportunity to study what is going on in a particular context, situation and community; the disciplined engagement with issues and persons in our professional work or religious communities; the searching out, delving into, probing and analysing of a situation or issue with a range of conversational partners – it is this that energizes, makes us feel we are in touch with reality and with our best selves. Field work, with its direct engagement with communities and individuals, is a particularly powerful expression of this interactive, conversational dimension of research, but it is not its only expression. Reading is another form of entering this conversation, although it may feel a more internalized form of it.

Both aspects of research – the withdrawal and engagement, the interiority and the externalized attention, the solitary and the communal – are important and worthy of attention. We may be more naturally and temperamentally inclined to one rather than the other dimension, but a good piece of research necessarily combines both, albeit there are many different ways of bringing together the inward and outward, the solitary and the communal – and this is partly what methodologies are for,[6] to provide frameworks for integrating and utilizing the full range of inward and outward attention required by research.

Research as disciplined endeavour

Research, like the life of faith, may begin with desire, but the desire is only sustained by the disciplined practice of study, just as the life of faith is sustained by the disciplined practice of that life in all its varied forms.[7] There is an inverse and mutual relationship between the desire and the discipline, each feeding, testing and honing the other, deepening the other.

Much of research, like much of the life of faith, is habit, or habitus, a daily discipline that we practise because we are committed to it, and want to desire it, even when we don't. We pray whether we feel like it or not. We do the next bit of the research process whether we feel like it or not; because it is there to be done and we will not fulfil our desire if we do not do it. Wendell Berry, in a lovely essay entitled 'Poetry and marriage: The use of old forms',[8] speaks of 'the acceptance of a form that is never entirely of one's own making' in the vocations of both poetry and marriage. 'When understood seriously enough, a form is a way of accepting and of living within the limits of creaturely life.'[9] Poetry, marriage and, we might add, research require a particular kind of faith, a faith in 'old forms' or conventions that have been developed by others over centuries and that constitute what it *means* to practise as a poet, a married person or a scholar. Of course, old forms can be reformed and transformed – as we see happening to marriage, one of Berry's examples of 'old forms' – in our own time. But we generally have first to understand, usually by inhabiting and practising, the form in its original givenness, before we can change it.

Research has its fair share of the tedious and mundane: wading our way through some book or article that does not excite us, akin perhaps to praying our way through the psalter or reading our way through the lectionary with all those dull or dodgy passages that test our patience and theology.

There are skills and methods that can only be learnt by practice, from systems of referencing and footnoting to techniques of transcribing, coding and analysing data, from the organization of a literature review to the development of the form of a convincing argument. These require painstaking, disciplined application and practice: a form of attention-giving that is sustained and honed over time.

The acquisition of scholarly skills is similar to the learning of the skills of a profession or trade, as well as the learning how to be a person of faith. In each case, there are quite specific *practices* that characterize the activity and the community that practices the activity. Over time, we learn these skills, initially by copying the way we see others practise: whether that practice is prayer, the analysis of a text, the preaching of a sermon or the way to bake a cake. In each community of practice there are levels or grades of performance, and we pass through one on to the next in order to become proficient in the discipline. The doctorate is generally regarded as an initiation into the community of scholarship through which the higher-level skills of academic learning are both acquired and tested. It depends on earlier foundations of academic learning but it is generally regarded as the benchmark for testing suitability to practise as a scholar or an academic. It is a lengthy, total immersion in the skills and the practices of scholarship, and its longevity is significant. You simply cannot become a scholar (or, by analogy, a mystic, a pastor, a preacher) overnight. Initiation takes time, as well as prolonged testing.

The testing of resolve: initiation as purgation

The practices of faith and scholarship necessarily take us into territory where, sooner or later, we discover that we are out of our depth, we do not see the way, we are no longer in control (if we ever were). It is a very common experience in research for the initial clarity we may have had about our project to evaporate as we get stuck into it and begin to recognize its inevitable complexity. When this happens, we may very well doubt our own capacity; our initial resolve and understanding of what it is we are about is put to the test. Now we enter the dark night of the soul, the vale of soul-making, the doctoral doldrums, the unmaking of research proposals, the unravelling of argument, the failure of nerve, the wasteland of chapters drafted, redrafted, abandoned and resuscitated (if they are). The oasis towards which we thought we were travelling turns out to be a mirage; all the paths in the woods disappear into a maze of labyrinthine ways and we despair of ever finding our path to the centre and out again.[10]

If we are not prepared for this process of undoing, it may come as a terrifying experience. Actually, it *is* terrifying, whether we are prepared for it or not, just as it is profoundly terrifying to lose the sense of God or to doubt God's good intentions, even though the saints and mystics tell us that such a stripping of our original naive notions of the divine is essential if we are to move beyond the foothills in the journey of faith.

As we get into our research, beyond the early stages, we begin to recognize how naive our original ideas and hunches were. The subject of our study becomes more nuanced, complex, capable of seemingly multiple forms of analysis and perspective, subject to endless qualification and critique. The path into the woods not only bends and winds out of view but endlessly divides; at every corner there seems to be a new crossroads and no signposts to show the way. Or, if there are signposts, they may be a bit like one infamous signpost in North Devon where all the signs point to the same village!

To put this more explicitly in research terms, I am talking about the multiplicity of philosophical and methodological questions and decisions we face as we go deeper into our research. They must be engaged with and settled one way or another, either wittingly or unwittingly (and it is considerably better for us, not least at our viva, if we make these choices deliberately and knowingly). In any research project, we face myriad questions, such as the following:

- What are my philosophical presuppositions and in what truth-claims are they embedded? Are they legitimate and, if so, how do I account for them?
- What individual scholars, texts, movements or traditions constitute my primary conversation partners? How do I choose them? How many do I need? What justification for their choice can I offer (including why I have excluded others)? Why Irigiray rather than Cixous, or Jung rather than Freud, for example?
- If I draw on multiple theorists, how much of their works must I read? And how far do I need to engage with secondary discussion and critique of my primary texts?
- How many different disciplines can or must I engage with in order to create a sufficiently robust and rigorous theoretical framework? How far can I be an 'expert' in more than one field? Must I sacrifice a degree of depth for breadth?
- How do I draw on perspectives from different disciplines or fields? Do they have equal weight or do I prioritize one over another as the primary framework and lens through which I 'read' the others?
- Which social science paradigm best suits my research aims and interests: qualitative or quantitative, or a mixture of the two?
- Which particular methodologies and methods should I choose from the bewildering array of possibilities – action research, ethnography, grounded theory or phenomenological enquiry? Longitudinal or cross-sectional research? Focus groups or interviews, and which sort of inter-

views – semi-structured, open ended, oral history, expert, and so on? Narrative, discourse or thematic analysis? And how many interviews or focus groups is enough? How long is a piece of string?!

These are only a few of the kinds of questions you will each be facing or will have to face as you move into your research. And each question posed will bring in its train a whole host of ideas, thinking, reading and pondering before you are able to come to some kind of answer, provisional as it inevitably will be. And each question answered will lead to another set of questions and choices. This is the nature of academic enquiry.

It gets difficult. It isn't meant to be easy! The doctorate is a measure of our capacity to engage with the challenges of academic, scholarly pursuit and come to some kind of satisfactory resolution of the multiple philosophical, methodological and practical issues that are entailed in the conduct of research. Our answers and choices will only ever be partial, provisional and personal. They are *our* answers and choices, and being able to own and justify these choices is part of what forms us in the journey of research. More than at any earlier stage of academic enquiry, we are required to be independent learners and this does not simply mean that we are self-motivated and self-disciplined enough to do the work on our own (it does mean that), but also that we are able to make and own the fundamental theoretical and methodological choices required by research and give some kind of convincing rationale for them. This is perhaps akin to the requirement in the religious life to be able to give an account of the faith that we hold; and for this account to be more than a learnt catechism, something taken on trust from others (though it will involve some of this). In research as in faith, our commitments need to be searched out, tested and scrutinized, with a measure of self-knowing and realism about the limitations of our stance. To come to a place of such conviction – Luther's 'Here I stand' – is the work of years, possibly decades, rather than months. Although the new convert often professes great assurance about what they believe, such beliefs have not been owned, tested or grounded in experience; it is only when they have been so tested over time that it is possible to judge their durability.

At the heart of the mystical way, as described by saints and mystics from many religious traditions, there is a central paradox: in order to save one's life one must lose it; in order to receive the knowledge of God one must be divested of all certainty and even lose the very sense of God at all. A profound unmaking of soul is necessary before the soul may become capable of receiving the mystery of God. Evelyn Underhill offers a five-fold schema describing this journey, which accords with the lives of many of the saints.[11] In the first stage of awakening, there is the dawning consciousness of absolute or divine reality, often in a sudden and dramatic manner. This leads on to purgation in which the soul senses its infinite distance from the divine reality and the need to purify the mortal self in preparation for the emergence of the spiritual self. Illumination follows, where there is a certain apprehension of the absolute, an awareness of the transcendent order, though not a complete union with it. In the dark night of the soul, the soul is purified, although the experience is one of confusion, helplessness, stagnation of the will and a sense of the withdrawal of God's presence. All of this paves the way for unification, the union of the soul with God and the realization of the spiritual self.

This way of purgation within the mystical journey has its parallels within the research process and our journeys towards academic recognition.[12] Just as the commitment to the life of faith requires us to strip away false images and idols of God, so the commitment to research requires us to let go of false images of ourselves, academia and the significance of what we are doing. In both cases, a fundamental stripping of ego is necessary as we recognize that our original motives – both in following God and in pursuing research – may be highly suspect. Our desires for affirmation, approval and recognition, whether from God, our supervisor or the academy, must be tested and purged. In the end, the driving force must be love of God, or love of scholarship, or love of art – whatever it is – for its own sake, and not for any rewards that may accrue. Grandiose ideals must be scaled back, over-reaching ambitions punctured and unrealistic research proposals honed. When we start a doctorate or a book project, it seems such a huge thing, a mountain to climb – and perhaps it is, symbolically, in terms of what it represents for us – but the more we go on with it, the more we come to realize what a little, modest thing it is; both how short and small a thesis actually is, and how modest any 'original' contribution to knowledge usually is. This may hurt our pride but at the same time can liberate us to jettison a lot of the unnecessary baggage we carry with us, the unrealistic expectations and projections that can stand in the way of the work itself.

The finding of form

How do we find the shape or form for our work? This is part of the process of ownership, the shaping and crafting of our work – never completely 'ex nihilo' but in relation to given forms that are part of the traditions we inherit. We do not entirely choose these forms; initially we will probably simply copy them, although over time we may learn to reshape and reform them.

Here is an extract from my journal in which I muse on my own efforts to 'find the form' of a recent piece of writing, and how this relates to 'finding a form' for my life:

Finding form, finding the form of a poem, an argument, a thesis, a day, a week, a sabbatical, a life – these are not separate things but one art, one work, one vocation. Learning the craft of shaping: shaping the line of a poem, the form of a thesis, the pattern of a life. How do we find it? It is gift, it is grace, and it is labour. It is a series of endless fallings and risings. It is a stab in the dark over and over that fails. It is a desire that does not live up to its own impetus, that peters out in disappointment or despair, yet will not give up, but starts again, looking to find or stumble upon a better fit. It is endless drafting and revision, moulding and breaking and refashioning to find a better fit.

How do we find the fit of a thing that is right? The fit of a shape that feels snug in the hand? The fit of a cloth that hangs perfectly on a body: the cut of fabric, sway of a skirt, the line of a well-made suit. The eye perceives it, knows it; we recognize a good fit, and a bad one. Just as we recognize an argument that works, that is convincing, that hangs together, that is of one piece. Or a poem that sits perfectly on the page, not a stanza over-length, with each word finding its rightful place in the line, each line contributing its part to the whole. Or an essay or book that has an integrity, a wholeness, knit together from its many component parts.

How do we learn this mysterious work of crafting, shaping, finding the form? There is a gift we do not earn or possess, whether that be a gift to write poems or make good arguments or cut and design clothes or cook or paint. Where does the gift come from? From genetics, from our DNA, from our histories and contexts and traditions. It helps enormously if we are born into a family, a society and a culture where these things flourish, seem 'natural', their organic forms at our daily disposal. But it is not essential. Many an artist grew up in homes where no one wrote, and barely read, or painted or played. Ultimately, the gift is from and of God, the gods: mysterious, transcendent, apparently random even, outrageously unfair both in its distribution and measure. Why is one person in a family or a village given a largesse of talent, opportunity and privilege when others in the same family or village have little or nothing? Is there a life that is given nothing? I think not. *Every* life is gifted with its own creative possibilities, however constrained or limited the gift or, more commonly, the limitation of its exercise.

But the gift is merely the seed, the root of the plant. It must be watered, nurtured, supported, fed – over weeks, months and years – if it is to flourish and find its true form. The gift must be recognized, accepted, exercised, practised, if it is to bring forth the promised fruits.

The shape of a life is a yet greater mystery. How do we find the fit that enables the life to flourish and fruit? How does the artist find the form of a life that enables the shaping of their art? How does a writer pattern and form her days? How does the Christian find a form that enables the shaping of a Christ-like life?

There must be order, pattern, rhythm, flow: the repetitions of the daily offices, the hours at the desk, the inhabiting of a room, a space. The shaping and form of a room have something to do with it. Is it possible to shape order from a space that is chaotic, uncared for, neglected? Some artists *do* create out of chaos, and that is the other side of the order, pattern and rhythm that most creativity requires. There must also be freedom, spontaneity, enough room for the gift to emerge, find its own way into the world, its own place at the table, its own shape on the page. There must be room for *play*, and play has an anarchic quality to it which always threatens the too-tight control of the ego, the adult consciousness. Creation is not *ex nihilo*, out of nothing, but out of the vast watery wastes of chaos. There has to be room for chaos in and around the artist's life. Too much control and the spirit is stifled, the gift stillborn.

There is, I believe, a profound connection between the process of finding a form for our work and finding a form for our life; but the connection is not straightforward. On the one hand, shaping our work, our thesis, our research, is a form of practising for the much larger task of shaping our life, finding our vocation; it is a form of experimentation on a smaller scale for what we want to do on the larger map. On the other hand, there is no neat parallel or symmetry between the work and the life. Often, there may be a very obvious disconnect. The work has shape, flow, order, while the life is chaotic and dishevelled. This may be because our intuition and creative selves 'know' things ahead of our conscious mind, which takes a while to catch up – and even longer for the will to act on what the conscious mind knows. I often say 'my poems know more than I do', and many poets express this notion. Thus Adrienne Rich says, 'poems are like dreams, in them you put what you don't know you know ... poems are more like premonitions than conclusive'.[13] So I may have the sense with some of my poems that they are way ahead of my life, that they know something I don't know yet except in my soul, and the challenge is to live into the truth of the poem. Again, Rich comments, 'the meaning of a poem becomes clear to me as I see what happens in my life'.[14]

What endures: metaphors of transformation

What is left when we have been purged by the long discipline of prayer/research, when we have learned to walk through the narrow gate, been sobered, tempered and aged by the limitations of our knowing, learned to let go of the false gods of certainty, pride, attachment to our own achievements? What endures and survives the apophatic fires?

Not necessarily the 'results' of our research or the fruits of our prayer – and who can ever say what the 'results' of our work or are prayer really are? We make whatever contribution we can to knowledge, practice and ongoing conversation. We are not in control of our work once it has been accomplished – if we can ever say it is 'completed'. There is a necessary letting go, taking our hands off the finished work, a trusting of what is no longer ours to go into the world and do its own work, whatever that might be. The work leaves us – like a child who grows up and becomes its own person, leaving the parental home. Our child may or may not look like us, may say and do all kinds of things we didn't know it had in them to do, travel to places we've never been and will never go. Our child – our work, our book, our research, our prayer – may or may not return to us, visit us from time to time, tell us of its exploits. Sometimes we will hear back – our work may be taken up, quoted, expanded, critiqued, replaced by others; our prayer may find an echoing return in the gratitude of those for whom we've prayed or a change in circumstances that seemed hopeless or impossible. We have little or no control on what may or may not come back to us – and this is as it should be.

What endures? Not necessarily the work, but what the work has accomplished – in us and in all the others (other people, other places, other contexts and lives) to which the work has travelled. Even if everything belonging to the work is lost (the thesis fails or is unfinished, the faith we thought we held evaporates or dies on us), we have been shaped and changed by the process, and perhaps others who have been involved with us in the research process have also been changed in some ways. I will end by offering a few metaphors of this transformation: not my own, but ones that I have found resonate with my own experience.

First of all, there is the metaphor of 'finding or claiming a voice'. Through our research, we learn new speech, new language; we are initiated into a new community and, over time, we become a spokesperson for that community. We learn to claim and speak out of a new voice. This much-used metaphor within feminism is precisely much used because of its power and resonance. It speaks of a process of self-actualization and self-authorship that is at the heart of the processes both of research and of the spiritual life as we discern our vocation and articulate it in the person we are as well as in the work we commit to.

We speak differently – often quite literally – as a result of the process of learning. We acquire a new tongue. We may begin by aping the speech of others – as poets practise by copying the style and form of established poets and as children learn to speak by copying adults around them – but as time goes on we develop our own distinctive syntax, vocabulary, tone and style: our own voice. We speak like no one else. It is not only *what* we say – though it is that – but the *way* that we say it that says who we are and what we know and what we are staking our life upon. As Seamus Heaney puts it:

Finding a voice means that you can get your own feeling into your own words and that your words have the feel of you about them; and I believe that it may not even be a metaphor, for a poetic voice is probably very intimately connected with the poet's natural voice that he hears as the ideal speaker of the lines he is making up.[15]

A little further on in the same essay, Heaney uses a striking image of how the development of the craft and technique of poetry marks the poet, akin to the way a watermark impresses itself on paper, and this is the second metaphor I want to offer. Just as a watermark is indelibly present on the page and cannot be erased, so our research as well as our faith practices leave their marks upon our bodies and minds, not to be erased. What endures may then be compared to 'the marking of the body'. Any labour we do over time leaves its impression on the body, although this is far more evident with manual labour than it is with intellectual or soul work. My grandfather's whole body bore the marks of his long years of farming, and as a child I remember in particular how extraordinary his hands seemed to my gaze: huge turnip hands, rough, earthen-coloured and textured, bloated by years of handling the soil and being out in all weathers. Scholarly work probably does not mark us as obviously as this, as the work of prayer or pastoral care or social engagement may not, but nevertheless we *are* marked, watermarked by it in subtle or not-so-subtle ways. It shows itself in our bearing, as well as in our speaking.[16] Janet Morley has a wonderful poem entitled 'The bodies of grown-ups', which expresses well the way in which the body shows forth its history, including the history of our struggles to bring forth our own creative work – whether that be in the form of biological or other kinds of life. She writes of the 'stretchmarks and scars', 'faces that have been lived in', 'relaxed breasts and bellies,/ backs that give trouble,/ and well-worn feet:/ flesh that is particular,/ and obviously mortal'. Morley praises the 'flood of beauty/ beyond the smooth-ness of youth' in 'bodies/ no longer straining to be innocent,/ but yearning for redemption'.[17] Yet, as I have put it elsewhere, such markings 'are not always obvious like/ tattoos, piercings, scars on visible parts, hair outra-geously coloured or dyed'. Rather, they may endure 'as faint scratches, fissures, blotches, lumps or imbalances'.[18] Whether visible or more subtle, our bodies show the imprint of our loves, our commitments, our labours, our yearnings and our desires. In our bearing, we may carry the weight as well as the liberation of our learning, and this may be evident in conscious and unconscious ways to others, even if we ourselves cannot see it.

Finally, what endures is perhaps a measure of 'faithfulness' in and beyond any particular commitment to work we make, learnt through the necessary keeping of faith with ourselves and our research that is required for the completion of any doctoral thesis. The capacity to keep faith with our research and to bring it to completion in a piece of work by which we are willing to stand, however imperfect or partial we know it to be, forges in us deeper qualities of resilience and a more enduring capacity for faithfulness that will stand us in good stead long after the research is complete and its findings superseded.[19]

Notes

1 Terry A. Veling, 'Listening to "The voices of the pages" and "Combining the letters": Spiritual Practices of Reading and Writing', *Religious Education* 102 (2007), pp. 206–22.

2 Mary Rose O'Reilley, *Radical Presence: Teaching as Contemplative Practice* (London: Heinemann, 1998), p. 3.

3 Simone Weil, 'Reflections on the right use of school studies with a view to the love of God', *Waiting on God* (Glasgow: Collins Fount, 1977), p. 71.

4 May Sarton, *Journal of a Solitude* (London: Women's Press, 1985), p. 1.

5 Weil, 'Right use of school studies', pp. 66–76.

6 By 'methodology' I mean the larger, epistemological (and, for persons of faith, theological) and hermeneutical framework which gives meaning and significance to discrete research methods. There can be a confusing variation of terminology in the literature on practical theology; what I term 'methodology' others, such as Elaine Graham, Heather Walton and Frances Ward, in their classic *Theological Reflection: Methods* (London: SCM Press, 2nd edn, 2019), term 'methods', or Stephen Bevans, in his classic *Models of Contextual Theology* (Maryknoll, NY: Orbis, 2nd edn, 2002), terms 'models'.

7 Maria Harris, in *Fashion Me a People*, identifies five primary practices in the life of the church that shape and embody faith – community, prayer, teaching, proclamation and service.

8 Wendell Berry, 'Poetry and marriage: The use of old forms', in *Standing by Words: Essays* (Berkeley, CA: Counterpoint, 1983), pp. 92–105.

9 Berry, 'Poetry and marriage', p. 93.

10 I have written about this process of getting lost in the woods, drawing on one of Berry's fine Sabbath poems, more extensively in Nicola Slee, *Sabbath: The Hidden Heartbeat of Our Lives* (London: Darton, Longman & Todd, 2019).

11 Evelyn Underhill, *Mysticism: A Study of the Nature and Development of Man's Spiritual Consciousness* (London: Dutton, 12th edn, 1961).

12 For a tongue-in-cheek model of the six stages of doctoral study – 'elated smugness', 'paranoid bemusement', 'domination', 'obsession', 'fear' and 'tranquillity', see Carol Haigh, Pip Hardy and Fiona Duncan, 'Six Stages of Doctoral Study: A New Model for PhD Students', *Nurse Researcher* 18.4 (2011), pp. 46–7, available at https://pdfs.semanticscholar.org/4018/51cb9aeb4b21e6750d9ac718c28b0 9182154.pdf (accessed 24.10.19).

13 Quoted in Peter Sansom, *Writing Poems* (Newcastle: Bloodaxe, 1994), p. 61.

14 Quoted in Sansom, *Writing Poems*, p. 61.

15 Seamus Heaney, from 'Feeling into Words', in *Finders Keepers: Selected Prose 1971–2001* (London: Faber and Faber, 2002), p. 16.

16 And, of course, education and learning can teach us to speak in words and accents that alienate us from our native backgrounds and set us apart from our kith

and kin. The changes that learning and research effect in us may be ambivalent, not all wholly positive.

17 Janet Morley, 'The bodies of grown-ups', in *All Desires Known* (London: SPCK, 1992), p. 113.

18 Nicola Slee, 'The markings of the body', in *Seeking the Risen Christa* (London: SPCK), p. 130.

19 See my poem 'Faithfulness', in Nicola Slee, *The Book of Mary* (London: SPCK, 2007), p. 17.

14

Reading and Writing as Transformative Spiritual Practice

Introduction

'You must write, and read, as if your life depended on it,' says Adrienne Rich in her essay 'As if your life depended on it'. And goes on:

> To read as if your life depended on it would mean to let into your reading your beliefs, the swirl of your dreamlife, the physical sensations of your ordinary carnal life; and, simultaneously, to allow what you're reading to pierce the routines, safe and impermeable, in which ordinary life is tracked, charted, channeled ...
>
> To write as if your life depended on it: to write across the chalkboard, putting up there in public words you have dredged, sieved up from your dreams, from behind screen memories, out of silence – words you have dreaded and needed in order to know you exist.[1]

In this chapter, I turn my attention to these two aspects of research that are so primary and fundamental as to be axiomatic – the practices of reading and writing – and yet, strangely, receive little attention in the standard literature on research. Perhaps because they are taken for granted – all students, it is assumed (particularly at doctoral level), know how to read and write – they are unremarked and unexplored. Or, where they are attended to, it is often from a functional angle: tips on how to read or write in an academic context and for an academic audience. These kinds of books can be helpful; reading and writing are difficult skills to learn and practise well. Lack of attention to their practice reinforces the idea one sometimes hears that good reading and writing cannot be taught; a mistaken idea, I think. More profoundly, lack of attention to reading and writing in the processes of research ignores the fundamentally formative nature of both practices and their potential as spiritual disciplines that shape us for life with God, as well as life in the academy. It is these formative and transformative aspects of the practices of reading and writing that I want to focus on in this chapter.

Reading as transformative practice

Of course, we read many kinds of different texts when we do research, and it is an interesting activity to call to mind the variety of texts we read within and around the processes of research. My main concern here, however, is to think about the activity of reading per se, perhaps particularly when we are engaging with hard theoretical texts that we find difficult to read.

Engaging with ideas *is* difficult. Following the thought of a dense, complicated thinker who writes in a dense, complicated way *is* difficult. I get impatient with reading that asks a lot of me. Why can't they say it more simply? I guess because it *isn't* simple, and if it were, what would be the need of study or analysis? Philosophical and theological thinkers, no less than poets and mystics, think and write what has not been thought or written before. They break new territory, mint new thought in new terms. Reading is like learning a new language, *is* learning a new language, getting our tongues and minds around words, terms and ideas that stretch both. Such terms are quite literally unpronounceable and indecipherable when we first come across them. It is only as we *use* them, take the risk of saying them, putting the words into our own sentences and speech, that we test out whether and how far we understand them. At first this can feel very self-conscious, like the first time you say aloud a word you've been reading for ages and have therefore often seen in print but don't quite know how to pronounce. Only gradually do we extend our vocabulary, and at the same time, stretch our thinking. Even more than the strange, technical and difficult terms, the complicated syntax and structure of a writer's thought on the page demands that we follow them in and out of the sinuous logic of their thinking, an activity that requires a cognitive as well as affective consent to the world of the writer, an act of trust as we give ourselves over to the strange world of the text.

Reading is foundational and formative. It shapes and forms our thinking, yes, but also our feeling, sensibility, awareness, our very sense of ourselves and the world. The best writing engages heart, brain, body and passions in one, integrated activity. We know the world differently when we are inside the book, and this is why we grieve over finishing some books that take us into a world we never want to leave. It is not as if reading is some kind of automatic, mechanical activity in which one person's ideas are passed through the neutral medium of language directly into the brain of another. It is something altogether more creative and mysterious, an interchange between writer and reader, which requires the concentrated attention of both.

The medium *is* the message. The texture, syntax, structure, sound and lexicon of the writer's language *is* their thought. If they could have said it differently, they would have – but then it would have been something different. We read not so much to understand as to learn how to think in the first place; how to see and sense and feel the world, through another person's intelligence, body and voice. The difficulty is the same kind of difficulty we experience when learning a foreign language and listening to a foreign speaker. It demands effort, exertion, repetition and acute listening. It is daunting but it is our passport to another country, in this case another country of thought, ideas and wisdom. Such reading trains the mind, stiffens the intellectual muscles, stretches the contours of thinking.

Nevertheless, we can approach reading in very different ways, and read for different purposes. Reading, like everything else we do, does not take place in a vacuum but is formed and shaped by the context in which we do it, and by the values and assumptions of that context or culture. Paul J. Griffiths distinguishes between three different ways of understanding and practising reading as a way of highlighting different theories of reading.[2] There is 'academic reading', which focuses on technical mastery and 'consumption-for-use', where there is no moral relation between book and reader and reading takes place in a disenchanted world. This is reading for explanation and analysis, 'whose principle tools are the concept deployed in coercive argument and the repeatable experiment'. Proustian reading, by contrast, is reading for pleasure, for reverie, for sensual, aesthetic and very likely sexual enjoyment. The content of the book is secondary to its style and its rhetorical and physical effects upon the reader. Reading is a tool of self-development, not so much training of the mind – as in the first approach – as inculcation of aesthetic sensibilities. The third type of reading, Victorine reading, is reading for moral and religious instruction, formation and value. This is akin to the ancient understanding of *lectio divina*, although formalized in a complex theory that I need not go into here. *Lectio divina*, holy reading, was practised by early Christian monastics, building on Jewish practices of reading scripture, in which communities of monks gave themselves to a slow, ruminative reading and rereading of the scriptures. This was part of their daily practice, a means of taking the words of scripture from the surface level of the eyes and the mind down into the heart, the seat of the will and of the affections. They understood that the word needs to be chewed slowly before it can be absorbed by the mind and the heart, and that this is the slow, patient work of years. The aim was for transformation of mind and heart, the development of the 'mind of Christ' in the believer, which not only informs thinking but also shapes action and disposition, forming a Christ-like character in the believer. Reading undertaken in this spirit and conviction is an act of prayer and devotion as much as it is an intellectual discipline.[3] For the early Christians, thought and prayer were not separate spheres; the theologian was a person rooted and grounded in scripture and prayer, and right thinking was the fruit of right living, right praying, right desire.

These different approaches to reading can be in real tension and conflict, and this can pose a dilemma for the researcher who is committed to the practice of research as part of their discipleship or spiritual life and yet is required to read comprehensively and exhaustively within the confines of limited time. Academic life is increasingly driven by models of consumption and production, and it is not surprising that, in this environment, reading becomes just another skill to master and to 'own', with the emphasis on speed, efficiency of recall and reproduction. This can foster a mechanical, mastery model of relationship to the text that is in conflict with models of reading for pleasure (the Proustian) or for contemplation and spiritual formation (the monastic and Victorine).

Religious traditions have always known the power of reading. Jewish, Christian and Muslim traditions, as religions of the book, hold a great reverence for the Word, which is so much more than the written or spoken word. In the Hebrew scriptures, God's *dhabar* is the creative life-force out of which the whole creation emerges. It is performative utterance; it brings into being that of which it speaks. It shows as well as telling (what every poetry workshop instructs the aspiring poet to do!); it is embodied utterance, rooted in matter and expressed as lived wisdom. It is not surprising that the earliest Christians spoke of Christ as the Word incarnate, the one who embodies most fully and vividly the lived Wisdom of God. The scriptures testify to that living Word but they only *become* Word of God when they are inbreathed by the Holy Spirit.

Mary, the mother of Jesus, is regarded in Christian tradition as first and foremost of readers, as the theologian par excellence: she hears and receives the Word in such a way that it quite literally takes flesh in her body and she gives birth to it in the form of Jesus, the Word made flesh. She is thus regarded as *Theotokos,* god-bearer, but also the model student or scholar of the word. Christian iconography often presents Mary at the annunciation absorbed in a book, the book of the scriptures; seated alone, in 'a room of her own', as Virginia Woolf's famous phrase has it,[4] beautifully dressed in silken garbs. Even though this is a highly anachronistic image of a working peasant girl who was almost certainly illiterate, it is a powerful image of Mary as what Margaret Hebblethwaite describes as 'quite an exceptionally booky woman':

> The Mary of iconography is an uncommon, cultured, learned lady, who is never seen doing housework, but is always seen – at the moment of the angel's interruption – nourishing her brain. Here is truly a Mary we can admire, the Lady of the Book, an exemplar for women's theology, a Mary who bears witness that educational aspirations are not a distraction from the duties of motherhood, but rather that the ideal mother – the kind of mother fitting for Christ – is a woman of letters.[5]

This idea of Mary as a woman cultivating her brain is continued in the tradition of Mary teaching her son Jesus to read, and we find this too in Christian iconography, as well as a matching iconographic tradition of Anna teaching Mary to read.[6] I have explored and celebrated this tradition of Mary as the first reader and Mary as theologian who teaches Jesus in *The Book of Mary*, whose very title focuses on Mary as reader and, implicitly, the composer of her own book.[7]

So Mary is the start of this tradition of 'holy reading', which the monastics continued in *lectio*. Terry Veling offers a helpful account of *lectio* as an active, embodied form of reading – with the lips and the ears as well as the eyes – through which monastics engaged with the *voces paginarum*, the 'voices of the pages', in an immersive, physically attentive practice that integrated study and prayer.[8]

Writing as transformative practice

Much of what I've suggested about the processes of reading could also be applied to writing, and, indeed, it is hardly possible to speak of reading without thinking about the activity of writing at the same time, what the writer as writer contributes to the process of reading. Thus Stephanie Paulsell, in an insightful essay, speaks of writing as a form of reading:

> Writing can be a kind of reading, a kind of thinking. A way of receiving and considering the work of others, a way of discovering what we think about particular questions. A way of articulating what we think in a way that invites others into the process of reading, thinking, and articulating.[9]

And Veling points out that, for the monastics, 'the process of writing grew out of the process of spiritual reading'.[10] First, the monks would copy out texts they enjoyed to savour them further. Then they would add their own comments to them, beginning to form the first commentaries on the scriptures. This is similar to the Jewish tradition of midrash, in which reading and responding to the text of scripture in writing are integrated in one activity. To read is already an act of interpretation, of response; to write is a form of reading, of imbibing and engaging with the tradition of which we are a part.

Just as reading is a learnt discipline that forms and shapes thinking, so is writing. I do know some people who say they do all their reading and thinking and *then* write what they have discovered, but I am not one of them. I do not know what I think or feel until I write it. I write in order to know what I think and feel about anything, and if I am not writing I do not know I am fully alive; some part of me goes underground or falls asleep. At the beginning of her *Journal of a Solitude*, May Sarton writes: 'I have written every poem, every novel, for the same purpose – to find out what I think, to know where I stand.' And then goes on immediately to say, 'I am unable to become what I see.'[11] It is precisely that tension between what one may know internally and what one actually embodies in one's life that drives one to write, to find a place of greater equilibrium and integration between inner and outer self, between the imagined life and the life lived.

Just as there are different ways of reading so, too, there are many different approaches to writing. There is no one right or wrong way of doing it, but it can be helpful to share others' experience and learn from what has worked for them. Research on how writers write suggests different categories of writers who each approach the task of writing differently. One study, by Torrance, Thomas and Robinson, distinguished between three kinds of writers: *planners* – students who prefer to have their ideas clear before starting to write, and who produce few drafts; *revisers* – students who prefer to start writing first before taking final decisions about content; and *mixed types* – students who planned but were then forced to change their plans by repeated revising.[12] Another study by Lewenthal and Wason distinguishes between 'serialists' who proceed one step at a time and 'holists' who think first about the big picture before committing to writing.[13]

We are also likely to experience the task of writing differently. Some people love the actual process of writing and find writing relatively easy; they may write quickly and do not find it difficult to produce material (but even these blessed individuals may have their 'down' days). Others struggle much more, find writing laborious, even tortuous, can be painfully slow in producing text, and experience many crises of confidence along the way. This is very common among research students (particularly among women students and some international students who are not working in their first language, as well as for students with dyslexia or other forms of learning needs); part of the challenge of doing research at postgraduate level is learning to manage one's fears, anxieties and blocks in the writing process.

Paulsell's essay suggests a number of ways in which writing may be formative as a spiritual discipline. First of all, its very difficulty – like the difficulties of reading – may engender in the student the twin virtues of audacity and humility, if we are not overcome by the sheer terror of committing anything to paper. Writing is inherently difficult, and the terror of the blank page that greets the writer at the beginning of any new piece is a widely recognized symptom of its challenges. Yet the writer of theology has a doubly difficult task: not only to get any words out at all, but to write authentically of divine truths, which requires even more than usual courage and daring. Audacity is necessary even to begin such an attempt – who are we to speak of God, and how can we know that our words are true? – yet humility is necessary to continue it, for whatever we write will only gesture towards the fullness of divine mystery and will constantly require revision. Second, Paulsell reinforces Weil's insight that writing can be a means of practising attention, as we search for the 'right words' to say what needs to be said and then come back to the first draft and revise it, probably a number of times. The process of revision is a significant one, in which 'we listen for the false notes, we watch for signs of an incomplete train of thought, we read with an eye for our own failures'.[14] The combination of attention and detachment required for editing our own work is a practice that may inculcate and embed these essentially moral values in us. Third, Paulsell speaks of the way in which writing offers a way of holding together a choice for solitariness with a profound sense of connection to others and responsibility to community. While writing is necessarily a solitary pursuit and requires willingness to close the inner door, at the same time 'practicing writing as a spiritual discipline means holding potential readers, and the other writers with whom we think and write, in our hearts'.[15] We write alone, but with others, responding to the work and thoughts of others through their writings, and we write towards others – the others who will read our words.

To come back to the work of editing and revising our writing, this is one of the practices that has taught, and continues to teach, me a great deal about discipline, loss and purgation. On the whole, I do not find it difficult to produce a first draft and very often, if the writing is going well (a big 'if'!), I positively enjoy the flow of words, the sense of thought forming as I write, the sensation of being carried on a stream of consciousness that is both me and not-me. There is an expansiveness and playfulness about the release of language in the first draft. I'm in love with words, float in the amniotic sac of the semiotic, the warm bath of the poetic/erotic, find myself seduced by the play of verbiage and relish the satisfaction of rhetoric. I'm someone who does not find it difficult to produce words – 'never knowingly underworded', as my partner affectionately describes my poems! I overwrite, and then have to hone the overblown prose back, and back again – like hacking at an overgrown rosebush. The process of editing and revision is often more difficult, for me, than getting the first draft out. It's hard work seeing what needs to go, not only the bad/dead wood but the gorgeous blooms that have to be sacrificed if the plant is to regain its shape and form. Editing would be easy if it were only a matter of excising what is bad, but we often have to lose what is good in order for the better to emerge. It requires a certain brutal astringency (one reason why it is often easier to edit someone else's work than one's own). Yet learning to excise what is unnecessary in order that the lines of one's argument may be clearer, or the poem speak more directly, is an exercise in courage and humility equal to the creation of the first draft. From it we learn, too, a greater respect and admiration for the fine writing of others whose work we read.

Conclusion

Our struggles, both to read and to write well – by which I mean not only 'well' as judged by academic standards of excellence, but morally and spiritually well as practices of justice and truth-seeking – are formative of who we are and who we may yet become. They are some of the primary places, within the processes of research, where we learn both to receive and shape wisdom, and to discover our own theological convictions and commitments in the process. Thus, choices we make in relation to our writing, as with our reading, are not merely intellectual or aesthetic choices, Paulsell argues, but moral, spiritual ones:

> The intellectual and aesthetic choices we make when we write are also moral, spiritual choices that can hold open a door for another to enter, or pull that door shut; that can sharpen our thinking or allow it to recline on a comfortable bed of jargon; that can form us in generosity and humility or in condescension and disdain.[16]

Notes

1 Adrienne Rich, *What is Found There: Notebooks on Poetry and Politics* (London: Virago, 1993), pp. 32–3.

2 Paul J. Griffiths, 'Reading as a spiritual discipline', in L. Gregory Jones and Stephanie Paulsell (eds.), *The Scope of Our Art: The Vocation of the Theological Teacher* (Grand Rapids, MI and Cambridge: Eerdmans, 2002), pp. 32–47. See also Paul J. Griffiths, *Religious Reading: The Place of Reading in the Practice of Religion* (New York: Oxford University Press, 1999).

3 For more on *lectio divina*, see Michael Casey, *Sacred Reading* (Liguori, MO: Liguori, 1995); Enzo Bianchi, *Praying the Word* (Kalamazoo, MI: Cistercian Publications, 1995); Mariano Magrassi, *Praying the Bible: An Introduction to Lectio Divina* (Collegeville, MN: Liturgical Press, 1998).

4 Virginia Woolf, *A Room of One's Own* (London: Penguin Classics, 2019).

5 Margaret Hebblethwaite, unpublished sermon, quoted in Nicola Slee, *The Book of Mary* (London: SPCK, 2007), p. 134.

6 For images of Mary reading at the annunciation, Mary teaching Jesus to read and Anna teaching Mary to read, Google Images has multiple examples.

7 See Slee, *The Book of Mary*, especially chapter 6.

8 Terry A. Veling, 'Listening to "The voices of the pages" and "Combining the letters": Spiritual Practices of Reading and Writing', *Religious Education* 102 (2007), pp. 206–22.

9 Stephanie Paulsell, 'Writing as a spiritual discipline', in Jones and Paulsell, *Scope of Our Art*, p. 24.

10 Veling, 'Listening to "The voices of the pages"', p. 213.

11 May Sarton, *Journal of a Solitude* (London: Women's Press, 1985), p. 2.

12 M. Torrance, G. V. Thomas and E. J. Robinson, 'The Writing Strategies of Graduate Research Students in the Social Sciences', *Higher Education* 27 (1994), pp. 379–92.

13 D. Lowenthal and P. C. Wason, 'Academics and Their Writing', *Times Literary Supplement*, 24 June 1977, pp. 782–3.

14 Paulsell, 'Writing as a spiritual discipline', p. 25.

15 Paulsell, 'Writing as a spiritual discipline', p. 27.

16 Paulsell, 'Writing as a spiritual discipline', p. 24.

15

Feminist Qualitative Research as Spiritual Practice: Reflections on the Process of Doing Research

This article first saw the light of day as a paper offered at the first meeting of the Symposium on the Faith Lives of Women and Girls in November 2010, subsequently published in the first book arising from the Symposium, co-edited with my colleagues Fran Porter and Anne Phillips, The Faith Lives of Women and Girls: Qualitative Research Perspectives *(Farnham: Ashgate, 2013, pp. 13–24). At the time, I was unaware of other literature reflecting theologically and from a spiritual stance on the activities of qualitative research, although I subsequently discovered Bernadette Flanagan's important essay, 'Quaestio Divina: Research as Spiritual Practice' (The Way 53.4 (2014), pp. 126–36), which put me in touch with wider literature on contemplative and heuristic research (for example, Clark Moustakas,* Heuristic Research: Design, Methodology, and Applications *(Newbury Park, CA: Sage, 1990); William Braud and Rosemarie Anderson,* Transpersonal Research Methods for the Social Sciences: Honoring Human Experience *(Thousand Oaks, CA: Sage, 1998); Robert Romanyshyn,* The Wounded Researcher: Research with Soul in Mind *(New Orleans, LA: Spring Journal Books, 2007)). Since the publication of my essay, a number of significant publications in this growing field have emerged, including Christian Scharen,* Fieldwork in Theology: Exploring the Social Context of God's Work in the World *(Grand Rapids, MI: Baker Academic, 2015); Zoë Bennett, Elaine Graham, Stephen Pattison and Heather Walton,* Invitation to Research in Practical Theology *(London: Taylor & Francis, 2018); Catherine Sexton, 'Method as Contemplative Enquiry: From Holy Listening to Sacred Reading and Shared Horizons',* Practical Theology *12.1 (2019), pp 44–57.*

Introduction

In this paper, I would like to reflect on some of the characteristic features of qualitative research, as represented in the work of feminist practitioners – including the work of the women contributing to this symposium – and consider how the practice of research both arises out of and feeds back into women's own ethical and spiritual lives.

Both qualititative and feminist researchers are fundamentally concerned with the process(es) of research as an integral aspect of the work, in opposition to certain malestream/patriarchal attitudes to research that we may find operative in the academy and elsewhere, where the emphasis is wholly or largely on the research product, conceived both as the new knowledge arising from research and as the enhanced qualification, status and reputation of the researcher earned through the process of completing a higher degree. Qualitative and feminist researchers from a variety of fields understand that process and content are integrally interconnected and cannot be easily separated; that feminists are after new ways of knowing – in our case, new ways of doing theology – as much as they are after new knowledge; that, as Audre Lorde famously put it, you can't dismantle the master's house with the master's tools,[1] or, as qualitative researchers might say, positivist research methods that assume objectivity, neutrality and detachment on the part of the researcher in the interests of control are not likely to yield liberating results for oppressed groups, and are highly likely to reinscribe the positivist vision of the researcher.

But even in qualitative and feminist research paradigms that pay explicit and detailed attention to the research process and to the importance of method, much of this concern is focused on methodology per se, the ethics of research enquiry and the effects of the research process on research participants – all right and proper concerns. There is much less in the research literature about the significance of the research process for the researcher herself, about research as a means of transformation for the researcher – and even less about the research process understood in essentially religious or spiritual terms, although Mary Clark Moschella is an important exception, who both acknowledges and explores 'the research process itself as a potential means of spiritual growth and social transformation'.[2] Both of these are significant and, I would maintain, interrelated; it is primarily the first that is my focus in this paper, but not without reference to the second.

For myself and, I think, for many other women researchers, the pursuit of research using qualitative methods has been a transformational process – not only in the way that it has contributed to our own knowledge and understanding of women's and girls' faith lives, but also in the ways in which the research process itself has embodied and enacted core ethical and spiritual values. I know I'm on hopelessly slippery ground by using such a vague term as 'spiritual' here – and I'm not at this stage going to become immured in a lengthy or learned excursus on various definitions of spirituality, and feminist spirituality in particular (though I have discussed this elsewhere[3]). Instead, I want to take a more concrete, analogical and narrative approach, by comparing the way in which feminist researchers use qualitative methods to research women's lives (in our case, women's

faith lives) to some of the classic ways in which people in religious traditions practise spirituality.

I want to try and describe the qualitative research process as I have experienced it, and as I have witnessed other women researchers experience it,[4] in
such a way as to evoke the lived experience of research and to bring to light
some of its core personal, ethical and what I will name spiritual characteristics and values. I want to suggest ways in which the research process itself
forms and shapes us as women of faith (however we understand that term),
challenges us to dig deep within our own spiritual resources (as well as
calling on the support and resources of others), teaches us how to discern
the sacred in other women's lives and in our own lives, and enables us to
grow in spiritual stature and wisdom. I shall attempt to do this, first, by
describing some of the features of the context in which many of us perceive
ourselves to be doing research, and then to go on to outline the various
stages of qualitative research, trying to show how each discrete aspect of
the research process presents its own spiritual challenges and, if we respond
faithfully, gifts us with its own particular spiritual graces.

The practice of research, I want to suggest, is one that can, when conducted within the theological framework of a faith perspective, not only
reflect but enact and enshrine core values of the faith community. Where
Elaine Graham speaks of pastoral theology in broad terms as 'transforming
practice',[5] I want to focus in particular on ethnographic and qualitative
research and show how they can be such transformative practices. Graham
articulates an understanding of praxis as a form of practical wisdom mediated and embodied in the church's activities of care, worship, social action,
formation and initiation, as much as in its formal theology. Although we
do not normally think of research as a fundamental characteristic of the life
of the church, perhaps we should. Mary Clark Moschella argues powerfully for 'ethnography as a pastoral practice', as the title of her book puts it,
in which the process of ethnographic research, undertaken with intentionality, care and skill, can be a form of pastoral care, prophetic critique and
spiritual discernment within the life of the church. She draws on doctoral
work by David Mellott, who describes the ethnographic encounter as 'an
act of primary theology', a means of being in relationship with God and
practising the core values of the faith community.[6]

Our location as women researchers using qualitative research methods to investigate the faith lives of women and girls

Before looking at the research process per se, it is important to acknowledge the context(s) in which we find ourselves conducting research and
the way in which we experience our location, for this impacts significantly
on the ways in which we experience the research process and the personal/

spiritual challenges it offers us. Without wanting to suggest that we are all located in precisely the same location – clearly we are not, and we need to acknowledge our different contexts, whether academic or pastoral, whether as lay women or ordained, as white, black or Asian, as younger or older, as more or less established in the church or academy – my experience is that many of us describe our location as researchers in similar terms. As Edwards and Ribbens describe feminist qualitative research into women's so-called 'private' lives (into which the category of religion or spirituality might fit) being on the edges of the social sciences,[7] so perhaps we perceive ourselves and our research to be located on the edges, at a liminal margin, a location that boasts little status, recognition or understanding from other theologians or social scientists. We may experience a variety of margins. Theology exists somewhere on the edges of the social sciences or the humanities, hardly considered mainstream by larger, secular disciplines. Within theology, both feminist theology in general and feminist practical theology more specifically, are marginalized discourses. Even within the small world of feminist practical theology – represented in the UK by such practitioners as Elaine Graham, Heather Walton, Zoë Bennett and Jan Berry, among others – we may experience ourselves as marginal as those who are choosing to use qualitative methods to research women's and girls' faith lives. Then there are other margins for some of us – if we're like Anne researching the experience of girls, or Abby, wanting to focus on older women, or like Deseta and Eun Sim, concerned with the faith lives of ethnic minority women and traditions. So it is not surprising if we experience ourselves as 'resident aliens', outsiders in an insiders' world, 'internal leavers', as Gwen tellingly describes the subjects of her research.

This is the location in which we find ourselves doing research, and it is a spiritual landscape every bit as much as it is an intellectual or professional one: a landscape that might be named in a wide variety of metaphors,[8] but certainly requires us to exercise courage, self-belief and tenacity. From such a location we conduct our research, drawing on deep inner resources of conviction, justice-seeking compassion and prophetic daring. Part of my offering to you who are gathered here is to reflect back to you what I see when I regard the way in which we, as feminist women of spiritual and Christian conviction, practise research.

Coming to the study of the lives of women and girls as on to holy ground

Whatever the precise focus of our respective research studies, we share an approach to the lives of women and girls as holy ground, a place where we expect to find and discern the presence and activity of the divine, however we name that. Moschella describes the reverence that undergirds all ethnographic research as 'profound respect and regard for the dignity of the persons and communities who allow us to see so much of themselves'.[9] While this attitude of reverence may indeed be required of all ethnographic research, I suppose we are particularly aware that, in studying the faith lives of women and girls, we are approaching a neglected site. We are cartographers of the spirit, charting maps that have not been made, until now.

I'm talking here, of course, about the fundamental feminist principle of women's experience(s). We deliberately privilege women and girls as the focus of our study, and while we need to face the myriad complex theoretical questions about the legitimacy of such a stance – what do we mean by 'women'? Which women and why? How far is gender a stable category and why focus on gender over and above other variables? and so on – we continue to operate a strategic feminism that insists on the prioritizing of women's lives. We do so because we want to hold up the holiness of ordinary women's and girls' lives, and I guess too because we want to say in and through our research that *our* lives, too, are sacred, our lives are worthy of reverence and painstaking study, our lives are revelatory of God. To put this theologically, our research becomes a praxis of the communion of saints, a way of insisting on the participation of very ordinary women and girls within the life of the people of God and of holding up their lives as those who, among the company of the faithful, are worthy of narration, visibility and reverence.

Listening to other women's lives as a practice of prayer and contemplation

Much has been written about the importance of listening within practical and pastoral theology and within the practice of ethnography, as well as within feminist theology. Nelle Morton's work on 'hearing into speech'[10] has become a classic text which enshrines a core value of listening to women's lives – and this, of course, is an expression of the conviction I've just been articulating of women's and girls' lives as sacred sites.

Listening is key at every stage of the research process. Long before the formal beginning of research we are listening to our own lives and the lives of others we know and hearing questions, stories, ideas, hunches, that shape themselves up into our research proposals. We listen to the literature, bringing our own lives and the lives of the women and girls we know into dialogue with it. We listen to our supervisor (hopefully!) and to peers and colleagues who may shed valuable light on our research. We listen with acute attentiveness to our participants in interviews or other settings. We listen again, over and over, when transcribing and analysing data. We listen, as we are doing here today, when we present our research to others and when we hear back from them. All the time we are listening at many different levels: to self, to the other, to the literature, to the Spirit at work in each of these.

It strikes me that the way we listen as women researchers is itself a form of spiritual practice that has many of the qualities of prayer, understood as the most attentive listening to self, other and God we can manage.[11] We listen with our lives. We bring our whole selves to the act of listening. Our listening is informed by scholarly reading, and that's vital, but it's informed by so much more. It's shaped by our own hunger to be listened to, by positive experiences of what it is to be listened to well, but also by the painful reality we all know of not being heard, of having our voices and lives silenced. We listen with our whole bodies, paying attention to feeling, memory, desire. We listen with emotional as well as intellectual intelligence, on the lookout for patterns, resonances, allusions. We listen to what is explicit in what we read or hear, to what is implicit but not directly said, and to what is null or absent – the inconceivable, unsayable, or not yet capable of being articulated.[12] We listen to tone of voice, sighs, stutters, laughter, tears, pauses, silences, body language, facial expression, the mood of the encounter, how it starts, shifts, changes, moves, circles, ends; how we feel as it's going on and after it's ended; using our feelings as a clue to how the other woman or girl may be feeling.

As in prayer, so in research, the practice of the discipline of waiting is a core gift and skill. We have to learn to focus all our attention on the other and to get ourselves and our egos out of the way. At the same time, we need to know how to use ourselves – feelings, body, intelligence, intuition – to assist our listening. We learn how to wait with, wait on, wait for the other, putting ourselves at their disposal, letting them speak as and when and where they will, sitting with them as they search for what it is they want to say, or remain silent, or stumble or stutter.

Turning life into text: transcribing as a practice of holy writ

The process of transcribing is often regarded as something of a chore (and best avoided, if possible, or passed on to someone else) or as a technical challenge of research (how do you turn verbal discourse into text?), but I have never come across transcription described as spiritual practice. I want to suggest it is, or can be, precisely that, and therefore is fundamental to the process of listening I've described above.

The act of transcribing is a painstaking, slow, laborious act, part of the ethnographer's craft, which can only be learned by practice. It requires the paying of minute attention to every word spoken by our research participants, and to the inflection, nuance, timing and timbre of voice, as well as to our own part of the dialogue and interchange. While there are different methods of transcribing and different levels of detail required according to the purpose of the research, the search for accuracy and authenticity is at the heart of all transcribing, and requires enormous effort. We have to play the tape again and again, especially going back to places where we can't make out words or phrases, or can't make sense of what seems to be being said. Finding a way for words on the page to bring alive the sound of a voice is an art. And I want to say it is holy and costly work; it is a way of enacting the giving of reverence to our subjects' lives that I described above. We can ask or pay someone else to do it, but, if we do, what does that say about our own commitment to listening, and what do we lose in the process?

Transcribing is a way of enacting listening in a wholly embodied, visceral fashion. As we listen and transcribe, we are employing ear, eye, hand (and often foot, too, if we are using a transcribing machine) in a coordinated manner to listen with every fibre of our being. We imbibe the words of the interview, we ingest them as holy sacrament; they enter our bodies and live inside us, where the voices continue to talk, to each other, as well as to us, generating their own internal conversations and meanings. Thus transcription becomes a kind of act of holy communion, a Eucharist of taking into our own women's bodies the stuff of other women's lives; an intermingling of women's and girls' lives that leaves us profoundly changed by the process: enriched, yes, but it's more than that. There's a sense in the act of transcribing and the profound listening it embodies, of our participants taking up residence within our bodies, becoming deeply enfleshed within us as a kind of community, an internalized ekklesia of women, as Fiorenza might describe it,[13] or an expression of Womenchurch[14] – and this internalized, embodied community of our participants becomes the place from which we do the research. The combined pain, struggle, wisdom, lived faith, insight and so on, of each of our participants, becomes part of our lives, part of our pain, struggle, wisdom and faith, and we enter into a kind of implicit covenant with them through the act of research. The formal procedures of consent and the conduct of the interview may be the obvious expression of this covenant, but I think the act of transcribing (followed up by the work of data analysis) seals and ratifies it in some mysterious way.

Handling the texts of our subjects' lives as sacred texts

Having turned our subjects' lives into texts that are amenable to analysis, we go on to read the texts of our subjects' lives with the same attention, reverence and expectation as characterized the earlier processes of the research. We pore over the pages of our transcripts like scholars poring over the pages of holy scripture. We bring the kind of attitude to the transcripts that monks, nuns and lay folk bring to scripture in *lectio divina*, the ancient practice of meditative, ruminative reading of scripture in which the believer seeks to go beyond a mere cognitive or analytical reading of the text to a profound inhabiting of the scriptures in such a way that they inform and form the heart, mind and will.[15] We read and reread the transcripts, searching beneath the surface for what is going on. We look for signs, patterns, repetitions, as well as gaps, contradictions, difference. We sift our subjects' lives, we go looking for meaning, for truth, for wisdom. We are like priests or preachers who break open the dense word of our subjects' lives and proclaim a liberating word that others can hear.

Losing in order to find: data analysis as a process of unknowing

So we move to the stage of analysing our data: a stage of research that can be at the same time the most exhilarating and exciting, and the most challenging and daunting. We work with our data in such a way that we can begin to come up with categories, themes and concepts that will lay the foundations for our research findings and conclusions. We do this in several stages, each one of which generates more data in addition to the data we already have from the transcripts. We make notes on each transcript, maybe equalling in quantity the data from the transcript itself. We start to compare transcripts and make more general notes from a broader perspective. We may use charts or graphs as a way of mapping some of the key patterns of the data. We may code data, using more or less sophisticated methods of coding. All of this is preliminary to the writing up 'proper' of our findings, and can take many weeks and months. Our research journals, where much of this work is done, are akin to an artist's sketchbook where many preliminary studies are made before a final painting is executed, or a poet's journal, where many different writing exercises are practised as foundational to the completion of a finished poem.

At this stage, we may experience something akin to a spiritual crisis. We may feel completely overwhelmed by the sheer amount of data we have gathered and our own detailed notes. We can no longer see the wood for the trees. We recognize that the whole subject we are investigating is so much more complex, nuanced and intricate than we ever imagined. We doubt our own original conception. We doubt our ability to handle the complexity of the data. We wish we could go back to our participants and ask them five more questions that would really give us what we need to make sense of what we have. We can't.

In this process, the landscape of our research has become the inner landscape of the dark night of the soul or the wilderness of unknowing. It is a place where the landmarks have disappeared and everything looks the same. The only thing to be done is to submit to the terror and confusion and walk by faith in the way of unknowing. The undoing of our own certainties and the falling apart of our original confident dream is probably a necessary part of any creative project, as well as of any spiritual commitment. It is a great test of resolve and trust, and many a research project founders at this stage.

At this stage, too, the role of the supervisor or mentor may be crucial, acting as someone, like a spiritual accompanist, who can stand by the researcher, metaphorically hold their hand and reassure them, 'It's OK. This is all part of the process. Others have been here before you and come through. Hang on. Stay with it. Don't panic.' (By the way, why is it so often assumed that once one is through one's doctorate there is no longer a need for a supervisor or mentor, as if we should be able to 'do it on our own'?) My experience, both of research and of prayer, as well as of other creative projects I have undertaken, is that, if we can hold on, don't lose nerve, let go and submit to the confusion, waiting patiently for we know not what, then, at a point and in a way that cannot be predicted, a turning point will come when, apparently miraculously, a new insight or direction begins to emerge out of the chaos and confusion. But it has to emerge organically, in its own time and way. It will not be coerced or controlled – and this is precisely what is scary, risky and lonely about the process. It requires of the researcher qualities of courage, faith and resilience to remain in the place of chaos and confusion without panicking, despairing or pushing to a hasty and unsatisfactory resolution – or, if it is not entirely possible to resist the forces of panic, anxiety or despair, at least to recognize them for what they are, temporary moments within a larger process of creativity, and to refuse to grant them the final word. And however much others can support us in this process, as they can, we have to find those inner resources for ourselves. As the supervisor, I may assure you that you will find a way through, and I may believe it – but you have to find that way for yourself.

The fact that we are all here today and we each have something to present to this symposium is testimony to the fact that we do come through and come up with some kind of coherent, ordered, patterned narrative to make sense of and communicate the findings of our research.

Writing up as a practice of mission and proclamation

The challenge of converting the entire research process into something that can be communicated to others – whether in the form of a conventional thesis or in other forms – is another praxis through which we enact our faith. Fundamental to our work as feminist practical theologians and social scientists is the conviction that our work is not just for us alone, but for others: the ones we have based our research upon, first and foremost, our research participants, but also for a wider audience, however we think about that wider constituency. Behind this sense of our responsibility and accountability to a wider community or communities lies another conviction, namely that feminist research is not only a matter of interpreting the world but of changing it.[16] At this point, our research practice is perhaps akin to the work of a preacher or an evangelist in a faith community, one who takes the core message of the community out to others, in the hope of convicting and converting others to her world view, and of changing both individual behaviours and social structures.

Out of our research is distilled a vision, a conviction, in continuity usually with the hopes and ideals that inspired the research in the first place but considerably refined, chastened, honed and strengthened as a result of doing the research, and more robustly rooted in the evidence we have gathered and the literature we have drawn upon. We usually have a passion to communicate that vision to others (although we can also experience a sense of boredom with the research, a kind of burn-out, that can be another challenge of research at this point, compelling us to dig deep and find a new energy for material that we may well have been working with for many years).

One of the key spiritual challenges at this final stage of research is that of completion itself: of committing to an end point and finishing the work. This can be difficult for some of us. As long as we are still writing the thesis, the book, the article, we can fool ourselves that perfection is possible, that we will manage comprehensive coverage or full systemization, that we will say all that needs to be said. But in the end, we realize we have to settle for 'as good as we can get it' – the imperfect provisional to which we're yet willing to commit. The more of a visionary we are, the higher the ideals we have for ourselves and our research, the harder this part of the process is likely to be. It requires confronting our own limitations, inadequacies and frailty. We'll always be the most severe critics of our own work because we'll know at first hand its flaws, and we'll know only too well what it was we aspired to – and didn't quite manage. (Is there a writer or artist alive who feels they fully achieved their ambitions?)

There's a sense, too, that as soon as we finish the work it becomes something else: it separates from us, becomes 'other', something external, objective, 'out there', available for others' critical scrutiny, reactions, indifference or applause – rather than only a part of our own internal psychic world. And, of course, as soon as we finish it, the research is out of date, obsolete in one sense. The final challenge of completion is to negotiate this transition from internal to external, from 'my' private research to something that has a life of its own in the external, public world (however small a world this may be), from the ideal fantasy of the piece of work as it could be when unfinished to the reality of what it is, for good and for ill, in its finished state.

Yet it is essential to let the work go and to let it be what it will. We have to learn to trust the work itself to do its own work in the world, separate from us. It is a strange relationship we have with our own work, akin to the relationship of parent to child, perhaps. It is our work, yet not ours. We no longer own it, we discover, once we have finished it (if we ever did). It came from others, was fed by others, motivated by them, and now we have to offer it back to them. In doing so, we have to let the work go, and risk it into the world. Sweet Honey in the Rock have a song, entitled 'Our children are not our children', based on words from Khalil Gibran's *Prophet*, which captures for me something of this quality we need to practise in relation to our work:

> Your children are not your children.
> They are the sons and daughters of Life's longing for itself.
> They come through you but not from you,
> And though they are with you yet they belong not to you.[17]

This is part of the research process as spiritual practice: learning to love our work, but also to let it go, to send it out into the public arena; learning to stand by our work, show up/stand up for it, be willing to be visible and accountable for what we have done; but also not being defensive about it, trusting it will do its own work. This is part of a process of claiming our power and visibility as women, claiming our place in the public arena and demanding that our voices be heard – and learning to take the flak alongside the praise and be thrown by neither.

Conclusion: the research process as a spiritual practice of empowerment and transformation

The research journey itself, then, is a kind of paschal process into which we enter: a sharing in the passion of God to make and remake the world, as Adrienne Rich might put it.[18] To this process of justice-making and the seeking of right relation we are willing to offer ourselves, our time, our skills, our bodies, our hearts, our whole selves. In the process, we ourselves are formed and transformed: losing and finding ourselves countless times in the messy, confusing, uncertain processes of research; labouring and struggling and suffering, as well as knowing elation, joy and excitement. We go on a journey in research, which takes us to places we couldn't have imagined at the outset, to landscapes as various as Hopkins' fields, 'plotted and pieced – fold, fallow and plough'.[19] We do not return the same. We are chastened and humbled by our research, discovering that we know much less than we thought we did. Yet we are also emboldened and empowered by it, and by the others with whom we share the process, to claim the truth of what we do know and to proclaim it where it can be heard and where it can make a difference to the world. So we move towards our own risenness as women, claiming an authentic, rightful authority to witness to what we have discovered, speaking into both academy and church (as well as other communities we represent) with conviction and without apology. As we do so, we discover we are not alone, but take others with us as we move together into a world where women and girls, alongside boys and men, can be all that they have it in them to be, and where all can be free.

Notes

1 Audre Lorde, 'The master's tools will never dismantle the master's house', *Sister Outsider*, in *The Audre Lorde Compendium: Essays, Speeches and Journals* (London: Pandora, 1996).

2 Mary Clark Moschella, *Ethnography as a Pastoral Practice: An Introduction* (Cleveland, OH: Pilgrim Press, 2008), p. 12.

3 See my essay, 'The Holy Spirit and spirituality', in Susan Parsons (ed.), *The Cambridge Companion to Feminist Theology* (Cambridge: Cambridge University Press, 2002), pp. 171–89.

4 In this paper, I am primarily addressing women researchers, but I do not wish to imply that *only* women researchers can or do work in the kinds of ways I describe or understand their research as ethical and spiritual practice.

5 Elaine Graham, *Transforming Practice: Pastoral Theology in an Age of Uncertainty* (London: Mowbray, 1996).

6 David Mellott, 'Ethnography as theology: Encountering the Penitentes of Arroyo Seco, New Mexico', unpublished PhD thesis, Emory University, 2005, in Moschella, *Ethnography as a Pastoral Practice*, pp. 90–1.

7 Rosalind Edwards and Jane Ribbens, 'Living on the edges: Public knowledge, private lives, personal experience', in Jane Ribbens and Rosalind Edwards (eds.), *Feminist Dilemmas in Qualitative Research: Public Knowledge and Private Lives* (London: Sage, 1998), pp. 1–23.

8 See the wide range of metaphors used by the women I interviewed to describe their experiences of alienation, including landscape and other natural imagery, in Nicola Slee, *Women's Faith Development: Patterns and Processes* (Aldershot: Ashgate, 2004), chapter 5.

9 Moschella, *Ethnography as a Pastoral Practice*, p. 85.

10 Nelle Morton, *The Journey is Home* (Boston, MA: Beacon Press, 1985), pp. 202–10.

11 Simone Weil, 'Reflections on the right use of school studies with a view to the love of God', *Waiting on God* (Glasgow: Collins Fount, 1977).

12 I owe this threefold distinction between the explicit, the implicit and the null to Maria Harris who, in her beautiful meditation on teaching, *Teaching as Religious Imagination: An Essay in the Theology of Teaching* (San Francisco, CA: Harper & Row, 1987), speaks of the three curricula taught by every institution in these terms.

13 Elisabeth Schüssler Fiorenza, *In Memory of Her: A Feminist Theological Reconstruction of Christian Origins* (London: SCM Press, 1983), chapter 8. Developed in Elisabeth Schüssler Fiorenza, *Discipleship of Equals: A Critical Feminist Ekklesia-logy of Liberation* (New York: Crossroad, 1994).

14 For a definition and discussion of Womenchurch, see Natalie K. Watson, *Introducing Feminist Ecclesiology* (Sheffield: Sheffield Academic Press, 2002), chapter 4.

15 For accounts of *lectio divina*, see note 3 in Chapter 14.

16 I am alluding here to Karl Marx's famous aphorism, 'The philosophers have only interpreted the world, in various ways. The point, however, is to change it.' *Theses on Feuerbach* 11, www.marxists.org/archive/marx/works/1845/theses/ (accessed 26.3.20).

17 Khalil Gibran, *The Prophet*, newthoughtlibrary.com/gibran-khalil/the-prophet/chapters/the-prophet-by-khalil-gibran-004.htm#TopOfText (accessed 26.3.20).

18 Adrienne Rich, 'Natural resources', in *The Dream of a Common Language* (New York and London: W & W Norton, 1978), p. 64. Mary Grey uses this idea of making and making again as a key component in her feminist reworking of atonement theology in *Redeeming the Dream: Feminism, Redemption and Christian Tradition* (London: SPCK, 1989).

19 Gerard Manley Hopkins, 'Pied beauty', in W. H. Gardner and N. H. Mackenzie (eds.), *The Poems of Gerard Manley Hopkins* (London: Oxford University Press, 4th edn, 1967), pp. 69–70.

PART 6

A Feminist Practical Theology
of the Christa

Christa, returning[1]

You think she has left
but she has not. She is resting.

You think she has gone underground
but she has not. She has veiled herself.

You think she is powerless
but she is gathering her power,
drawing it back to herself from where it has been dispersed, scattered.

You think she is not speaking
only because you do not hear the language of her silence.

You think she is alone
but she has never been.

You think she has lost all her names and seasons
but there have always been those who have kept her ways.

You think that the pattern is broken
but see, she spins the chaos into waves and whorls
you can't yet decipher. Keep looking.

She has never left, though you couldn't find her:
it is we who are returning.

Note

1 Originally published in Nicola Slee, *Seeking the Risen Christa* (London: SPCK, 2011), p. 119.

16

Re-imagining Christ as the Coming Girl: An Advent Experiment

The ideas in this piece were first explored in a lecture I gave at Vancouver Cathedral, at the invitation of the Vice-Dean, the Revd Canon Dr Ellen Clark-King, in December 2014. The piece was subsequently published in Jonny Baker, Steve Collins and Cathy Ross (eds.), Future Present: Embodying a Future World Now *(Sheffield: Proost, 2018).*

Introduction

I want to insist on the urgency of dreaming as an imaginative work to which Christians are called and, in this essay, to engage in an experimental act of dreaming of the coming of God in female form, entering our world as a girl. If this strikes the reader as a bizarre or even improper experiment, I crave your indulgence as I seek to make my case for this being a proper theological endeavour, grounded in scripture and Christian tradition, and one that may make a significant contribution to Christian faith and practice today.

First I will sketch out the central role of dreams and imagination in Christian life, after which I will trace the notion of God coming in female flesh in Christian theology, not only in contemporary feminist theology but also in more ancient times.[1] I will suggest that the eschatological dimension of Christian faith – particularly evident in the Advent season, but a core strand of biblical faith – invites us to look forward with anticipation and expectation to the coming of Christ in novel and unexpected ways. I will suggest that, while the Jesus of history was male, Jewish, Palestinian and young, the Christ/a of faith can – and, indeed, must – manifest in a much more expanded repertoire of human faces and forms, if different groups of people throughout the world are to know themselves 'made in the image of God' and access the truth of the incarnation in their own flesh and lives. While the idea of a female Christ figure – the so-called Christa – has been developed over a number of decades in feminist theology out of its more ancient lineage, the notion of Christa as a *girl* is rarely heard or developed, reflecting the lack of attention to the lives, needs and gifts of girls in feminist theology, as well as in theology more broadly. I will argue that there are particular political and theological reasons for developing the notion of Christa as a girl,[2] not least as a contribution to a more authentic theology of childhood within the Christian community.

The urgent work of dreaming

Common parlance tends to speak of 'dreamers' as those who are not in touch with reality, drifting and dreaming their lives away, living in a fantasy world of make-believe. Yet Christian faith holds dreaming in high esteem. From Jacob to Daniel, from Joseph of Nazareth to Pilate's wife, the Bible is full of stories of dreams and dreamers; it is a primary means by which God communicates to people – and not only to people of faith. While Jesus does not speak of dreaming directly, many of his parables have the quality of intense, surreal dreams.

Throughout the ages, poets and theologians, among others, exemplify this work of dreaming: they are those who imagine the world, God and human beings not merely as they *are* but as they *might be*. Imagination is a profoundly prophetic faculty – the vision of what might be critiques and judges the corruption of the present and the failures of the past. Our imagination is the faculty of transcendence, that capacity within us for reaching above and beyond the limitations of the present. While the body can be imprisoned, tortured and killed, the imagination cannot be owned by anyone, which is why totalitarian regimes tend to fear and seek to eliminate artists, poets and people of religious faith. They know that imagination is a dangerous faculty of freedom.

Imagination is vital for feminists and for any group who do not wish to put up with present political reality. Patriarchy, colonialism, racism and every other system of oppression will not be overcome by brute force, strategy or intellectual argument so much as by a radical reclaiming of language, symbol and story to articulate an alternative reality. Feminists are those who dream that the world might be different from its present rule by male power and its endemic violence and misogyny. They seek to tell new stories, or to articulate old stories in new ways, in order to imagine what the world might look like if women's experiences were taken seriously, if women and girls were assumed to possess agency to claim and use their own power, if women and girls were made, equally with men and boys, in the image of God – as Christians surely believe they are.

So I invite you to come with me, in this essay, in an exercise of feminist imagination, a work of dreaming of how God might come to us in new forms and ways, and specifically as a girl. I offer this experiment in both playful and deadly serious mode. It is an invitation to perceive God incarnate among us in new ways and to glimpse anew the sacral nature of human flesh; specifically, it is an attempt to lift up the bodies and lives of girls as holy and precious, capable of imagining and reflecting the incarnate God. I intend this experiment to be subversive of tired and stock ways of thinking about the advent of God in Christ, an exercise in free thinking, which may be challenging, critical and hopeful.

In many ways, the idea that God may be among us in female form is hardly a novel idea. Yet the specific notion that Christ/a might be born among us as a girl, and attention to the image of the girl as a symbol for Christ, is more unusual. As Anne Phillips and others have pointed out,[3] the faith lives of girls have been neglected in feminist as well as mainstream theology until very recently; attention to the specific needs and experiences of girls, as well as the gifts they might bring to Christian faith, has been rare. I hope this experiment in imagining Christ/a as a girl may help to reverse this trend.

'It's a girl!'

There's a cartoon which I've seen both online and in various versions as a Christmas card; it shows Mary and Joseph in the stable, with the crib centre stage. Mary has a startled look on her face as she gazes into the crib, and the speech bubble declares, 'It's a girl!' Here's my version of this, as a poem:

> The news spread like wildfire.
> Sages were perplexed.
> Astronomers recalculated their stars.
> Shepherds sloped back to their charges.
> Only the midwives smiled their knowing smiles.
> And the angels crowded round,
> singing 'Glory! Glory!'[4]

The cartoon works precisely because it is amusing, if not shocking, to imagine Christ coming as a girl. But why is it such a startling idea? There's another, rather less well-known version of this joke, which tells how God *did* come as a girl, and no one took the slightest bit of notice of anything she said or did, nothing got passed on or written down, so God had to start again and send a boy. And the rest is history.

> Come as a girl.
> *I did. Nobody noticed.*

> Come as a girl.
> *I do. Open your eyes, your mind, your stoppered ears.*

Come as a girl.
I will. I am still arriving among you,
looking for a safe place to be born,
a welcome, a home.[5]

What if?

Could God have come as a girl? While to some Christians this seems a ludicrous notion, and I have met those who suggest it is blasphemous even to
ask the question, the issue was taken seriously by early theologians and was
a matter of considerable debate, particularly among medieval theologians.
As Janet Martin Soskice puts it, 'The conclusion, that it was fitting that
Christ be born a man, was never in doubt, yet the arguments are worth
noting by anyone interested in the symbolics of sex.'[6] After reviewing a
variety of these arguments, Soskice comes to the most common one, typified
by Aquinas in the *Summa Theologiae*: 'Because the male excels the female
sex, Christ assumed a man's nature' – though this is balanced by the addi-
tional comment, 'So that people should not think little of the female sex, it
was fitting that he should take flesh from a woman.'[7] Even while the great
theologian attempts to retain respect for female flesh, paralleling the body
of Mary with the infant Christ-child's flesh, it is clear that he still thinks, as
does the little girl in her letter to God, that 'boys are best'.[8]

I want to suggest that it is not a ludicrous idea that Christ might have
come – and might yet come – as a girl, but is, in fact, an idea expressive of
some core Christian theological principles. In particular, the eschatological
dimension of Christian faith orients us towards the endless future coming
of Christ in forms and ways that will take us by surprise and for which
we are not prepared. Christianity is, of course, a historical tradition with
roots in a specific history – the history of Israel, as well as the history of
Jesus of Nazareth and the early church; there is nothing in what I wish to
propose that denies or seeks to undo that specific history. Yet the notion
that Christianity is a historical tradition does not *only* point to its rooted-
ness in the past; it also expresses its dynamic unfolding over time and its
openness to future development. History is not only about the past, it is
also about the emergent and the future forms that a tradition might take
and, indeed, must take if it is not to ossify in the past.

Advent eschatology

The eschatological dimension of Christian faith comes to the fore particularly in the Advent season, when the liturgy of the church looks forward
to the second coming of Christ in glory and judgement, as well as offering

a period of preparation for the celebration of the first coming of Christ as a vulnerable child.

Advent is a time of preparation for the 'second' coming of Christ; and I want to say, for the third, fourth, fifth, fiftieth and hundredth coming of Christ, not in some future apocalyptic end-time but in the real historical future that is just around the next corner, the next day or month or year. Advent is a looking forward as well as backward: it is a time to anticipate newness rather than mere repetition of the gospel story we (think we) all know and love. Above all, Advent is a dynamic period of expectation, arousal and awe for the coming of that which we do not yet know: the Christ who is not yet born among us, the Christ who is strange and unfamiliar to us, the Christ who comes in ever new forms, as the stranger, the incognito, the unrecognized and unwelcomed, the neglected and the marginalized.

The notion of the Christ incognito is a strong biblical theme. Jesus' teaching is full of stories about the coming one who is unexpected and unprepared for, whether this is the master who returns unexpectedly at midnight (Mark 13.35) or the bridegroom who appears when the bridesmaids are asleep (Matthew 25.1–13). Paul speaks of the coming of Christ as a 'thief in the night' at a time and an hour when he is least expected (1 Thessalonians 5.2). But it is not only the *time* that is unexpected; the form, too, of the future Christ is strange and unexpected. This is particularly evident in the resurrection narratives in the Gospels. A recurring theme in these strange stories is the fact that the risen Christ is not recognized by his disciples (for example, Luke 24.13–35; John 20.1–18; John 21.1–8) and I want to suggest that this is a theme of core theological significance. It is more than the lack of recognition by those who are unprepared to meet one whom they believe to be dead, returned to life in their midst. There is the strong suggestion, in many of the narratives of the resurrection that the risen Christ is strange and different from the earthly form of the historical Jesus. (S)he is the same and yet not the same. They fail to recognize him (her?) and do not know how to respond to him (her). A BBC and HBO film of Christ's passion, produced in 2008, reflected this feature of the resurrection narratives by showing different actors appearing very briefly in different episodes, suggesting the fluidity of the risen Christ.[9]

This is deeply significant. The risen Christ is in continuity with the historical Jesus yet is so much more expansive. Whereas the historical Jesus was male, Jewish, Palestinian, young (yet we do not know what he looked like), the risen Christ is none of these – or all of them and more. Whereas the historical Jesus walked among us in one specific and utterly unique human body, affirming the closeness of God to all human flesh, the risen Christ cannot be confined by particularities of gender, race, age or bodily form. The forms the Christ will take are novel, strange, unrecognized, subversive, pushing the boundaries of the known and familiar. Christ may, indeed does, manifest as African, Asian, Polynesian, as well as European, appearing as black and not only white (so often we think of Jesus as white, and the image of the white Christ has reinforced white supremacy). Christ may manifest as old (something the earthly Jesus never experienced), as disabled, blind, with mental health issues; as gay, trans or queer – and as female, as well as male. If Christ incorporates all human life and experience, and 'saves' humanity by his flesh-taking, then it must be possible to imagine Christ as female, gay, black, blind. If not, we might as well stop baptizing women, blacks, gays and disabled people (and there have been times in history as well as in the present when, of course, some of these groups have been excluded from the fellowship of the church and denied access to God's welcome table).

Thus, at Advent most particularly, but at any time of the year, we are invited to welcome the Christ who continues to be born among us: black and white, young and old, male and female (and gender queer), in likely and unlikely places. And, as the historical Jesus was born a poor refugee among an oppressed and despised people, to parents whose sexual relationship was at the very least unconventional, so Christ/a continues to be born among us as the vulnerable, unprotected and unnoticed one dwelling among the poor, the despised and oppressed. It just turns out that, in our own time, this is most likely to be a girl child.

The girl child in our own time

Both at the time of Jesus and in our own world, the child remains the most powerful symbol of those who are most radically powerless and dispossessed – and the girl child very particularly. In a global setting, girls are still those most likely to be aborted or abandoned at birth, deprived of education, healthcare and basic rights, at risk of sexual and physical abuse and trafficking. There are plenty of statistics to prove it,[10] and daily on our TV screens we see and hear examples of the vulnerability and abuse of women and girls around the world. In times of war, women and girls are most likely to be raped and displaced from their homes; in so-called 'peace' time, women and girls are most at threat from domestic violence, malnourishment and slavery in their own homes.

In such a world, looking and longing for the coming of God as a girl is not simply a wishful fantasy, a joke or a feminist whim, but an urgent desire for liberation and healing for these vulnerable little ones. It is a cry to the God who identifies with the little ones and the least among men to come among us anew as a young girl, sharing the danger and the delight, the potential and the immense risk of female flesh.

As previously mentioned, the girl is a neglected site in theology – hardly visible in scripture or tradition or in contemporary theology. Anne Phillips reviews the relevant scriptural texts on girls, demonstrating how scant the material is and how, even where girls are present in scripture, they are almost always unnamed and passed over as insignificant.[11] Even feminist theology has ignored girls until very recently, perhaps due to the critique of women's identities and value being limited to marriage and motherhood in patriarchy (so also, motherhood has been neglected within feminist theology).[12] Boyhood has been more visible in Christian tradition, far more imaged in paintings, stained glass and other forms of iconography through the boyhood of Christ and other significant male figures such as Moses, Samuel, David and so on. Of course, much of the iconography of childhood in Christian tradition is deeply problematic: images of Christ as a boy are frequently sentimental and idealized, and hardly offer helpful resources for thinking about the faith lives of children, including boys, today. There is undoubtedly an urgent need to consider the faith lives of boys and to relate newly emerging masculinities to our thinking about the changing needs and gifts of boys and men within the life of the church.[13] Yet the even greater degree of invisibility of girls within Christian faith, in a global setting of risk and danger to girlhood, points to my focus in this essay on girls specifically, rather than children more generally.

The girl as a symbol of the be-coming God

In a highly suggestive article, Marcella Althaus-Reid (one of our most daring and original theological dreamers) speaks of the girl as 'the becoming of the becoming woman, and of all becomings'.[14] The girl is poised on the threshold of womanhood, in the liminal state of pure potential, embodying the manifold choices and possibilities that lie before every human being at birth, yet may be most vulnerable to being squashed in the female child. Research conducted into the development of girls has painted a fairly consistent picture of the ways in which the freedom and experimentation of early childhood become increasingly constrained for girls as they grow closer to puberty and to taking on the expectations of adult femininity. Some research suggests that girls quite literally lose their voices as they approach puberty and become prey to adult pressures to 'tone down' their style, their bodily gestures and movements, as well as their opinions (young girls may run, climb trees, shout and swagger freely, yet this is not how 'young ladies' are expected to comport themselves).[15]

The enormous pressures on young women to look and dress in particular ways, to be small and thin and to take up little room in the world, may manifest in anorexia and other eating disorders,[16] as well as in a lack of academic and other kinds of confidence. Some girls experience a sense of dread, anxiety and depression as they approach puberty and recognize that they will be expected to conform to notions of femininity with which they do not identify. Of course, boys are also subject to very considerable social pressures to conform to dominant notions of masculinity, although these generally enshrine more agency and power than dominant notions of femininity. And of course, too, the lives of girls in many parts of the world where such research has not been conducted are even more at risk from other, more basic, denial of human rights (shelter, education, food, privacy and healthcare, and so on). In so many ways, the potential of girls to become all that they have it in them to become – the full flowering of their humanity and the potential to contribute in novel and original ways to their communities and world – is threatened and undermined.

The symbol of the Christa who comes as a girl speaks into this reality at a number of different levels. First, it expresses the identification of God in Christ with the experiences of girls and, most particularly, with their struggles and suffering. God is not indifferent to such life-threatening suffering but enters into it, taking the risks and threats to life experienced routinely by girls, into God's very own flesh and being. Second, the symbol of the Christa who comes as a girl expresses the longing of God for the survival of girls, and the commitment of God towards the salvation and flourishing of girls. Rachel Starr has recently argued for a model of salvation as survival, suggesting this is a more authentic and helpful model of salvation than many existing models rooted in violent theologies of atonement or sacrificial suffering.[17] The Christa who comes as a girl and survives all the threats to her well-being is a powerful symbol of the capacity of girls to withstand all that threatens their survival and flourishing in the world. The God who is for us stands with and alongside girls in their vulnerability and potential as they struggle against the forces of denial and death that would abort their potential before it has even begun to be released. Third, the symbol of the Christa who comes as a girl affirms the girl as a symbol of the be-coming God. Our images and models of God function deeply at both the psychological and sociological level, as well as theologically, to model what we believe about human nature. As Mary Daly put it decades ago, 'if God is male, then the male is God';[18] and, conversely, if God is never imaged in female terms, then women and girls do not know themselves to be made in the image of God. So the symbol of Christa as a girl speaks very powerfully of the ways in which girls may incarnate and represent God present and at work in the world.

So what?

What might it mean to take seriously the notion that young girls can represent and symbolize the coming of Christ/a in our midst? It would mean taking the gifts and experiences of girls seriously in the worship, theology and life of the church more generally; it would mean listening to them seriously and regarding them not only as 'future church' but as present church. It would mean expecting to learn and receive from girls, and not only seeing ourselves as those who teach and nurture them. It would mean committing to their full visibility in the life of the church, searching for scriptures and stories and images of girls that are positive and affirming of the potential of girls.[19] It would also mean taking seriously the risk and danger to girls in our society and world, and having courage to name these realities in Christian worship and teaching. It would mean regarding girls, as well as children generally, as theologians who might teach us, as well as disciples who learn with us in the lifelong process of becoming what we are called to be.

And it would mean praying to God in female language, imagery and symbols, as we actively look for the myriad ways in which Christ/a comes to us afresh. Thus I end this essay with one such prayer, which I invite readers to try praying in the season of Advent – or, indeed, at any other time of the year.

Christa, our sister,
come to us in female flesh,
tasting the danger and delight of any young girl's growing;
bleeding as we bleed,
loving as we love,
learning to claim our womanly power
as God's redemptive presence in the world.[20]

Notes

1 For a much fuller exploration of the notion of the Christa, see Nicola Slee, *Seeking the Risen Christa* (London: SPCK, 2011).

2 In this essay, I shall use the term 'Christa' to refer to the female Christ form, while 'Christ/a' is an attempt to incorporate both male and female (and gender ambivalent) forms of the Christ.

3 Anne Phillips, *The Faith of Girls: Children's Spirituality and Transition to Adulthood* (Farnham: Ashgate, 2011), is a landmark text that breaks new ground in the study of the faith of girls, and I owe much to Anne for my own developing awareness of the significance of the theological study of girlhood. Most of what is in this essay is directly dependent on Anne's work. See also Dori Grinenko Baker, *Doing Girlfriend Theology: God-Talk with Young Women* (Cleveland, OH: Pilgrim Press, 2005), and Joyce A. Mercer, *Girl Talk, God Talk: Why Faith Matters to Adolescent Girls – and Their Parents* (San Francisco, CA: Jossey Bass, 2008).

4 Nicola Slee, 'It's a girl', in Gavin D'Costa, Eleanor Nesbitt, Mark Pryce, Ruth Shelton and Nicola Slee, *Making Nothing Happen: Five Poets Explore Faith and Spirituality* (Farnham: Ashgate, 2014), p. 38.

5 'Come as a girl', in Slee, *Seeking the Risen Christa*, p. 33.

6 Janet Martin Soskice, *The Kindness of God: Metaphor, Gender, and Religious Language* (Oxford: Oxford University Press, 2008), p. 85.

7 Thomas Aquinas, *Summa Theologiae* 3a, 31, 4 (London: Eyre & Spottiswoode, 1964).

8 In *Children's Letters to God*, ed. Stuart Hemple and Eric Marshall (London: HarperCollins, 1976), Sylvia's letter goes, 'Dear God, Are boys better than girls? I know you are one, but try to be fair.'

9 'The Passion', by Frank Deasy, directed by Michael Offer, BBC Productions and HBO Films, originally broadcast on BBC1 in March 2008.

10 See, for example, www.unwomen.org/en/news/in-focus/commission-on-the-status-of-women-2012/facts-and-figures and www.worldbank.org/en/topic/gender/overview (accessed 5 January 2018).

11 See Phillips, *The Faith of Girls*, pp. 1–3, 73–4, 163–5.

12 An important exception is Bonnie J. Miller-McLamure, *Also a Mother: Work and Family as Theological Dilemma* (Nashville, TN: Abingdon Press, 1994).

13 See, for example, Mark Pryce, *Finding a Voice: Men, Women and the Community of the Church* (London: SCM Press, 1996); David Anderson, Paul Hill and Roland Martinson, *Coming of Age: Exploring the Identity and Spirituality of Younger Men* (Minneapolis, MN: Augsberg Fortress, 2006).

14 Marcella Althaus-Reid, 'The bi/girl writings: From feminist theology to queer theologies', in Lisa Isherwood (ed.), *Post-Christian Feminisms: A Critical Approach* (Aldershot: Ashgate, 2008), p. 112.

15 For a comprehensive review and discussion of relevant research, see Phillips, *The Faith of Girls*, chapter 2.

16 Lisa Isherwood, *The Fat Jesus: Feminist Explorations in Boundaries and Transgressions* (London: Darton, Longman & Todd, 2008), provides a strong critique of the slimming industry aimed at young girls and endorsed by Evangelical religion, particularly in the USA.

17 Rachel Starr, *Reimagining Theologies of Marriage in Contexts of Domestic Violence: When Salvation is Survival* (London: Routledge, 2018).

18 Mary Daly, *Beyond God the Father: Towards a Philosophy of Women's Liberation* (London: Women's Press, 2nd edn, 1986), p. 19.

19 This is not easy; as already mentioned, there are very few stories about girls in the Bible and even when girls are mentioned, they are often nameless or passive objects in a male world. However, Anne Phillips highlights some possibilities, such as Hosea and Gomer's daughter Lo-ruhamah (Hosea 1.6, 8), Namaan's (unnamed) servant girl in 2 Kings 5, the daughters of Zelophehad (Numbers 27), Jairus' daughter (Mark 5.21–43 and parallels), the servant girl Rhoda (Acts 12.13–15) and, of course, Mary the mother of Jesus, who was likely to have been little more than a teenager when she became pregnant (see Elizabeth Johnson, *Truly Our Sister: A Theology of Mary in the Communion of Saints* (New York: Continuum, 2003), part 4, for a helpful account of Mary's young life).

20 Slee, *Seeking the Risen Christa*, p. 148.

17

#Me Too: A Reflection on Edwina Sandys' *Christa*

This is the text of a sermon preached at Jesus College, Cambridge, February 2018, which formed part of a series for the Lent term reflecting on a variety of visual images of Christ. I am grateful to the Revd Dr Paul Dominiak, Dean of Chapel and Fellow of the College, for this invitation, which gave me the opportunity to reflect anew on the 'original' Christa, the sculpture created by Edwina Sandys.

Sometimes it takes the shock of a radical displacement for us to see what we think we know well, as if for the first time.

Figure 1: Edwina Sandys' *Christa* sculpture, in the Cathedral of St John the Divine, New York. Photo by Nicola Slee.

Gazing at Edwina Sandys' sculpture of the suffering, crucified Christ in female form, what do we see?[1] How do we react to the passion of Christ displayed in female flesh? With confusion? Anger? Revulsion? With a sense of attraction, or recognition, as if we have understood and received something for the first time which we knew somewhere deep down but had not fully realized until now? All of these – and more – are possible. There is no 'right' response. If we have never encountered the idea or the image of a female Christ form before, we might want to take particular note of our reactions and consider what they tell us – about ourselves, about our assumptions about God and whether or not we are able to recognize God in female flesh.

Marcella Althaus-Reid, one of Britain's most creative and daring theologians, much missed by many of us, speaks about the way in which certain images of Christ can 'undress' or make visible our deepest, instinctual reactions.[2] So a black Christ, if we react to such an image with horror or shock, reveals to us our own unthinking racism; a gay Christ similarly undresses our internalized homophobia; and if our instinctual reaction to a female Christ is of something blasphemous, perhaps our own fear or hatred of female flesh is being laid bare. In such ways, the naked, vulnerable Christ of the passion exposes and probes our own vulnerability and nakedness, invites us to confront aspects of ourselves and our values that we may prefer to leave in the dark.

If you *have* come across the figure of the female Christ, it's very likely you know this image – although there are others, scores of them in fact. Edwina Sandys, a British artist living in New York, created this sculpture in 1975, without pre-meditation – she got the idea in a traffic jam! It was shown first in London, then exhibited in Rome, Toronto, New York, Washington and Kansas City. It was when the sculpture was displayed at the Cathedral of St John the Divine, New York, during Holy Week 1984, that the work came to widespread public attention through intense media coverage, evoking visceral and vociferous reactions. After 11 days, amid a raging controversy, *Christa* was taken down and banished from the cathedral.

I've long known this image, until recently in reproductions only, often quite bad ones. To tell you the truth, in contrast with some other images of a female Christ figure, I've never felt particularly drawn to this one. Something about the muscularity of the form and the shaded face, which is difficult to see well in photographs, left me always feeling at a distance, unable to connect to the form. That is, until I saw the sculpture 'for real', 'in the flesh' so to speak, around this time last year. The Cathedral of St John has reinstalled Sandys' *Christa* permanently in the Chapel of St Saviour, one of the many chapels that fringe the main body of the church. It is displayed centrally against the magnificent stained-glass window in the chapel, hanging over the altar in the chapel.

Figure 2: Close-up of Edwina Sandys' *Christa* sculpture, in the Cathedral of St John the Divine, New York. Photo by Nicola Slee.

I find it difficult to put into words the impact of seeing the *Christa* at last, after decades of knowing about her; not in some art gallery or educational venue, but in sacred space, in a cathedral, in *the* most sacred space possible – over the altar where the Eucharist is celebrated, where Christ's passion, death and resurrection are honoured and remembered, where the body and blood of Christ are blessed, broken, shared and consumed. Here is a poem I wrote, which tries to capture something of my experience:

On seeing Edwina Sandys' *Christa*

Chapel of St Saviour, Cathedral of St John the Divine

She is here
at last
over the altar

this body I have known
all my life
but did not receive 'til now

the strange beauty
of her dark, muscular form
her shadowed, lowered face

She hangs solid as any human body
her bronze form glinting in light
from the February sky

The pilgrims come and go
kneeling before her
or sitting long in her presence

Suspended, wide open
body of woman
given for us

She is the one
raised, reviled, rejected
risen among us

She will never cease
her witness
within and beyond us

The mass that is only just beginning
will never have an ending
at last we may go in peace

There is a profound theology at work in this sculpture, developed not in words but in bronze, in the body of the naked, suspended woman. In the very place where, for centuries, women have been forbidden to break the holy bread and even denied access when menstruating, in *this* very place, the body of a woman over the altar tells us that God abhors no flesh. As the Christmas hymn puts it, God did 'not abhor the Virgin's womb'; on the contrary, God took flesh within the body of a woman, was born from a bleeding woman's vagina and suckled at her breast. Henceforth, all female flesh is holy and worthy of the highest honour. When the priest at the altar proclaims, 'this is my body, this is my blood', we can hear it as an affirmation of all bodies and all bleeding as essentially sacred, not simply the one body and shed blood of the man Jesus.

In particular, Edwina Sandys' *Christa* speaks of women's pain and suffering, both now and in the past, as God's suffering and pain. Every girl child aborted before birth, or thrown out naked at her birth and lying uncovered in her blood, *is* Christ, Christa, crying out to God for redemption – as the extraordinary passage from Ezekiel 16 which we heard as our first reading described. God is the one who sees the abandoned infant and lifts her up, washes and clothes her, covers her nakedness, and tells her to 'live' and 'grow up like a plant in the field' (Ezekiel 16.6–7). Every teenage girl trafficked across borders and sold for sex, every woman raped in war or in her own bed, every student or actress harassed or abused, *is* Christ, Christa, and wherever the bodies of women and girls are systematically or randomly attacked and violated, there the body of God bleeds.

If we think the idea of Christ as an abused woman is far-fetched, perhaps we need to go back to the scriptures and study the gospel accounts of the passion of Christ again. In our second reading (Mark 15.15–27) we heard the well-known account of Christ's trial before Pilate, his mocking and stripping and crucifixion. It is so well known that we don't see or hear it for what it is: a brutal display of the power of the state in an act of sexual humiliation as well as extreme physical torture. Professor David Tombs, a scholar based at Otago University, has made a close study of the gospel account of Christ's passion and argues convincingly that crucifixion, as employed by the Romans, was a form of sexual torture and violence. He describes the scene we have heard read as follows:

> An adult man was stripped naked for flogging, then dressed in an insulting way to be mocked, struck and spat at by a multitude of soldiers (note that Jesus is brought before Pilate *and the cohort*, i.e., up to 1,000 armed soldiers, in a huge arena) – before being stripped again and reclothed for his journey ... only to be stripped again and displayed to die while naked to a mocking crowd.[3]

We don't see the scene in all its sexual aggression and humiliation because almost all representations of the crucifixion show Jesus wearing a loincloth rather than naked, with only a few soldiers standing around Pilate, rather than displayed naked before a vast crowd of soldiers. We have only to think of some of the ugly scenes of torture and humiliation inflicted on captives in our day, or the way in which rape is used routinely as a weapon of war, to get a sense of what was going on at Jesus' crucifixion. For the soldiers, off duty and able to let down their guard for a few hours, this was an occasion of sport, a way of venting their own sexual frustration and, at the same time, enjoy the ritual humiliation of a representative of one of Rome's vassal provinces.

The notion that Jesus was sexually assaulted, possibly even raped, in the lead-up to his crucifixion, may be as startling and shocking to us – more, perhaps – than the idea of a female Christ. Yet it underlines what Christians have always claimed about Christ's passion: that God in Christ has experienced and borne the worst that humanity can do to its own. The figure of the Christa, Tombs suggests, is one of the few places where we can begin to glimpse the horrific and sexual nature of Christ's crucifixion, since the naked crucified female form evokes for most viewers the reality of women's sexual abuse and humiliation. It is the place, if you like, where we can hear God saying, 'Me Too'. 'I have been there with you, whenever and wherever women's bodies have been aborted, humiliated, assaulted, abused, raped and then blamed and shamed.'

Yet we can't stop here. There is a danger, as some critics of the *Christa* have suggested, that such images of naked female suffering will simply reinforce the sexualization and victimization of women, if we do not also hear God saying 'No more!' The passion of the Christa speaks, first, of God's absolute identification with all human – and most especially, all female – suffering, oppression and abuse; but we also need to understand it as the divine protest against all unjust suffering. God in Christ/a has suffered the most appalling humiliation and death precisely so that no one else need do so. All the violence and hatred and aggression, whether sexual or of other kinds, needs to stop right here – in the body of God, who absorbs it all into Godself and refuses to give back anything but love.

Edwina Sandys has said, 'I like looking up at Christa and seeing her look down on me in a compassionate way.'[4] As we gaze on the Christa and make our own responses – which will be as varied as we are – my prayer is that we will be able to receive something of the compassion of God for our vulnerability, suffering and brokenness, and that we may exercise that same compassion on the bodies of all suffering, vulnerable flesh – whether human, animal or even vegetable and mineral, since we know that the body of the earth and of the seas suffers and bleeds at our abuse. As we identify with the passion of the Christa in many hidden ways and places, may we also have the courage to say 'No more'; to proclaim to all who suffer and are humiliated, 'Live and grow like a plant in the field'(Ezekiel 16.6–7).

Notes

1 Reproduced in a number of places on the web, including www.stjohndivine.org/art/the-christa-project; https://happylutheran.blog/2017/02/05/the-christa-project/; https://twitter.com/stjohndivinenyc/status/970774557794631682 (accessed 27.3.20).

2 Marcella Althaus-Reid, *Indecent Theology: Theological Perversions in Sex, Gender and Politics* (London: Routledge, 2000), pp. 110–16.

3 David Tombs, 'Crucifixion, State Terror, and Sexual Abuse', *Union Seminary Quarterly Review* 53 (1999), p. 104.

4 Edwina Sandys, in Caroline Seebohm, *Edwina Sandys Art* (New York: Glitterati, 2011), p. 58.

18

The Crucified Christa: A Re-evaluation[1]

This is the most recent piece in the book, written as a contribution to Jayme R. Reaves, David Tombs and Rocío Figueroa Alvear (eds.), When Did We See You Naked? Acknowledging Jesus as a Victim of Sexual Abuse (London: SCM Press, forthcoming). I first met David several decades ago, when he came to teach at Roehampton University (then Institute of Higher Education), just as I was leaving; I have got to know Jayme more recently, as one of a number of honorary research fellows at Queen's. Their joint work on Jesus as a victim of sexual abuse is of wide-ranging theological significance and I am glad to have the opportunity in this essay to engage with it from the perspective of Christa and feminist Christology.

Introduction

There is a compelling body of evidence to suggest that the historical Jesus was sexually assaulted and very possibly raped as part of the state machinery of crucifixion.[2] That the idea of Jesus being a victim of sexual abuse remains scandalous and abhorrent to the majority of Christian believers is due, in large part, to the falsification of visual representations of the death of Jesus in Christian art, which, as Jayme Reaves and David Tombs argue, 'misrepresent the historical scene and suppress the disturbing truth'. By covering up Jesus' nakedness, and in other ways, Christian art tends 'to suppress the sense of violence and threat in the scene'.[3]

One place where the nakedness, sexual humiliation and abuse of Jesus *do* come together in public view – albeit in an unexpected, re-gendered form that is not well known by the majority of Christian believers or even theologians – is in the so-called Christa, or the female Christ figure.[4] In multiple images of the Christa, found in a wide variety of media by a wide range of artists, she is fully naked on a cross or in cruciform shape, suggestive of the sexual humiliation, abuse and victimization of women, and associating sexual violence against women with the Christ event. In their recent article, Reaves and Tombs note the possible significance of the Christa in passing, referring to the work of Elaine Heath who, in her book *We Were the Least of These*, calls attention to Edwina Sandys' sculpture, *Christa*, as a shocking and controversial image that 'links Jesus's crucifixion with the sexual abuse of women'.[5] Yet neither Reaves and Tombs nor Heath pursue the topic or consider the ambivalence of a suffering and crucified naked woman as a religious symbol. This is the remit I set myself in this chapter, drawing upon and extending my earlier work on the Christa[6] in order to consider how the image of the Christa might express and reflect the sexual abuse of the historical Jesus as well as that of countless women, children and men throughout history and in our own time. I want to critically interrogate images of the crucified Christa in order to explore the ambivalence of this symbol, particularly in relation to the key features of nakedness and sexual abuse which are prominent features of most (but not all) such images.[7]

I shall argue that, while images (and associated theologies) of the Christa are important in exposing and bringing to judgement sexual abuse, in all its various historic and contemporary forms (including that of Jesus of Nazareth), such representations may also be problematic and are as a genre therefore ambivalent. As others, including myself, have previously argued, notions of the Christa that fuse the violent suffering, abuse and death of women into a central image of a crucified woman may reinforce cultural tropes of woman as helpless suffering victim, as object of male sexual voyeurism, and as responsible for (sexual) sin, rather than challenging and reworking patriarchal representations of the female body. Replacing the idealized, youthful and covered body of a European male Jesus with that of a young, thin, white naked female form, in visual representations of Christ, may also mask the racism and ableism of much cultural and theological thought, as well as the necrophiliac obsession with suffering and death that feminists such as Mary Daly[8] and Grace Jantzen[9] have critiqued. At the same time, the symbol of a naked, crucified female Christ figure may deflect attention away from the historical reality of Jesus' sexual abuse and make it more difficult for contemporary believers to confront the scandal of Jesus' passion and death. It may thereby unwittingly deny and protect male nakedness from being incorporated into a contemporary religious imaginary. The figure of the Christa, while an important and necessary corrective to the Christolatry that has reified masculinity in Christian thought and practice and denied the feminine divine, will only be a potent religious symbol if it finds a wide range of forms beyond that of a suffering and/or dying Christa *and* if the male Christ symbol is also reworked in significant ways that embrace male sexual vulnerability and that show forth the ethnic as well as sexual diversity of contemporary masculinities.[10]

My argument will proceed in a number of stages. First, I will review visual representations of the Christa to demonstrate both the wide range of such images and their tendency to reinforce certain dominant tropes, such as passive suffering, sexual victimization, nakedness, white privilege, youthfulness and idealized versions of the (white) feminine form. Next, I will consider ways in which nakedness has been gendered in Christian thinking, culture and representation, in order to investigate different meanings of a male and female naked Christ figure. I will propose that a naked male Christ does not carry similar or parallel meanings to that of a naked female Christa; they function very differently in the cultural and religious imaginary in ways that challenge any equivalence of forms. This will bring the discussion back to some specific images of the Christa, in order to consider different renderings of female subjectivity, sexuality and agency. I will suggest that, while some images and readings of the Christa may contribute positively towards a reworked feminist imaginary, others have no useful place in contemporary religious thought or practice. I will conclude with a sequence of statements or hypotheses that attempt to summarize the wide-ranging argument.

The crucified Christa in feminist art and theology

The figure of the female Christ or the Christa has been a recurring motif in Christian feminist theological writings[11] since the 1970s (although the idea and image of a female Christ figure have a much older history[12]), provoked by the creation of a sculpture of that name by Edwina Sandys in 1974 for the United Nations Decade for Women: Equality, Development and Peace (1976–85).[13] The sculpture – a nude woman wearing a crown of thorns with arms outstretched in the form of a crucified figure – was originally displayed in the Cathedral of St John the Divine, New York, during Holy Week 1984, but quickly removed by the Dean of the cathedral in response to the strongly divided reactions from those who viewed it. Only recently, in 2017, has the sculpture been reinstated in the cathedral, in the Chapel of St Saviour, forming the focal point of a large exhibition entitled 'The Christa Project' and now on permanent display over the altar in one of the side chapels. In the catalogue for the exhibition, there is a short statement by Edwina Sandys about the sculpture, in which she states: '*Christa* means many things to many people. To me, Christ on the cross symbolizes sacrifice – *Christa* symbolizes the sacrifice of woman.' She describes the making of the sculpture as a 'largely subconscious act' that was 'not a conscious feminist statement', although she 'wanted to make it as womanly as possible'.[14]

At around the same time as Sandys' creation of *Christa*, a second sculpture, *Crucified Woman*, was made by Almuth Lutkenhause-Lackey in 1974,[15] and displayed in the chancel of Bloor Street United Church, Toronto, during Lent, Holy Week and Eastertide 1979. Lutkenhause-Lackey was initially hesitant about lending the sculpture to a church, 'arguing that my message was merely a portrayal of human suffering'. Yet 'being asked, "Can you see Christ in a Chinese man? Can you see Christ in a black man? Can you see Christ – in a woman?" made [her] change [her] view.' The artist comments: 'I was deeply touched by the many women who told me that for the first time they had felt close to Christ, seeing suffering expressed in a female body.'[16] She subsequently offered the work as a gift to Emmanuel College, Toronto, and the sculpture was installed in the grounds in 1986.

A third graphic sculpture, *Christine on the Cross*, by James M. Murphy, was exhibited in James Memorial Chapel, at Union Theological Seminary in New York, Easter 1984, at the same time as Sandys' *Christa* was on display in the cathedral (Union is only a few blocks away from the Cathedral of St John the Divine).[17] Murphy's sculpture shows a woman pinned to an inverted cross, with her legs spread-eagled and her feet nailed to the arms of the cross, such that her whole body is more exposed than in the other two sculptures. Stephen Moore describes it as a 'highly unsettling sculpture of a cruelly tortured woman symbolically spread-eagled on a cruciform bed of pain'.[18] Murphy himself has described the sculpture as:

> a vehicle for acknowledging the world's crucifixion of women by denigrating them, dehumanizing them, and placing them in the state of being an animal or a sex object ... 'Christine' is a symbol of the world's abuse of women. She is humiliated, demeaned, tortured, raped, and murdered. She is spread apart and mounted on the cross. She is slaughtered sacrificially. She is the object of the patriarchal world's morbid sadomasochistic sexuality. She is the bearer of the world's contempt and disgust toward lower-realm beings.[19]

While these three works are some of the best known of the so-called Christa figures, there are multiple forms of the crucified or cruciform woman in art, literature and film, as well as in feminist theology. I have found dozens of images, well over one hundred, in my quest for images of a *risen* Christa.[20] Mary Grey offers literary as well as visual examples of the Christa from early Christian martyr narratives, from Asian and African iconography and in Chaim Potok's novel *My Name is Asher Lev*, in which Asher Lev paints an image of his mother on a cross.[21] Julie Clague has reviewed representations of the Christa, highlighting in particular *Crucifixion, Shoalhaven* by Arthur Boyd (1979–80) and *Bosnian Christa* by Margaret Argyll (1993), alongside the works by Sandys and Lutkenhaus-Lackey.[22] Kittredge Cherry brings together a range of images of the female Christ, alongside those of a gay Jesus, by Jill Ansell, Robert Lentz, Janet McKenzie, William McHart Nichols and Sandra Yagi, in her book *Art that Dares: Gay Jesus, Woman Christ, and More*.[23] Kim Power discusses various images of the crucified Christa, including *Crucifixion* by Eric Drooker and *Woman Crucified (On Her Own Reproductive System)* by Maggi Thickston, which, as Thickston's title indicates, depict a crucified woman hanging from a cross that is her own fallopian tubes, uterus and ovaries.[24] As well as paintings and sculptures, a number of photographic images of the Christa figure have appeared recently, including reworkings of the Last Supper depicting a female Christ and female disciples,[25] and more examples of the crucified female Christ,[26] as well as film and video versions.[27] Anne-Marie Korte calls attention to Madonna's staging of a crucifixion scene for her 'Confessions on a Dance Floor' tour in 2006, in which the pop idol was suspended on a huge shining silver cross wearing a crown of thorns.[28]

The vast majority of the images of the Christa depict a suffering if not crucified woman, almost always naked, sometimes nailed or impaled on a cross; at other times in cruciform shape, suggestive of the cross even when there is no cross as such (as in Sandys' *Christa* and Lutkenhause-Lackey's *Crucified Woman*). There are a few images of a risen Christa, for example Jill Ansell's *Missa solemnis*, depicting a naked Christa surrounded by animals and other aspects of creation,[29] Robert Lentz's icon of *Christ Sophia*,[30] and Emmanuel Garibay's various female versions of the Emmaus Christ,[31] but these are the exception rather than the rule. Interestingly, where almost all images of the crucified Christa show her naked, the risen Christa is generally clothed.

The figure of a crucified woman – and, occasionally, of a child – continues to emerge in new contexts and situations, as a powerful and shocking symbol of violence against women but also as protest against other forms of injustice against a variety of dispossessed and marginalized individuals and groups. For example, Stephen Burns draws attention to a powerful art work entitled *Deterrence*, by Uniting Church in Australia deacon John Tansey.[32] This installation of three crosses, exhibited outside St Paul's Anglican Cathedral in Bendigo, rural Victoria, in Passiontide 2017, places three figures, twined from barbed wire, on the crosses – that of a man, a

Figure 3: John Tansey's *Deterrence* sculptures. Photo by John Tansey.

child and a pregnant woman. Each cross bears a sign, showing the names of off-shore Australian detention centres – Christmas Island, Manus, Naura.

Tansey has spoken of the sculptures being intended 'to explore the questions and links between the crucifixion, the way the Romans used crucifixion as a deterrent and how the Australian Government has become obsessed with the harsh treatment of asylum seekers'.[33] Burns contextualizes Tansey's piece within wider instances of the Christa, as well as within the reality of 'crucified children' in our contemporary world, citing the deaths of children at sea (such as that of Aylan Kurdi, 'whose limp body washed up on a beach near Bodrum, Turkey, on September 2, 2015, stirr[ed] up international attention'), the sexual abuse of children by clergy and other authority figures, and the beheading and burning alive of children by ISIS/Islamic State/Daesh. Burns compares Tansey's sculpture of a crucified child to Erik Ravelo's 'difficult images, *Untouchables* (2013)', a series of six photographs showing children and adolescents slung against the backs, in turn, of a Catholic priest, a sex tourist, a soldier, a medic, a young man bearing guns and a fast-food worker, variously symbolizing paedophilia in the church, sex child tourism in Asia, the death of children in the Syrian war, the trafficking of children's organs on the black market, the death of children in gang violence, and via obesity fuelled by fast-food companies.[34] If the image of a crucified woman on the cross is shocking, images of crucified children are probably even more disturbing to viewers for whom childhood represents powerlessness, dependence and vulnerability most acutely in any society.

Images of the female Christ figure (and images of a crucified child) are produced by a wide variety of artists and cultural commentators; some may have an overt theological agenda or linkage to religious practice, but many, perhaps the vast majority, know nothing of feminist theological debates about Christ and the cross and appear to be motivated (so far as one can tell) by broader socio-political trends and debates. While feminist theologians have taken up the suggestive notion of the Christa and developed it in a range of ways,[35] the visual images of the Christa appear to both reflect and speak into a wider, more popular cultural milieu created by and within film, music videos, pop culture, street art and so on. They are examples of contemporary artists and cultural commentators employing the historic symbol of Christ on the cross, in shocking, subversive and/or paradoxical ways, variously parodying, critiquing and re-imagining the central Christian symbol of the cross to represent female and child suffering, sexuality and victimhood in patriarchal religion and society. As Rachel Anderson suggests:

> images of crucified women are necessarily potent; they combine two of the most intensely evocative motifs of Western culture, the image of the

Crucified Christ and the image of the alluring Female Body. The result of their combination yields an extraordinarily freighted image.[36]

Anderson suggests that the image of a crucified woman, per se, is likely to cause a 'complicated and confusing morass of emotions' in the viewer because of the inherently paradoxical, contradictory frisson of bringing together the holy and the erotic in one symbol.[37]

This leads into the question of how to assess the meaning and value of images of the Christa (in particular, those of a crucified female figure). We might ask, in Kim Power's words, 'Are the Christa images proliferating in contemporary fine arts an obscene modern fad or a new leading of the Spirit, challenging old certainties that assert a false obscenity against her?'[38] Or, more tersely, 'Does the Christa perpetuate the abuse of women?'[39] Or, to turn the question around, and given the largely negative reactions to many images of the Christa, we might ask, with Ivone Gebera, 'Why should the naked body of a crucified man be an object of veneration while that of a woman be judged pornographic?'[40]

Nakedness, gender and representation: what does a naked Christa signify?

In order to assess the various meanings of a naked crucified Christa – especially, but not exclusively, in visual representations and three-dimensional form – we need first to consider female nakedness and religious meaning more widely, in western culture and religious tradition. Margaret Miles' authoritative study, *Carnal Knowing: Female Nakedness and Religious Meaning in the Christian West*,[41] shows how nakedness has been a significant feature of Christian practice, theology and representation, from the earliest times onwards. In early Christian practice, naked baptism was the norm and held a range of rich religious meanings, from imitation of Christ in his nakedness on the cross (as acknowledged by Cyril of Jerusalem and others), through various associations with death and rebirth, the stripping off of the world or the old life, to a form of quasi-martyrdom, and so on.[42] Baptism was also a gendered ritual; one that, for women, was both empowering and, at the same time, confirmed their confinement to supportive roles in Christian churches and communities. In a rite that could not be conferred by women but in which naked women were anointed by male clergy, and baptized last, after children and men, the symbolic enactment of secondary status is clear.[43]

What was begun in the practice of naked baptism was amplified and extended in subsequent theology and in visual representations of male and female nakedness. In ascetic practice and martyrdom, the tension already noted between gender equality and female subservience continued in the meanings ascribed to the naked female body. Female nakedness could be used as a symbol of a religious self characterized by 'courage, conscious choice, and self-possession' in narrative accounts such as *The Acts of Paul and Thecla*, and *The Martyrdom of Ss. Perpetua and Felicitas* and, at the same time, as an object of the male gaze in which women's appearance and its effects upon men become the primary concern. As Miles asserts, 'Female beauty created temptation for male Christians'; and therefore 'women were to obscure their beauty to protect men's salvation'.[44] The female body both was and was not a site of female subjectivity and agency, and herein lay a contradiction that continued throughout Christian history and arguably continues still.

This contradiction becomes most evident in readings and representations of Adam and Eve, in which the naked body of Eve became seen 'as symbol of sin, sexual lust, and dangerous evil',[45] while the naked body of Adam, although sharing in the fruits of Eve's fall into sin and therefore partaking of shame, was generally read in a more positive light as signifying superior and heroic strength, enlightened reason and a 'glory and prestige' far beyond female beauty.[46] Such meanings were discussed and elaborated in theological texts but, above all, they were disseminated in religious images. Alongside the dominant image of Eve as the symbol of 'every woman', images of other naked or semi-naked biblical women, such as Susanna and Mary Magdalene, reinforced the range of meanings of the female form for the male voyeur as representing 'simultaneously threat, danger, and delight'.[47] Figures of the ideal woman, pre-eminently the Virgin Mary, helped to solidify such readings by offering a binary of female good and female evil.[48] By contrast, figures such as Michelangelo's David, as well as many representations of Adam and Christ (the Second Adam), demonstrate how 'male nakedness represented spiritual discipline and physical control and order – the body as perfect vehicle and expression of the difficult and committed work of the creation and cultivation of religious subjectivity'.[49] In Renaissance painting and imagery, Leo Steinberg argues that there is a new emphasis on the naked genitals of Christ, displayed by the Virgin in scenes of mother and child, or on display in images of the crucified and dead Christ.[50] Drawing on Steinberg's scholarship, Miles argues that 'the heroic male nakedness of athletic asceticism adds visual associations to Christ's nakedness, constructing a richly complex visual symbol in which strength and weakness, triumph and vulnerability are resolved'.[51] Thus, in the naked female form, frailty and strength, sexuality and holiness are in unresolved tension, while in the naked male form the tensions are held together and resolved.

Having surveyed female nakedness throughout Christian art and tradition, Miles concludes that 'female bodies, in the societies of the Christian West, have not represented women's subjectivity or sexuality but have, rather, been seen as a blank page on which multiple social meanings could be projected'.[52] 'Men have figured "woman" as a frightening and fascinating creature whose anger and rejection could deprive them of gratification, delight, and, ultimately, of life and salvation.'[53]

In the final chapter of *Carnal Knowing*, Miles turns to the question of whether 'more equitable' public images of women can be produced in our own time, in light of the problematic inheritance of Christian theology and symbolism. She queries whether 'the female body [can] be a usable symbol for women's articulation of themselves as subjects?' Miles is sceptical about the possibilities of 'turning the symbols', to use Janet Martin Soskice's evocative phrase.[54] She considers, briefly, Edwina Sandys' *Christa*, regarding it as an image that 'makes vivid the perennial suffering of women' and that, 'as a private devotional image … may have great healing potential for women who have themselves been battered or raped'.[55] Yet, she considers the sculpture problematic as a public image, because of the way in which, according to her, it 'fetishizes suffering women'. 'The *Christa*, by its visual association with the crucified Christ, glorifies the suffering of women in a society in which violence against women has reached epidemic proportions.'[56]

While Miles is right to recognize the enormous challenge of undoing and revising existing patriarchal representations of the female body and the inherent difficulties of 'turning the symbols' and making new religious meaning out of female nakedness, I suggest that the figure of the Christa *may* be one place where meanings of female suffering, nakedness, sexuality and subjectivity can be revised and represented. I do not claim that any or all versions of the Christa are useful or liberating; some (perhaps many?) of them reinscribe a voyeuristic male gaze and thus undermine female subjectivity and agency, employing an authoritative religious symbol to endorse and baptize familiar tropes of the naked female body as a site of the male gaze, heteronormative sexual desire and masochistic voyeurism. In such cases, the symbol of a naked female Christ figure may be superficially novel, but in every other way is only too familiar as a pornographic image. The most obvious instances of such Christas are the multiple photographic and filmic versions created by Ramon Martinez.[57] Although there are multiple versions, his Christa is in essence the same image repeated from different angles and in different postures, all of which assume the voyeuristic male gaze and reduce the naked female form to an object of male arousal, pleasure and violence. The fact that the exposed female body is superimposed on a cross only heightens the frisson of dangerous pleasure, giving religious legitimacy to sadomasochistic fantasies and practices. Such images merely reproduce and reinforce a tired, jaded but still potent pornographic rendering of the female body.

In light of such representations of the female Christ figure, we are right to be cautious about the significance of the Christa. Yet the crucified Christa cannot be reduced to such pornographic readings. Other symbolic renderings are possible, ones in which women represent themselves in ways that claim female subjectivity and agency even as they demonstrate and protest against the sexual violation of women. Thus, I would offer an alternative reading of Edwina Sandys' *Christa*, particularly in its replaced positioning above the altar in the Chapel of St Saviour in the Cathedral of St John the Divine. Positioned in the place where Christian celebration of the Eucharist is publicly and regularly enacted and highlighted against the rainbow colours of the enormous stained-glass window in the chapel, Sandys' *Christa* is capable of evoking a wide range of reactions and readings: not only ones that affirm Christ's identification with the suffering and abuse of women, but also those that read women's bodies and blood – in birth, as well as in life and death – as a primary symbol of the divine feminine. There is an ambivalence about the female form, too, which resists conventional readings; whatever Sandys intended by her endeavour to create an image that is 'as womanly as possible', this is not a conventionally beautiful female form. It is muscular in ways that may confuse gender expectations. Its naked form hides as much as it reveals sexuality. The bowed face cannot easily be gazed into, resisting occupation or colonization.

Tansey's barbed-wire figures that form his *Deterrence* installation, in different ways, also resist conventional or voyeuristic responses. The fact

that the bodies are composed of barbed wire is a potent symbol of imprisonment and allows many readings but also disallows literalistic interpretations of the bodies. Faceless and lacking detailed features, the bodies take on a wider symbolic meaning and do not permit a voyeuristic gaze.

In the same way, images of the Christa that are more suggestive or abstract in outline, such as Arnulf Rainer's *Wine Crucifix*[58] – where the outline of a pregnant body can be seen within the explosion of dripping colour on the canvas – refuse to allow the viewer to reduce the female body to sexual function or availability. Despite its explicit sexual morphology, Margaret Argyll's *Bosnian Christa*[59] – a textile work, showing the faint outline of a female form on a cross within the opening of a vulva, worked in blood red – refuses pornographic

Figure 4: John Tansey's *Deterrence* sculptures, detail. Photo by John Tansey.

appropriation by being both explicitly representational of women's sexual organs and, at the same time, lacking detail. As in Arnulf's *Wine Crucifix*, colour and shape represent women's sexualized suffering (in Argyll's case, the multiple rape of Bosnian women in the Bosnian war), yet this is clearly not a realistic portrayal of a woman's sexual organs.

The attempt to represent the crucifixion as a symbol of female healing and empowerment is a risky undertaking, and every Christa – particularly every naked, crucified or cruciform Christa – walks a dangerous tightrope between reinscribing patriarchal renderings of the female form and forging new, liberationist, readings. Each representation must be considered on its own terms, and viewers will differ in their judgements, according to their own contexts, interests and agendas. Power proposes that 'principles of justice, inclusiveness and respect for women's bodies be the touchstone of discernment for the legitimacy of the Christa',[60] although she does not spell out how these might be applied. While open to wide application, such criteria may be helpful in assessing the variety of renderings of the Christa.

Alongside a wide range of images and theologies of the Christa, including renderings that move away from a fixation on the cross, more is needed. However various and rich, the image and concept of Christa cannot do all the work that Christian theology and representation needs to do around understandings of human sexuality, violence and salvation. We need renewed attention to the male body of Jesus and to theologies and images of the man Jesus on the cross (and off it!) that reveal his nakedness and his wounded, abused sexuality. As Clague argues:

> Jesus has been systematically stripped of his sexuality throughout art history. A lifetime of seeing his male form on the cross has inoculated us against its sexual impact. The male Jesus on the cross is gendered but not sexual, because the viewer has unwittingly castrated the Christ.[61]

A number of male theologians have explored and sought to reclaim the nakedness and the sexuality of Jesus for new theologies of masculinity. For example, in his 1996 article, 'Does Jesus have a Penis?', Robert Beckford appeals for 'the production of images of Jesus that symbolize the quest for a black socio-political sexual wholeness' (such as Robert Lentz's portrayal of Jesus as a squatting Maasai warrior with visible testicles).[62] In his fascinating study of nakedness and clothing in the Bible and early Christianity, Dan Lé develops an atonement theology based on the nakedness of Christ on the cross, what he calls the *Christus nudus* model.[63] These are two instances of a much wider project of reconfiguring masculinity in the light of a rereading of Jesus' own sexuality and masculinity.

Only by reclaiming the naked body of the man Jesus as a central symbol within Christianity can the reality of Jesus' own suffering of sexual abuse be grasped and reflected upon by theologians and ordinary believers alike while, at the same time, the objectification and sexualization of women's bodies in the male gaze is challenged and corrected. Only such a reclamation of the sexed, male body of Jesus can offer a potent symbol to men seeking new forms of masculinity, *and* convey to women the solidarity of men with their sexual victimization and abuse.

Conclusion

My discussion of the Christa has ranged round a number of interconnected themes concerning female embodiment, representation and subjectivity; sexual and other forms of violence against women; readings and renderings of the cross of Christ/a and whether the Christa has a place within a renewed feminist religious imaginary. I will now try to bring together the various themes and restate my argument in a series of statements or hypotheses.

Images of the Christa are multiple, and have an ancient pedigree; scholars continue to unearth previously neglected ones, as artists continue to create new ones. The image of a crucified woman continues to be potent in our time. The vast majority of images of the Christa are of a suffering, crucified or cruciform woman on a cross or suggestive of a cross. Nevertheless, there are other images of a female Christ figure (and I have argued elsewhere that these may be particularly significant for women seeking their own subjective agency and 'risenness'[64]).

In so far as they function on the symbolic plane, ideas and visual representations of the Christa qua symbol are multivalent, capable of more or less endless interpretation, and cannot be reduced to one reading or meaning. By bringing together the central symbol of Christianity, the cross of Christ, with the image of a suffering and naked female body, the Christa functions as a highly charged symbol that tends to elicit strong, visceral and emotive reactions, tapping into deep human experiences of sexuality, suffering and subjectivity and uncovering unconscious attitudes towards gender, sexuality, holiness, nakedness, sin and shame. It is in this sense that Althaus-Reid speaks of the Christa as an 'obscene' image, in its capacity to uncover or undress the obscenities of sexism, racism and other unconscious prejudice in the viewer.[65]

While readings of the Christa are multiple, and cannot be reduced to any particular meaning, certain interpretations appear to be common or recurring. Thus, for many, the Christa is a symbol of the physical and sexual abuse of women, both historically and in our own time, including and focusing particularly the abuse of women perpetuated by the Church in the name of Christ. The Christa brings to light violence against women in a potent way, drawing on the authority of the cross of Christ to do so. This is clear in the statements from Edwina Sandys, Almuth Lutkenhause-Lackey and, most obviously, James M. Murphy, above, in discussion of their representations of the Christa. As such, the image of a crucified woman may be therapeutic, liberating and healing for women, most particularly women who have suffered physical and sexual abuse at the hands of men, especially where this has been perpetuated or endorsed by male religious authorities. There is a good deal of anecdotal and pastoral evidence that women viewers do, indeed, find the Christa such a potent therapeutic symbol, capable of expressing and conveying the theological claim that God is present to redeem and save all those victimized by oppressive structures and all victims of sexual violence.

The Christa, as a regendering of the cross of Christ, may also shock viewers into recognizing the historic violence perpetuated against Jesus, including sexual violence, in ways that more familiar images of the male Christ on the cross generally fail to do, viewers having become habituated to such imagery. The Christa is one of the few symbols that makes visible the sexual abuse of Jesus on the cross, even as it hides it by placing the reality of sexual violence in the naked bodies of women. It is thus a paradoxical symbol, which may generate both disruption and confusion, both of traditional understandings of the cross of Christ and of meanings associated with the naked bodies of women.[66]

By associating sexual violence against women with the suffering of Jesus on the cross, the Christa is an ambivalent symbol, which can be read both as a protest against sexual and other kinds of violence against women *and* as a reinforcement of female victimization and suffering. Theologians, art critics and cultural commentators alike are divided in their reading of the symbol of the Christa. Where some see the image as a powerful symbol of the feminine divine, claiming and reworking a traditional patriarchal symbol to invoke new religious meaning and sacralizing female bodily experience, others regard it as reinscribing patriarchal readings of the female body as symbolic of sin, suffering, sexuality and shame. Feminist theologians who have critiqued the dominance of theologies of death and violence in Christian tradition are particularly concerned that the figure of a suffering, dying Christa may reinforce, rather than challenge, the centrality of death, suffering and violence at the heart of Christian theology and iconography. Thus Mary Grey asks pointedly: 'If the central symbol of Christianity contains with it a message which keeps women impaled on that cross, with societal approval, what message of resurrected hope and redemption can it bring?'[67]

For these, and other reasons, a number of theologians and artists have developed theologies and images of the Christa that do not focus on the cross or on the suffering of women/Jesus. My own search for a theology of the risen Christa is one such example;[68] Kim Power's reworking of theologies of Eucharist via the Christa in order to relocate suffering as part of the painful labour of birth,[69] and Karen O'Donnell's reconfiguring of Eucharist through the lens of incarnation, Marian theology and maternal experience,[70] are two others, each of which seeks to shift the balance of Christian theology away from death and violence towards natality and fecundity. Within these theologies, as Power asserts, the Christa 'can be considered the Easter dawning of a divine horizon for women through the sacrality of the female body, embraced in all its fluidity and fecundity'.[71]

The symbol and notion of a crucified woman, however multivalent, is not capable of bearing or expressing the whole range of theological, political and ethical terms necessary for a renewed theology of human sexuality, suffering and redemption in our time. We also need new imaginings and new theologies of the male Christ that affirm his naked vulnerability and sexuality. By stating the need for new masculine and feminine images of Christ on the cross, I do not wish to reinscribe a gender binary that reinforces tired notions of biological essentialism. Gender-ambivalent and gender-queer images of Christ/a are also needed and, indeed, already exist.

In conclusion, I suggest that *neither* the image of a naked female body on the cross *nor* the reclaimed sexual body of a male Jesus on the cross, however potent and liberating these may be, can do all the work required for a 'turning of the symbols' and a renewed religious imaginary. Nevertheless, to develop such new (or reclaimed) iconographies in parallel and in dialogue with each other – as well as in conversation with alternative images of a risen Christ/a – may go some way towards reconfiguring the relationships between nakedness, gender, sexuality, subjectivity, redemption and holiness, endorsing new forms of practice, thought and action.

Notes

1 I am grateful to Stephen Burns for his helpful comments on an earlier draft of this article, and for putting me in touch with John Tansey, to whom I am also grateful for permission to include photos of his Deterrence sculptures.

2 For a summary of the evidence, see David Tombs, 'Crucifixion, State Terror, and Sexual Abuse', *Union Seminary Quarterly Review* 53 (1999), pp. 89–109; and Rocío Figueroa and David Tombs, *Recognising Jesus as a Victim of Sexual Abuse: Responses from Sodalicio Survivors in Peru* (University of Otago: Centre for Theology and Public Issues, 2019); https://jliflc.com/wp-content/uploads/2019/06/Figueroa-and-Tombs-2019-Recognising-Jesus-as-a-Victim-of-Sexual-Abuse.pdf (accessed 13.1.20).

3 Jayme R. Reaves and David Tombs, '#MeTooJesus: Naming Jesus as a Victim of Sexual Abuse', *International Journal of Public Theology* 13 (2019), pp. 387–412.

4 For a summary and discussion of the emergence and development of the idea and image of the Christa, see Mary Grey, 'Who do you say that I am? Images of Christ in feminist liberation theology', in Stanley E. Porter, Michael A. Hayes and David Tombs (eds.), *Images of Christ: Ancient and Modern* (Sheffield: Sheffield Academic Press, 1997), pp. 189–203; Julie Clague, 'The Christa: Symbolizing My Humanity and My Pain', *Feminist Theology* 14.1 (2005), pp. 83–108; Nicola Slee, *Seeking the Risen Christa* (London: SPCK, 2011), chapter 1; and Kim Power,

'Embodying the Eucharist', in Anne Elvey, Carol Hogan, Kim Power and Claire Renkin (eds.), *Reinterpreting the Eucharist: Explorations in Feminist Theology and Ethics* (Sheffield: Equinox, 2013), pp. 152–85.

5 Reaves and Tombs, '#MeTooJesus', p. 402; Elaine A. Heath, *We Were the Least of These: Reading the Bible with Survivors of Sexual Abuse* (Grand Rapids, MI: Brazos Press, 2011), p. 124. Heath's book is republished as *Healing the Wounds of Sexual Abuse: Reading the Bible with Survivors* (Grand Rapids, MI: Brazos Press, 2019).

6 See Slee, *Seeking the Risen Christa*; Nicola Slee, 'Visualizing, Conceptualizing, Imagining and Praying the Christa: In Search of Her Risen Forms', *Feminist Theology* 21.1 (2012), pp. 71–90; Nicola Slee, 'Reimaging Christ as a girl: An Advent experiment', in Jonny Baker, Steve Collins and Cathy Ross (eds.), *Future Present: Embodying a Future World Now* (Sheffield: Proost, 2018), pp. 45–60; and chapter 16 in this book.

7 I am by no means the first to interrogate images of the Christa theologically. See, in particular, Grey, 'Who do you say that I am?'; Clague, 'The Christa'; Susannah Cornwall, 'Ambiguous bodies, ambiguous readings: Reflections on James M. Murphy's "Christine on the Cross", in Zowie Davy, Julia Downes, Lena Eckert, Natalia Gerodetti, Dario Llinares and Ana Christine Santos (eds.), *Bound and Unbound: Interdisciplinary Approaches to Gender and Sexualities* (Newcastle: Cambridge Scholars Publishing, 2008); and Stephen Burns, 'Deterrence', in Carolyn Alsen (ed.), *Feminist Fractures and Intersections* (Lanham, MD: Lexington, 2020).

8 Mary Daly, *Beyond God the Father: Towards a Philosophy of Women's Liberation* (London: Women's Press, 1986), and *Gyn/Ecology: The Metaethics of Radical Feminism* (London: Women's Press, 1979).

9 Grace Jantzen, *Becoming Divine: Towards a Feminist Philosophy of Religion* (Manchester: Manchester University Press, 1988).

10 As Robert Beckford argues in 'Does Jesus have a Penis? Black Male Sexual Representation and Christology', *Theology and Sexuality* 5 (1996), pp. 10–21, to which I shall return.

11 In this article I am focusing primarily on visual representations of the Christa, rather than the theologies that have developed in dialogue with Edwina Sandys' original *Christa* sculpture.

12 See Grey, 'Who do you say that I am?' and Slee, *Seeking the Risen Christa*, for ancient examples of the idea and image of a female Christ.

13 See www.edwinasandys.com. The image is also included in the study pack, *The Christ We Share* (London: USPG, 2nd edn, 2000).

14 Edwina Sandys, 'Christa: A statement from the artist', in *The Christa Project: Manifesting Divine Bodies* (New York: The Cathedral of St John the Divine, 2016).

15 At www.dittwald.com/torontosculpture.

16 Cited in Bobbie Crawford, 'A Female Crucifix?' *Daughters of Sarah* 14.6 (1988), pp. 24–7.

17 Images of *Christine on the Cross* can be found in Clague, 'The Christa', p. 92; and Cornwall, 'Ambiguous bodies', pp. 101, 104. I have not been able to find out if the exhibition of Murphy's sculpture was planned to coincide with that of Sandys' *Christa*.

18 Stephen D. Moore, *God's Beauty Parlor: and Other Queer Spaces in and around the Bible* (Stanford, CA: Stanford University Press, 2001), pp. 158.

19 James M. Murphy, 'A Female Christ for Men and Women', unpublished manuscript, 1990, pp. 67–8. Quoted in Clague, 'The Christa', p. 94.

20 See Slee, *Seeking the Risen Christa*.

21 Grey, 'Who do you say that I am?'

22 Clague, 'The Christa'.

23 Kittredge Cherry, *Art that Dares: Gay Jesus, Woman Christ, and More* (Berkely, CA: AndroGyne Press, 2007). See also her website, www.jesusinlove.org, especially 'Alternative images of Christ and Mary' under 'Links'.

24 Power, 'Embodying the Eucharist', pp. 175, 177.

25 For example, Renée Cox's *Yo Mama's Last Supper*, a five-panel colour portrayal with Cox herself as a naked Christ figure surrounded by twelve black apostles – at www.reneecox.org/yo-mamas-last-supper – and François Girbauld's portrayal of the Last Supper with a female Christ and eleven female disciples, one male, at adsoftheworld.com/media/print/marithe_francois_girbaud_last_supper.

26 For example, a whole sequence of stylized photographs of a female crucified Christ can be found on the Passion of a Goddess site, at www.passionofagoddess. com and https://ramon-martinez.pixels.com/. Warning: some of these may be considered pornographic in content and approach.

27 Linda Mercadatne proposes Bess, in Lars von Trier's 1996 *Breaking the Waves* film as a female Christ figure, in 'Bess the Christ Figure? Theological Interpretations of *Breaking the Waves*', *Journal of Religion and Film* 5.1 (2001), pp. 1–14, https://digitalcommons.unomaha.edu/cgi/viewcontent.cgi?article=1795&context= jrf (accessed 18.1.20). Arnfrídur Gudmundsdóttir considers Beth alongside Sister Helen Prejean in Tim Robbins' 1995 *Dead Man Walking* as female Christ-figures, in 'Female Christ-figures in Films: A Feminist Critical Analysis of *Breaking the Waves* and *Dead Man Walking*', *Studia Theologica* 56 (2002), pp. 27–43.

28 Anne-Marie Korte, 'Madonna's crucifixion and the woman's body in feminist theology', in Rosemarie Buikema and Iris Van Dertuin (eds.), *Doing Gender in Media, Art and Culture* (London: Routledge, 2007), pp. 117–33.

29 At https://jesusinlove.org/artthatdares/atd1-ansell-z.html (accessed 20.1.20).

30 At www.pinterest.co.uk/pin/346003183845537302/ (accessed 20.1.20). Also in Robert Lentz and Edwina Gateley, *Christ in the Margins* (Maryknoll, NY: Orbis, 2009), p. 112.

31 Garibay's *Emmaus* exists in a number of versions, one of which can be found at https://imagejournal.org/article/recognizing-the-stranger/ (accessed 20.1.20) – and forms the cover image of my *Seeking the Risen Christa*. Other versions can be found online.

32 Burns, 'Deterrence', p. 1.

33 In Burns, 'Deterrence', p. 3.

34 See themicrogiant.com/the-untouchables-erik-ravelo/ (accessed 18.1.20).

35 See Slee, *Seeking the Risen Christa*, chapter 1, for a survey of theological discussions of the Christa.

36 Rachel Anderson, 'The Crucified Woman: A Paradox of Prurience and Piety', research paper, 21 May 2007, p. 2. https://digital.lib.washington.edu/researchworks/ bitstream/handle/1773/3101/anderson_project.pdf?sequence=1&isAllowed=y (accessed 14.1.20).

37 Anderson, 'Crucified Woman', p. 2. Note her assumption that the naked female body is an erotically charged image in western culture, in ways that are not commonly suggested of the representation of the naked male.

38 Power, 'Embodying the Eucharist', p. 159.

39 Power, 'Embodying the Eucharist', p. 160.

40 Ivone Gebara, *Out of the Depths: Women's Experience of Evil and Salvation* (Minneapolis, MN: Fortress, 2002), p. 117.

41 Margaret R. Miles, *Carnal Knowing: Female Nakedness and Religious Meaning in the Christian West* (Tunbridge Wells: Burns & Oates, 1992).

42 Miles, *Carnal Knowing*, p. 35. For further consideration of the significance of nakedness in baptism, see Frank C. Senn, *Embodied Liturgy: Lessons in Christian Ritual* (Minneapolis, MN: Fortress, 2016), pp. 53–89.

43 Miles, *Carnal Knowing*, p. 45.

44 Miles, *Carnal Knowing*, p. 70.

45 Miles, *Carnal Knowing*, p. 81.

46 As in Luther's account. Miles, *Carnal Knowing*, p. 107.

47 Miles, *Carnal Knowing*, p. 124.

48 Miles, *Carnal Knowing*, p. 139.

49 Miles, *Carnal Knowing*, p. 142.

50 Leo Steinberg, *The Sexuality of Christ in Renaissance Painting and Modern Oblivion* (New York: Pantheon, 1984).

51 Miles, *Carnal Knowing*, p. 143.

52 Miles, *Carnal Knowing*, p. 169.

53 Miles, *Carnal Knowing*, pp. 169, 170.

54 Janet Martin Soskice, 'Turning the symbols', in Daphne Hampson (ed.), *Swallowing a Fishbone? Feminist Theologians Debate Christianity* (London: SPCK, 1996), pp. 17–32.

55 Miles, *Carnal Knowing*, p. 177.

56 Miles, *Carnal Knowing*, p. 177.

57 See https://ramon-martinez.pixels.com/ (accessed 19.1.20).

58 See www.tate.org.uk/art/artworks/rainer-wine-crucifix-t03671 for Rainer's *Wine Crucifix* (accessed 17.1.20).

59 An image of Argyll's *Bosnian Christa* can be found at https://efecwomen.com/2017/12/13/date-announced-lecture-in-partnership-with-luther-king-house-12-february-2018/ (accessed 19.1.20).

60 Power, 'Embodying the Eucharist', pp. 164–5.

61 Clague, 'The Christa', p. 103.

62 Beckford, 'Does Jesus have a Penis?', pp. 10–21.

63 Dan Lé, *The Naked Christ: An Atonement Model for a Body-Obsessed Culture* (Eugene, OR: Pickwick Publications, 2012).

64 Slee, *Seeking the Risen Christa*.

65 Marcella Althaus-Reid, *Indecent Theology: Theological Perversions in Sex, Gender and Politics* (London: Routledge, 2000), pp. 110ff.

66 Clague, 'The Christa', pp. 99–100.

67 Grey, 'Who do you say that I am?', p. 193.

68 Slee, *Seeking the Risen Christa*.

69 Power, 'Embodying the Eucharist'.

70 Karen O'Donnell, *Broken Bodies: The Eucharist, Mary, and the Body in Trauma Theology* (London: SCM Press, 2018).

71 Power, 'Embodying the Eucharist', p. 179.

19

In Praise of God as Feisty Crone

Although I have been preaching, on and off, for many years, I had never preached on Luke's parable of the unjust judge (so called) until September 2016, when I found myself down on the rota at Queen's to preach and this was the set Gospel. I am glad to be able to pay tribute, in print, to Ianthe Pratt, a pioneering prophet whose life has been an inspiration to me and to many others, along with a number of other women in their eighties and nineties whose persistence in working for justice and inclusion gives me hope for my own old age and cronedom. I'm not there yet, but perhaps I'm on my way. It seems a fitting piece to end this book: a fragment from a particular time and place which I hope bears witness to some core values of the Christian gospel.

I'd like to introduce you to my friend Ianthe Pratt. I'm not quite sure how old she is – in her late eighties at least, possibly now in her early nineties. She's one of a number of feisty, radical, Catholic crones (I don't think it's an accident that many of them are Catholic) I feel immensely blessed to know. They are all slightly mad, they no longer care – if they ever did – what the hierarchy or their husbands (if they have them) think of them, and I love them to bits. They have thrown caution to the wind and are using every last bit of their remaining energy working for radical change in the Catholic Church and for wider social justice.

For decades, Ianthe and her husband Oliver were a formidable team, deeply involved in many radical Catholic lay movements ('We Are the Church', the 'St Joan's Alliance', the 'Association for Inclusive Language', to name but a few), many of them run from their house. They wrote books together, campaigned and ran a feminist theology bookshop from their large house in Dulwich, which must have resourced thousands of research studies – from school RE projects to PhDs – long before feminist theology books and journals were widely available in shops and libraries.

Around thirty years ago, Oliver died. And Ianthe just carried right on doing what she's always been doing: speaking out, writing, running workshops and lugging Lumen Books around to any and every feminist event. In the 1990s, many Catholic women were part of the Anglican Movement for the Ordination of Women and, when in 1992 General Synod finally voted for women priests, Ianthe and a number of others founded the Catholic Women's Ordination (CWO) movement, to campaign for the ordination of women in the Roman Catholic Church. Week after week, year after year, they have gathered outside Westminster Cathedral with banners saying 'Ordain Women Now'. When Pope Benedict visited the UK in 2010, CWO paid for large advertisements on London buses that said 'Pope Benedict: Ordain Women Now'. Although the Catholic Church shows no signs of ordaining women any time soon, or of making even the most modest changes to the liturgy to signal the inclusion of women, these women (and some doughty men) don't give up, but carry on turning up and demanding justice.

And we might think of any number of other women across the world – and they are often old women – who demand justice in the face of what looks like implacable refusal. There are the Mothers of the Plaza de Mayo in Argentina who march in the Plaza to protest the 'disappearances' of relatives under the military dictatorship; and numerous other groups – you'll have to look them up for yourselves, but just to name some of them: 'the Saturday mothers' from Istanbul, the 'Mourning Mothers' in Iran, the Ladies in White in Cuba, the Tiananmen Mothers in China, the Mothers of Srebrenica, the Women of the Wall who protest against women's exclusion from the Western Wall in Jerusalem, and others I have never heard of and we will never know about.

All of these women and groups might take inspiration from the widow in our parable, who seems to me the epitome of the feisty crone who is determined to get justice, come what may, and who will not give up in her efforts to achieve it, even when the odds are stacked against her. The judge is corrupt, with no fear of God or respect for persons. The only reason he grants her justice is for his own peace of mind; the text here is quite startling. What is usually translated as 'pestering' or 'bothering' ('because this widow keeps bothering me, I will grant her justice so that she may not wear me out by continually coming', Luke 18.4) has the more usual meaning of 'hit in the face'; so the judge is really afraid that the widow is going to come and give him a black eye, which is why he relents in the end.[1]

We're used to the notion that widows are among the most vulnerable of Israelite society; the Bible frequently charges its readers to have a special care for the widow, the orphan and the stranger – because these are all groups of people who are peculiarly defenceless, who exist outside the normal social structures of the patriarchal family. Yet by the same token, precisely because widows were no longer under the authority of either their husband or father, they were at least potentially the most radically free and independent of women. Widows were the only class of women who could act on their own, with the same autonomy granted to men. It seems likely that some of Jesus' women disciples were wealthy widows who were freed from the demands of family life and who were able to travel with him and help finance the men.

Maybe it's easier for us to think of the widow in the parable as a poor, vulnerable, defenceless woman (and I don't want to deny the fact that plenty of widows at the time of Jesus must have been in this situation) because this image conforms to our own – or at least our society's – stereotypes of old women. For all of the successes of feminism, old women are frequently caricatured as lonely, frustrated, shrivelled and sexless; as ineffectual, dependent and passive. Terms for old women are frequently pejorative and hateful: hag, shrew, spinster, witch, even crone – which is precisely why that arch-feminist Mary Daly took many of these terms and turned them into positive appellations. In her *Websters Intergalactic Wickedary of the English Language*, Daly defined the crone as the 'Great Hag of History, the long-lasting one, one who has survived and who therefore has discovered depths of courage, strength, and wisdom in her self'.[2]

So maybe this parable challenges us to rethink our stereotypes of old people, and old women in particular – of whom our churches are full. Do we regard them as 'the little old ladies; God bless 'em', the sweet, charmless, harmless old biddies? Or perhaps as the tiresome, nagging tittle-tattlers (and the stereotype of the nagging old woman is not far beneath the surface of this parable)? Yet every one of these old women and men have survived long lives and most have extraordinary histories if we would care to listen to them. I remember reading somewhere – I can't remember where – that anyone who survives into their eighties is almost certainly living with several health conditions, maybe many. As I approach my sixties, I begin to understand that saying, 'Old age is not for cissies.' Just getting up every morning and greeting the world with a smile requires an enormous effort of energy and will – let alone, like Ianthe and her many sisters, taking on the establishment and marching for justice.

What if just such a feisty crone is offered to us in the parable as an image of God? We've probably been taught to think of the judge as the God figure in this parable, and indeed Luke himself seems to make this connection: 'And the Lord said, "Listen to what the unjust judge says. And will not God grant justice to his chosen ones who cry to him day and night?"' (Luke 18.6). The logic seems to be: if even a corrupt and wicked human judge will grant justice to an old woman who refuses to give up, how much more will the righteous and loving God give justice to God's children?

But what if God is not so much like the judge but much more like the widow? I want to end with a poem by Carola Moosbach, entitled 'Inversion',[3] which suggests precisely this possibility:

Inversion (Luke 18.1–8)

Just imagine
that God was the widow and not the judge
in this story
begging persistently angry whatever
she came running along
demanding rights her rights from us
for the odd ones out and those without means
for the refugees victims of torture and street kids
just imagine
we were those in power
corrupt complacent and arrogant like that judge
indifferent with regard to others and God
but she would simply not give up
would bend our ears with her justice
a complete pain in the neck just imagine
which one of us would want to hear
that?

Notes

1 Elisabeth Schüssler Fiorenza translates the verse as, 'I will grant her justice so that she may not give me a black eye (bruise, batter down, or wear me out) by her non-stop coming.' Fiorenza goes on to comment: 'The soliloquy of the judge expresses a typical sentiment of those who act violently; the judge blames the wo/ man victim for "battering" him although she only seeks her rights and vindication whereas he acts violently by denying justice to her.' *Sharing Her Word: Feminist Biblical Interpretation in Context* (Edinburgh: T&T Clark, 1998), p. 155.

2 Mary Daly with Jane Caput, *Websters First New Intergalactic Wickedary of the English Language* (Boston, MA: Beacon Press, 1987), p. 114. Although I feel I'm not yet fully into my cronedom, I take great delight in an exquisitely needle-worked square poster made for me by one of my PhD students, Jelly Morgans, which sits in my study at Queen's and proclaims, 'Prof Slee at 60: Catty Old Crone, Sinister Sibyl'. I only have myself to blame, since I encouraged Jelly to read the *Wickedary*!

3 Carol Moosbach, 'Inversion', in *Traces of Heaven*, trans. Natalie K. Watson and Giles C. Watson (London: SPCK, 2002), p. 82.

Acknowledgements of Copyright Sources

Liverpool University Press for publication of 'Poetry, Psalmody and Prayer in Feminist Perspective', originally published as 'Getting God through Poetry', *Modern Believing* 59.3 (2018), pp. 209–17.

Taylor and Francis for publication of 'God-language in Public and Private Prayer: A Place for Integrating Gender, Sexuality and Faith', originally published in *Theology and Sexuality* 20.3 (2014), pp. 225–37.

Taylor and Francis also for 'A Spirituality of Multiple Overwhelmings', originally in *Practical Theology* 10.1, pp. 20–32; and 'Theological Reflection *in extremis*: Remembering Srebrenica', originally in *Practical Theology* 12.1 (2019), pp. 30–43.

Taylor and Francis also for '(W)riting Like a Woman: In Search of a Feminist Theological Poetics', originally published in Gavin D'Costa, Eleanor Nesbitt, Mark Pryce, Ruth Shelton and Nicola Slee, *Making Nothing Happen: Five Poets Reflect on Faith and Spirituality* (Farnham: Ashgate, 2014), pp. 9–47. And 'Feminist Qualitative Research as Spiritual Practice: Reflections on the Process of Doing Research', originally published in Nicola Slee, Fran Porter and Anne Phillips (eds.), *The Faith Lives of Women and Girls: Qualitative Research Perspectives*, edited by (Farnham: Ashgate, 2013), pp.13–24.

Wild Goose Publications for Kathy Galloway, 'The Crack', in Kathy Galloway, *The Dream of Our Shared Language* (Glasgow: Wild Goose Publications, 2003), p. 42.

Darton, Longman & Todd for Rosie Miles, 'So here we are', in Geoffrey Duncan (ed.), *Courage to Love: An Anthology of Inclusive Worship Material* (London: Darton, Longman & Todd, 2002), pp. 78–9.

SPCK for 'Presiding in the Classroom: A Holy Work', originally in Nicola Slee and Stephen Burns (eds.), *Presiding Like a Woman* (London: SPCK, 2010), pp. 156–65. Also for Carola Moosbach, 'Inversion', *Traces of Heaven*, trans. Natalie K. Watson and Giles C. Watson (London: SPCK, 2002), p. 82.

Proost for 'Re-imagining Christ as the Coming Girl: An Advent Experiment', originally in Jonny Baker, Steve Collins and Cathy Ross (eds.), *Future Present: Embodying a Future World Now* (Sheffield: Proost, 2018), pp. 45–60.

John Tansey for photos of his *Deterrence* sculptures in Chapter 18.

Index of Biblical References

Index of Names and Subjects